THE
OLYMPIC
FACTBOOK

THE
OLYMPIC
FACTBOOK

A SPECTATOR'S GUIDE
TO THE WINTER GAMES

Martin Connors   **Diane Dupuis**

Marie J. MacNee   **Christa Brelin**

DETROIT • WASHINGTON D.C. • LONDON

The Olympic Factbook

CONTENTS

WINTER GAMES

A Lifetime Ago:
1980's Team USA
137

LUGE

Duncan Kennedy
148

Cammy Myler
151

SKIING—ALPINE

Marc Girardelli
164

A.J. Kitt
165

Tommy Moe
167

Alberto Tomba
168

Julie Parisien
171

Vreni Schneider
172

Katja Seizinger
174

Picabo Street
175

Toni Sailer
180

SKIING—FREESTYLE

SKIING—NORDIC CROSS-COUNTRY

Bill Koch
219

SKIING—NORDIC SKI JUMPING AND NORDIC COMBINED

Matti Nykänen
238

SPEEDSKATING

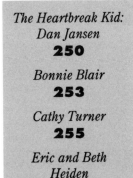

The Heartbreak Kid:
Dan Jansen
250

Bonnie Blair
253

Cathy Turner
255

Eric and Beth
Heiden
262

▼
INTRODUCTION

The Olympics capture our attention like no other sporting event. Front page of the news, splashy magazine covers, prime-time television. An international festival, the Games celebrate a gathering of the finest athletes from around the world. This winter in the arctic spendor of Lillehammer, Norway, thousands will compete in ten sports and more than forty separate events, a smorgasbord of athletic delight for both the ardent and casual spectator. And two years hence in Atlanta, Georgia, thousands more will compete in twenty-six summer sports and some 250 separate events.

Used to be that we had to wait four years to renew our acquaintance with the Olympic Games. Beginning with these 1994 Winter Games, though, we'll be able to watch the grand spectacle every other year, alternating between Winter and Summer Games. One hundred hours of television will cast this Winter's version of the modern Games as a televiewer's paradise, providing high drama, tragedy, and glory at the touch of your basic remote control. More than two weeks—morning, noon, and night—of televised Winter Olympic glory await.

fact: Also-rans outnumber medalists by a ratio of 17 to 1.

Thousands of amateur athletes with names unfamiliar are competing in sports you rarely see, their images captured by hundreds of zig-zagging broadcast and cable network cameras. The Olympics are the candy store of sports, with something for everyone's taste and aisle after aisle of impulse items. Yet where do you turn for information on *hopefuls in the luge competition?* Rules for ice dancing? *Freestyle skiing roots?* Winners of the two-man bobsled in 1952? *Scoring a ski jump?* Where do you turn for the facts?

The *Olympic Factbook* is designed to be your companion to the Winter Games, counterpointing the commentary, fleshing out the images on the television screen, guiding you to points past and present on the Olympic map. The background information will help you fully enjoy individual events, providing context and detail. We call it a *Spectator's Guide* because it truly is; the *Factbook* is designed to answer questions you may have as you watch the Olympics on television or on-site in Lillehammer.

fact: IOC rules forbid the host city from staging any sporting events not officially authorized for the Games.

The *Factbook* is *the* convenient reference source on rules and procedures, history and highlights, hopefuls and legends. Traditional Olympic sports are covered, as are the many new and relatively new events, such as short track speedskating, women's biathlon, and freestyle skiing.

Finding Your Way Through the Factbook

The *Factbook* presents information in three parts: **Opening Ceremonies, Winter Games,** and the **Index. Opening Ceremonies** is, as you might guess, concerned with the preliminaries. It begins with an insightful examination of what draws us to the Winter Olympics, written by veteran sports journalist Tom Callahan. Next, **Opening Ceremonies** presents a chronology of the Winter Olympics ranging from the first official Winter Games of Chamonix, France, to the Lillehammer Games. A timeline of Olympic-related events occurring between the last Winter Games in Albertville and 1994's Games follows. Then *Factbook* correspondent David Yntema examines the shifting definition of amateurism as it relates to the Olympic Games. A CBS television schedule concludes the **Opening Ceremonies.**

Next, the **Winter Games** section is organized alphabetically by sport, each of which includes:

➤ The **Warm-Up:** How and where did the sport begin, and who invented it? Some of the sports started by implementing surrogate clubs and rocks (like hockey), others developed as means of defense (biathlon), and then there are the basic transportation modes: skating, skiing, bobsledding. We'll tell you about those very first games, who played them, and how the games came to be played the way they are today.

➤ **Spectator's Guide:** How do you play the game? How do you win? The Olympics feature many sports that the average fan may not follow on a regular basis (luge, for instance), including some with very unique scoring procedures. The scoring for several events—freestyle skiing, figure skating, and ski jumping among them—approaches a sort of mystical mathematics. The **Spectator's Guide** clears up the confusion fast, enabling you to grasp the essentials and get on with the most enjoyable part of Olympic viewing— watching the athletes perform. Our overview of the important rules, procedures, equipment, terminology, and technical demands of each sport enables you to better appreciate the spectacle at hand, and more accurately predict the medal winners.

➤ **Hopefuls:** For each event, who has the best chance of bringing home a medal? Based on pre-Olympic competitions held worldwide, our preview supplies the names of the favorites.

➤ **Schedule:** In which we answer the question, "When do they play?" The **Schedule** lists a full events calendar for each sport.

➤ **Highlights:** The Olympics have always invited a walk through history. Every time a medalist takes the stand, he or she is compared to the greats of past Olympics. From the first Winter Games in 1924 to the present, the **Highlights** trip back through the history of the event, relating notable wins, ignoble defeats, famous victors, favorite losers.

➤ **Medalists:** Who's won the event in the past, and by what margin? We provide a complete list of all gold, silver, and bronze winners, along with sponsoring country, winning times, and point totals or other scoring data.

➤ **Trivia Quiz:** What is an *axel* in figure skating, and why is it called that? Which American scored the game-winning goal against the Soviets in 1980? How do luge sliders steer? Which came first: the giant slalom or the super-G? Test your knowledge (and that of fellow Olympic fans) with each sport's trivia quiz.

Sprinkled throughout the regular features on these pages you'll find the odd fact, the tantalizing tidbit of lore that makes you want to accost your friends and co-workers with, "Did you know ..." You'll recognize these time-out morsels because they announce themselves like this:

> **fact:** At the alternative Summer Games held in boycotting Eastern bloc countries in 1984, more than 20 athletes posted better marks than those in the Los Angeles Olympics, and at least seven set new world records.

And like this:

> **fact:** A large proportion of China's Winter sports stars come from Manchuria.

They're part of the fun of appreciating the Games in a broader context, with a perspective on all the momentous and trivial threads woven into the fabric of the Olympic flag.

And finally, the *Olympic Factbook* is about people—all of whom can be found in the *Factbook*'s comprehensive **Index.**

The *Factbook* reports on dozens of past, present, and future Olympic stars, from Italian slalom king Alberto "La Bomba" Tomba to American speed-skating queen Bonnie Blair to Norwegian ice angel Sonja Henie. The *Factbook* also answers numerous "whatever happened to" questions, including:

➤ Stars of the 1980 gold-medal hockey team

➤ Legendary speedskater Eric Heiden and sister Beth

➤ The figure skaters who changed the sport—Ulrich Salchow, Richard Button, and Tenley Albright.

As you treat yourself to Olympics action with this *Factbook* in hand, you may read while you watch, watch while you read, or read, then watch (or just watch—and look it up later). No matter what your personal style, you'll have scored a perfectly enriching Olympic experience, and possibly set a record for amateur sports enjoyment.

You're ready for a personal best.

Acknowledgments

Our thanks to:

Mike Boyd, for his tireless typesetting efforts; Mary Krzewinski, for peerless design; Keith Reed for his efforts in securing photographs; Michael Harris for his legal expertise; and all the contributors, for writing well and meeting their deadlines. We would also like to thank the following organizations and, in particular, their media and communications people, for so cordially accommodating our pursuit of the facts:

United States Olympic Committee
International Olympic Committee
USA Track & Field
United States Biathlon Association
United States Bobsled and Skeleton Federation
United States Figure Skating Association
USA Hockey
United States Luge Association

United States Ski Association
United States International Speedskating Association
US Olympic Training Center, Colorado Springs
US Olympic Training Center, Lake Placid
United States Olympic Education Center, Marquette

CONTRIBUTORS

Tom Callahan: Dubbed a "writer's writer" by *Golf Digest*, veteran sports columnist Tom Callahan has covered 10 Olympics, 20 World Series, and 20 Super Bowls. An award-winning columnist for the *Washington Post* and contributing editor for *U.S. News & World Report*, Tom also spent 10 years as a senior writer for *Time* magazine and is currently on a round-the-world adventure writing a book about his favorite sport, golf.

George Cantor: One of the deans of Detroit sports writing (yet, he hastens to add, a man still in his prime), George Cantor is a *Detroit News* general columnist. George began his career with the *Detroit Free Press* in 1963, where he worked the baseball beat and served as travel editor. Prior to assuming the general columnist position at the *News*, he wrote a sports column for that paper. Cantor is the author of *Historic Black Landmarks: A Traveler's Guide, North American Indian Landmarks: A Traveler's Guide, The Great Lakes Guidebook,* and *Where the Old Roads Go.*

Eric Kinkopf: Eric is a former sports writer for the *Detroit Free Press* and, most recently, a sports columnist for the *St. Paul* (Minnesota) *Pioneer Press.* In 1990, Eric took first place in the Minnesota AP competition for human interest reporting and was nominated by the *Pioneer Press* for the Pulitzer Prize in feature writing (in 1986, he was nominated for a Pulitzer by the *Free Press*). Eric published his first novel in 1993, *Shooter,* based on his experiences as a police reporter for the *Detroit Free Press.* A resident of Shaker Heights, Ohio, he currently makes his living as a freelance writer.

Brian Lysaght: Brian is a veteran reporter, world traveler, and avid Olympics watcher who is currently working as a freelance writer. He lists Shane MacGowan as one of his major influences.

Marie MacNee: A resident of Grosse Pointe, Michigan, Marie is a freelance writer and editor. A contributor to the 1992 ***Factbook,*** she claims she had nothing to do with rearranging the Olympic schedule to suit her professional designs. Marie has contributed to numerous publications on a wide variety of topics, including two editions of *Videohound's Golden Movie Retriever* and *She Said, He Said.*

Pat Schutte: A hired hand with the AP award–winning *Ann Arbor News* sports staff, the ***Factbook*** ski correspondent spends his spare time sliding down mountains on skis, snowboards, and—more often than not—the seat of his pants.

Les Stone: Les is an Ann Arbor–based freelance writer and contributor to several reference books, including *The World Encyclopedia of Soccer, Newsmakers,* and *Videohound's Golden Movie Retriever.* His favorite pastimes involve watching things on screens, including Olympic broadcasts and motion pictures (particularly those with subtitles).

David Yntema: A historian of American culture, David has been involved with the "Made in America" project for Dearborn, Michigan's Henry Ford Museum and Greenfield Village and is currently teaching history at Wayne State University in Detroit. An avowed curling fan and Blackhawks devotee, Davis swears that Lloyd Pettit's is the greatest voice in broadcasting.

OPENING CEREMONIES

On Your Marks

▼

TOM CALLAHAN

ecause they originally exercised in the nude, Greek Olympians probably never envisioned Winter Games. But there must be a charm to chilblains, for the more appealing of the quadrennial conventions in the Olympics' two-party system is often the younger, smaller, more mysterious winter segment. Just the thought of a global snowball fight is amusing, but think of it as a happier reason for the world to shiver....

US reporters have their most penetrating questions ready (How tall do you have to be to qualify for the giant slalom?), having just reminded themselves that luge is the French word for Flexible Flyer. At Sarajevo in 1984, intent on seeing those marvelous birdmen sail off their 90-meter sliding boards, two sportswriters hopped an unattended ski lift. Halfway up the foggy mountain, the one from Atlanta asked the handsomer one from New York, "Is this more dangerous than you thought?" The chair seemed to tilt away, leaving them hugging the frame and dangling in the sky. It wasn't until a rider passed by going the other way that they glanced straight up and pulled down the crossbar that holds you in.

Other handy things to know: the Alpine skiers are the ones showing their trademarks to the cameras; the Nordic skiers have the icicles in their beards. Slaloms are perfectible, downhills only survivable. The best biathlete is one whose pounding heart won't betray his rifle's aim. And the speed skaters are the kind dressed like frogmen....

The athletes in these sweet, neglected sports have been up at dawn polishing their dreams, and are ready now to show us how far, how fast, how beautifully they can go. We so seldom drop by their world, and yet are made welcome.... "I am alone with the mountain," Jean-Claude Killy used to murmur, but the golden skier of Grenoble was also known to drop his pants in midair and park his Volkswagen in the hotel lobby. This is serious stuff, but it promises to be fun.

Olympic representatives parade through Chamonix, France, before the first Winter Games.

Faster, Higher, Colder: The Evolution of the Winter Games

▼

Winter is icummen in,
Lhude sing Goddamm,
Raineth drop and staineth slop,
And how the wind doth ramm!
Ezra Pound

The Games of Winter are bastard children of the Ancient Games; Theogenes might have known boxing, but he didn't know the bobsled. None of the winter sports can trace its lineage to the ancient Games—except, perhaps, hockey, which might convincingly demonstrate a pugilistic patrimony—thanks to the simple fact that the Greeks weren't into winter sports. For that matter, they weren't into winter.

But that's not to say that the Winter Games don't share in the Olympic spirit. In fact, the Olympic motto—*citius, altius, fortius* ("faster, higher, stronger")—couldn't suit the cold Games better. The Games of Winter are largely games of speed, where the athlete's greatest competition comes not from other athletes but from the laws of nature. The snow sports are gravity sports: athletes attain speeds so high that there's something transcendental to it all. Sights and sounds become an impressionistic blur, and gravitational pull can magnify a minute miscalculation to herculean proportions. A certain degree of danger is part of the climate of winter, where the agony of defeat is sometimes grieved posthumously.

In many of the winter sports, time is all. It's measured in increments unfathomable to most mortals—to the hundredth and even to the thousandth of a second—and merely tensing a muscle at the wrong moment can relegate a record-threatening time to middle-of-the-pack anonymity. In these events, the margin of error has an inverse relationship to speed. And where there's speed, there's technology; "faster, higher, and stronger" may be the Olympic motto, but "aerodynamics" is the Olympic mantra.

And, finally, the Winter Games are those of counterpoint. There's no more objective measure than the stopwatch, nor is there a more subjective judgement

5

than that of a panel of partisan judges quantifying "style" and "artistic impression." True, figure skaters may be getting stronger and jumping higher, but the philosophy behind the discipline would have been as foreign to the Ancient Games as chariot races are to us now.

In short, the Winter Games are in some ways pedigreed descendants of the Ancient Games and of Baron de Coubertin's Olympic vision. In other ways, they share little or nothing with their classical predecessors. But one thing is sure: they always entertain and inspire.

A Brief History of Winter

Winter sports were no stranger to the Olympics before the Winter Games were christened in 1924. Skating first figured into the Olympic roster—with men's, women's, and pairs events—at the London Games in 1908. The men's winner that year, Sweden's Ulrich Salchow, enjoys a certain immortality, having had a jump named after him. Hockey's first Olympic moment came at the Antwerp Games in 1920, when the Canadian team captured the first of the six gold medals maple leaf players would reap over the course of the next seven Games.

Although the first official Winter Games were held in Chamonix in 1924, they weren't official at the time: the Scandinavian countries objected to the idea of a Winter Olympics, fearing that they'd interfere with their Nordic Games. Not that they had any reason to object: the Nordic countries—together with the Soviets, in their various incarnations—have hoarded the Winter Games' precious medals from the start. Norway, with a population just about equal to Minnesota's, has accrued more Winter medals than any other country.

Originally called the "International Sports Week," the Chamonix Games were grandfathered into Olympic status in 1926, two years after they took place. Only sixteen countries—Austria, Belgium, Canada, Czechoslovakia, Finland, France, Great Britain, Hungary, Italy, Latvia, Norway, Poland, Sweden, Switzerland, the US, and Yugoslavia—competed. Norway and Finland set the stage for years to come, taking four of the fourteen gold medals each.

Joining the veteran favorites of figure skating and ice hockey, four other sports—bobsled, nordic skiing, ski jumping, and speedskating—debuted at the 1924 Games. Since then, sports have been added, events have been included, dropped and transmuted, and women—the Winter Games' sometimes neglected sex—have been increasingly, and in some cases begrudgingly, included.

Alpine skiing was first included on the Olympic roster in 1936, the same year it received IOC recognition, and only twenty-five years after the staging of the first downhill race. Women's alpine events have kept pace with the men's, which hasn't always been the case with other sports in the Winter Games. Freestyle, skiing's most recent addition, first enjoyed medal status in 1992.

Nordic events, although included in the Games from the start, have been slower to include women: the 1952 Oslo program added the first women's nordic event (a 10km), and it wasn't until 1984 that a longer women's event was added (a 20km). While Albertville put the women's biathlon on the Winter program in 1992, ski jumping/nordic combined medalists still belong to a men-only fraternity.

So do bobsledders. Four-man teams charged down the bahn at Chamonix in 1924, but two-man teams didn't compete in the Games until the Lake Placid Games in 1932, when the US team grabbed top honors in both events.

Speedskating, always popular among the Scandinavian countries, has been part of the Winter Games from the beginning; it was speedskater Charles Jewtraw, in fact, who garnered the first official Winter Games medal. Women's events weren't added until much later: although the 1932 Games included one women's speedskating event, women sat on the sidelines another twenty-eight years before women's speedskating became a medal sport. Short track speedskating, an equal-opportunity sport, proved its mettle at Calgary as a demonstration sport; both men's and women's individual and relay events gained medal status at the 1992 Games.

Luge events, although staged on bobsled bahns, didn't appear in the Games until 1964, when both men's and women's events were added to the Olympic program, in spite of critics' protests over the sport's danger. While men compete in both double and single sleds, women compete in singles only. The skeleton—a sled ridden in a head-first, prone position—has found its way into the Games on exactly two occasions, in 1928 and in 1948; by order of the Olympic poohbahs, skeleton events appear only when St. Moritz hosts the Games.

1924

Chamonix

The First Olympic Winter Games

cold facts: Countries competing: 16
Guys: 281
Gals: 13
Most Medaled Country:
Norway (17)
Uncle Sam's rank: 3rd

The International Sports Week—later dubbed the Winter Games—is at first not supported by the Scandinavian countries, whose Nordic Games are thought to be in conflict with the Winter Games. The Games nonetheless receive a go-ahead. Norway and Finland own the Chamonix Games, which include figure skating, ice hockey, bobsledding, speedskating, nordic skiing, and curling; meanwhile, alpine skiing waits in the wings for its Olympic moment. The IOC—which had also opposed the introduction of Winter Games—approves the official addition of a winter cycle at the Congress of Prague in 1925, and Chamonix is retroactively given the title of the First Olympic Winter Games.

- American Charles Jewtraw speeds to the first gold of the Winter Games, out-muscling his speedskating competition despite his mother country's lukewarm sentiment for the sport.

- 30-year-old Finnish speedskater Clas Thunberg captures the 1500m, the 5000m, and the "all around" title, an event contested only in 1924.

- In women's figure skating, last place falls to an eleven-year-old unknown from Norway named Sonja Henie.

- Cross-country skiers from Scandinavian countries nab the first eleven places in the 15km event.

- Switzerland finds gold on the bobsled run, but the US team fails to prove its mettle.

- Norwegian-born American Anders Haugen garners fourth place in the large hill ski jump. Decades later, at the age of 83, he is awarded the bronze medal when an error in the scores is discovered.

- Military patrol—the grandfather of the biathlon—is demonstrated for the first time, with repeat exhibitions in 1928, 1936, and 1948.

- Two days before the closing ceremony, The International Ski Federation (FIS) is formed.

1928

St. Moritz

The Second Olympic Winter Games

cold facts: Countries competing: 25
Guys: 366
Gals: 27
Most Medaled Country:
Norway (15)
Uncle Sam's rank: 2nd

Not for the last time, weather wreaks havoc on the Winter Games: two of the four bobsled runs and a speedskating event are canceled due to unseasonal weather. Norway continues its Winter Games hegemony, taking six golds, four silver, and five bronzes back to the land of the Midnight Sun. The definition of "amateur"—an issue at the Congress of Prague in 1925—continues to plague organizers.

- Comely Sonja Henie—the youngest member of the class of '28—wins her first gold for her "Dying Swan" routine, kicking off a new era in figure skating.

- Sweden's Gillis Grafström grabs his third straight gold in men's figs.

- Speedskater Irving Jaffee loses out on a gold medal when the 10,000m race is cancelled due to thawing ice.

- Clas Thunberg earns his fifth speedskating gold medal, and is the most gilded Winter Olympian until Eric Heiden comes along.

- Five-man bobsled teams make their first—and only—appearance. The golden era of American bobsledding begins: from the late 1920s through the 1940s, US sled teams medal 14 times, including five golds. The 16-year-old US driver is the youngest gold medalist at St. Moritz.

- The Canadian ice hockey team—a reincarnation of the 1926 Toronto University team—decimates the competition, shutting out Sweden, Great Britain, and Switzerland in the final round.

- Sweden sweeps the 50km cross-country event, which begins with near-zero temperatures and concludes in balmy 70-degree weather.

- Norway's Jacob Tullin-Thams proves he'd do anything to defend his ski-jumping gold, crashing at the end of a 73m jump. Tullin-Thams's jump far exceeds jump course designers' expectations.

1932

Lake Placid
The Third Olympic Winter Games

cold facts: Countries competing: 17
Guys: 277
Gals: 30
Most Medaled Country:
US (12)

Lake Placid hosts 17 gaming nations, despite a spate of warm weather. With snow brought over from Canada, a last-minute chill provides favorable conditions, although the four-man bobsled event is postponed until after the closing ceremony. New York State Governor Franklin D. Roosevelt opens the ceremony, while First Lady Eleanor bobs down the sled run.

- 1920's golden pugilist Eddie Eagan medals on the 1932 bobsled team, becoming the first Summer–Winter medalist of the Games.

- 52-year-old American pairs skater Joseph Savage slides into the geriatric hall of fame as the oldest contestant ever in the Winter Games.

- Blond bombshell Sonja Henie—once again the youngest competitor at the Games— charms her second figure skating gold at Lake Placid.

- Figure skating moves indoors, and women's speedskating is introduced as a demonstration sport (but must wait 28 years for full-metal status). Unaccustomed to mass—or pack— starts, the European speedskating men are decidedly disadvantaged under the American rules.

- Scandinavian skiers repeat their 11-top-place sweep of the cross-country 15km, and the 50km racers battle a blizzard.

- A dozen seven-dog power sled teams pull canine sled racing—as a demo sport— into the public eye.

1936

Garmisch-Partenkirchen

The Fourth Olympic Winter Games

cold facts: Countries competing: 28
Guys: 680
Gals: 76
Most Medaled Country:
Norway (15)
Uncle Sam's rank: 5th

Weather again troubles the Winter Games, this time due to blizzard conditions in southern Germany. A record 28 countries participate, while record crowds attend, despite rumors of a boycott to protest the German government's racist policies. The Games are not the sole attraction: Adolph Hitler draws quite a crowd, swelling the daily population of Garmisch-Partenkirchen to nearly 75,000.

- Thrice-gilded Sonja Henie skates away with one last gold before heading to the Hollywood hills.

- Europeans dominate the victory stand when speedskaters return to the continental style of racing against the clock.

- The alpine combined event is added to the Olympic roster at the German Games, and homeboy Franz Pfnur nabs the first gold.

- Norwegian Birger Ruud successfully defends his ski jumping title—the first such Olympic success—and finds more gold on the slopes in the men's combined Alpine event.

- Rudi Ball—one of two Jewish athletes recalled from France by Germany—laces up for the German ice hockey team.

- Puckish Brits surprise all with an ice hockey win, although most of the team was born under the Maple Leaf.

1940 & 1944

Gone Ice Fishin'

Sapporo says *sayonara* to the 1940 Winter Games when the Sino-Japanese war breaks out in 1937; the Games are rescheduled for St. Moritz, but when the Swiss insist that ski instructors don't count as professional athletes, the IOC says *au revoir* to the alps. Garmisch-Partenkirchen plans to host a second go-round, but the German invasion of Poland in 1939 back-burners all talk of fun and Games. The 1944 Games—scheduled for Cortina d'Ampezzo—are cancelled due to war.

1948

St. Moritz

The Fifth Olympic Winter Games

cold facts: Countries competing: 28
Guys: 636
Gals: 77
Most Medaled Countries:
Norway, Sweden, and
Switzerland (10)
Uncle Sam's rank: 4th

After much voting and shuffling, the IOC determines to hold the Games on neutral slopes, in Switzerland. Twenty-eight countries participate, while the Japanese and German teams are invited to stay home. Post-war woes dampen the public's enthusiasm, and poor weather cooperates not at all with the spirit of fair play. Debates over amateurism take on hockey-brawlish proportions, and Sunday competition is again hotly contested.

- American Dick Button—the year's youngest champion—ices the competition in the men's division by landing a double axel and eight out of nine judges' votes.

- John Heaton slides the US to victory two times in two decades in the skeleton toboggan—an event held only when St. Moritz hosts the Games.

- The hockey tournament causes tempers to flare when the IOC bans the American teams from competing because of commercial affiliations. After disowning the tournament, the IOC agrees to approve the results provided that the American teams be excluded from the rankings.

- Gretchen Fraser grabs a silver for the US in the women's alpine combined.

- Birger Ruud—now a concentration camp veteran—concludes his ski-jumping career, at the age of 37, with a silver.

- Swedes prove themselves gluttons for punishment in the 3500m winter pentathlon exhibition.

1952

Oslo

The Sixth Olympic Winter Games

cold facts: Countries competing: 30
Guys: 624
Gals: 108
Most Medaled Country:
Norway (16)
Uncle Sam's rank: 2nd

No strangers to winter sports festivals or winter sports medals, the Norwegians—who once objected to the Winter Games—stage the first Olympics to be hosted by a Nordic country. Seasoned by the Scandinavian Nordic Games, and sharing in the Scandinavian countries' massive medal haul—tallying 352 Winter medals at Games' start—the Norwegians put on a show that's touted as the best Winter Games to date. 700,000 spectators turn out despite the fickle arctic weather, while up to 150,000 ski-jump groupies line the slopes of Holmenkollen Hill—a record attendance for an Olympic event, in winter *or* summer. The crowds aren't confined to the Olympic venues: on February 18, 1952—an especially profitable day for the mother country, precious metal-wise—Oslo workers pour into the streets to toast their country's victors.

Basking in its moment in the sun, Norway collects seven gold medals, three silver, and six bronze: it is the most medaled and the most gilded nation of the 1952 Games. Homeboy Hjalmar Andersen collects three gold medals in as many days, winning both the 5,000m and 10,000m speedskating events by a whopping margin of victory that has yet to be equaled. Downhill skier Stein Eriksen picks up the giant slalom gold for the mother country en route to fame and fortune, capturing the first alpine Olympic gold to be awarded to a skier from outside of the alps. Together with the Finns, the Norwegians sweep the cross-country medals, garnering top honors in the 18km and in the nordic combined. And to no one's surprise, they collect both ski jumping golds; by Games' end, Norway owns 14 of the 18 Olympic ski jumping medals.

- Germany and Japan return to the Olympic flock, but the Soviet team declines to attend, while British athletes sport black armbands in respect of King George VI's funeral.

- Dick Button sews up another gold, wowing the judges with a triple loop in his figure skating routine.

- French boy skater Alain Giletti garners fame not for his twelfth-place finish but for being the youngest-ever male athlete in the Winter Games, at the ripe old age of 12 years and 5 months.

- Silver-skiing Martin Stokken—a nordic skier from the host country—is one of not-too-many athletes to compete in the Winter and Summer Games in the same year.

- The fairer sex kicks and glides into their first Winter Olympics when women's nordic ski races are added to the program.

- Andrea Mead Lawrence shreds the competition in Oslo to become the first US skier in Olympic history to slide to two gold medals in Alpine events.

- The Canadian hockey team grabs another gold medal, with a daunting Olympic record of 37 wins, one loss, and three ties between 1920 and 1952.

- Germany's two-man bobsled team slides to victory, even though their sled is sixteen years old.

Cortina d'Ampezzo

The Seventh Olympic Winter Games

cold facts: Countries competing: 32
Guys: 687
Gals: 132
Most Medaled Country:
USSR (16)
Uncle Sam's rank: tied
for 4th

For the first time, the Winter Games hit the silver screen. Sunshine melts snow imported to the spanking-new ski runs, causing practice runs to be canceled. A stadium built to hold 10,000 spectators—in a town of 6,000 or so—showcases the skating and hockey events. Crown Prince Olav, Prince Harald, and some 32,000 of the hoi polloi attend, and many of the teams from the 32 participating nations go on to Oslo for the World Championship Winter Games the following month.

- Italian skier Giuliana Chenal-Minuzzo is the first female oath-taker in Olympic history.

- Soviets enter the Games for the first time since 1908, sweeping the medals not for the last time.

- The 1956 Games mark the end of the US bobsledders' winning streak. 47-year-old Italian Giacomo Conti bobs to victory and his place on the geriatric rolls, as the Winter Games' oldest gold medalist.

- Speedskaters set chilling records on the fastest Olympic ice ever—at an altitude of 1755m.

- Finns soar to victory with a new ski jump technique, shutting out erstwhile Norwegian champs in the first six events.

- Austrian skier Toni Sailer does a broom job on the slopes, making the first clean sweep of the three men's alpine events.

Squaw Valley

The Eighth Olympic Winter Games

cold facts: Countries competing: 30
Guys: 521
Gals: 144
Most Medaled Country:
USSR (21)
Uncle Sam's rank: 2nd
TV Rights: CBS/ $50,000/
15 hrs

Following on the heels of the 1959 Pan-American Games in Chicago, the climate is right for the 1960 Winter Games. Except for the blizzard. The Disney-directed opening ceremonies start off in cartoon-catastrophe fashion: driving snow delays the festival, prop-laden trucks sit in traffic in some faraway place, the Master of Opening Ceremonies is called to stay an execution, and the vice president (Richard Nixon) acts as his stand-in. Awarded to Squaw Valley over Innsbruck by a less-than-landslide IOC vote (32-30), the Olympics host competitors from some 30 nations who boldly go where no athlete has gone before. Thanks to landowner Alexander Cushing—and nearly $9 million in IOC funds—Squaw Valley is the first Winter Games venue to be constructed on demand, in what had been a town of 300 inhabitants. What's more, a new Olympic age dawns as television seizes the day.

- American Carol Heiss makes good on her vow to capture a figure skating gold, garnering unanimous first-place votes from the judges.

- Women's speedskating is made official, only 28 years after it was first demonstrated at the Games.

- Metal alpine skis debut at the Games, and no skier medals twice.

- East and West Germany compete as one. The national anthem: Beethoven's Ninth.

- Soviet speedskater Yevgeny Grishin skids and stumbles in the final stretch, but still manages the gold by one second.

- The underdog US ice hockey team cleans up on the ice, winning every one of its games; the final match between the US and the Soviets concludes with the 8500 spectators delivering a standing ovation.

- Cross-country skiers whistle "Gunsmoke" as biathlon joins the Winter Games as a medal sport.

- Bobsledding is 86'd from the

Games due to the prohibitive cost of erecting a bob run.

Innsbruck

The Ninth Olympic Winter Games

cold facts: Attendance: 36 countries
Guys: 986
Gals: 200
Most Medaled Country:
USSR (25)
Uncle Sam's rank: 7th
TV Rights: ABC/
$597,000/ 17 hrs

The Games come of computer age as microchips help officials to judge and time events. Having missed hosting the 1960 Games by the seat of their lederhosen, the Austrians are primed for the event, which is introduced by the first Winter torch relay. Over one million spectators attend the festivities, where a new record of 36 countries compete. The weather again plays the master of ceremonies, and 3,000 soldiers from the home country haul snow by the ton to the Olympic venue.

- Soviet skaters Ludmila Belousova and Oleg Protopopov introduce classical ballet to skating.

- Soviet speedskater Lydia Skoblikova brushes off the competition, nabbing a gold medal in all four of the women's events.

- Over strenuous objections about the danger of the sport, luge is added to the Olympic program. The German Democratic Republic makes a clean sweep of the medals, not for the last time.

- Italian bobsledder Eugenio Monti earns the Pierre de Coubertin Fair Play Trophy for supplying the replacement bolt that allows the Brit team to bob to victory.

- Skiers at Innsbruck are clocked to the hundredth of a second for the first time at the Games. The sisters Goitschel, from Val d'Isere, France, place one–two in the slalom, and switch roles to place one–two in the giant slalom.

- India enters its first Winter Games, Korea competes as two teams, and the Swiss team—in atypical form—returns home *sans* medals.

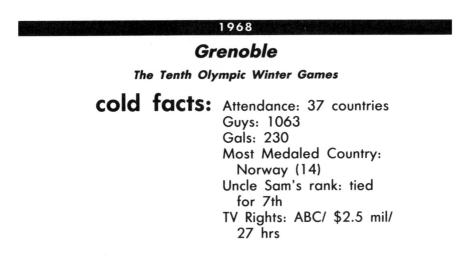

Grenoble

The Tenth Olympic Winter Games

cold facts: Attendance: 37 countries
Guys: 1063
Gals: 230
Most Medaled Country:
Norway (14)
Uncle Sam's rank: tied
for 7th
TV Rights: ABC/ $2.5 mil/
27 hrs

Charles de Gaulle opens the 1968 Winter Olympics, which, for the first time, recognize the East-West rift in Germany. A mere 70,000 spectators weather the snowy Games—whose organizers are criticized for a lack of logistical acumen—while another 500 million watch a celluloid spectacle from the comfort of home. Thousands of paper flowers drop from the sky during the opening ceremonies, and a microphone broadcasts the torchbearer's heartbeat as he runs up the stadium steps. Three months after Games' end, France is embroiled in chaos as the student riots begin.

- Nineteen-year-old American figure skater Peggy Fleming shimmers in gold, while the women's speedskating silver splits three ways among US women.

- French heartthrob Jean-Claude Killy storms the men's downhill competition to capture three gold medals.

- The men's slalom winner is hotly debated. Given a re-run when a mysterious French "worker" interferes with his second pass, Austrian Karl Schranz outscores Killy, but race officials refuse to accept his winning time.

- Italy's Franco Nones bests the Scandinavians in the 30km, becoming the first cross-country gold medalist to hail from a non-nordic country.

- Italy's Eugenio Monti—the previous Games' good sport—gets his just desserts with the bobsled gold.

- East Germany's three leading women lugers are disqualified

17

by the Jury of Appeals for illegally warming the runners of their sleds.

- Sex is tested at the Games: female competitors undergo sex tests for the first—and not the last—time.

1972

Sapporo

The Eleventh Olympic Winter Games

cold facts: Attendance: 35 countries
Guys: 927
Gals: 218
Most Medaled Country:
USSR (16)
Uncle Sam's rank: 6th
TV Rights: NBC/ $6.4 mil/
37 hrs

The first Winter Games to be held in Asia (originally scheduled for 1940), the 1972 Winter Olympics become the Sapporo inquisition. The argument over the definition of amateurism reaches new heights in semantic gymnastics, and Austrian ski-god Karl Schranz is DQ'd for the indiscretion of openly endorsing a ski manufacturer. The paparazzi flock to the event in record droves, outnumbering the athletes two to one, and some 54,000 spectators attend the $55 million hoopla.

- Austrian Trixie Schuba figures for gold in spite of her mediocre free skating performance. Scoring is soon revised to weight freeskating more heavily than compulsories.
- Dianne Holum muscles her way to a 1500m Olympic record and the first American gold in women's speedskating.
- Canada fuels the debate over professionalism, refusing to play hockey in protest of state-sponsored Eastern bloc teams.

- The GDR's female lugers recover from their Grenoble debacle, sweeping Sapporo of precious metals.
- American Barbara Cochran gets the edge on her slalom competition by the closest-ever margin—.02 seconds—winning the first US alpine gold in 20 years.
- Diminutive Soviet skier Vyacheslav Vedenine earns his country's first individual cross-country gold, winning the 30km by almost one minute.

18

Innsbruck

The Twelfth Olympic Winter Games

cold facts: Attendance: 37 countries
Guys: 1013
Gals: 218
Most Medaled Country:
USSR (27)
Uncle Sam's rank: tied
for 3rd
TV Rights: ABC/ $10 mil/
44 hrs

The Olympics are awarded to the Tyrolean venue in 1973 after the state of Colorado vetoes a $5 million bond issue to finance the Games in Denver. Innsbruck makes use of many facilities from the 1964 Games, constructing a new bob run for their second stint as Winter host. Athletes are again outnumbered almost two to one, this time not by the paparazzi but by the Austrian police. The flu makes a surprise appearance at the Games, striking 25 percent of the athletes and inspiring a drug-testing nightmare. In attendance are 1.5 million spectators, while millions of international viewers enjoy the Games up close and personal thanks to $4 million of television equipment. Interviews, background vignettes, and expert commentary bring the Games to new heights of infotainment.

- Dorothy Hamill—singlehandedly changing the hairstyle of American girl-teens—pirouettes to the women's gold in figure skating.

- Champion cyclist Sheila Young thrice medals—in speedskating—to become the first American woman to medal three times in a single Games, and the only person to be a world sprint champion in cycling and skating in the same year.

- Smashing Olympic records at 102.828 km/h, Austrian skier Franz Klammer nails the men's downhill gold.

- Hanni Wenzel brings home Liechtenstein's first medal, a bronze in the women's slalom, while West German Rosi Mittermaier misses becoming history's first grand dame of all three alpine races by twelve-hundredths of a second.

- Returning home with the 30km silver, Bill Koch is the first American to garner a nordic ski medal.

- With a less-than-enthusiastic reception by the IOC, ice dancing takes its place in the Games.

19

Lake Placid

The Thirteenth Olympic Winter Games

cold facts: Attendance: 37 countries
Guys: 1012
Gals: 271
Most Medaled Country:
East Germany (23)
Uncle Sam's rank: 3rd
TV Rights: ABC/ $15.5
mil/ 53 hrs

Following on the heels of mega-bucks media-blitz Winter Games, the Lake Placid Games are touted as "an Olympics in perspective"—that is, an event for the participants, not the entertainment seekers. But Lake Placid is entertainment, although not always intentionally, and the 1980 Winter Games are rife with gaffs and imbroglios of Olympic proportions. So much so that the New York State governor is forced, a week into the Games, to declare a limited state of emergency: the Adirondack hamlet is virtually frozen in state by a paralyzed bus system, leaving scores of shivering spectators out in the cold. Rebuilt from the 1932 Games, the Village becomes a post-Games, tundra-like penal institution.

- American skating pair Tai Babilonia and Randy Gardner—dubbed the "star-crossed lovers" by the press—figure to medal but are sidelined by injury.

- Eric Heiden shuts out the competition, becoming the first speedskater to nab all five golds.

- In the women's events, Beth Heiden takes home a bronze for the US in the 3000m.

- Willie Davenport and Jeff Gadley from the US, and Canadian Bob Wilson—all bobsledders—are, as far as records indicate, the Winter Games' first black athletes.

- The US hockey team does a zamboni on the 16-year Soviet winning streak en route to victory against the Finns.

- Finishing in 19th place in the two-man bob, and in 21st place in the four-man, Sweden's 53-year-old Carl-Erik Eriksson is the first athlete to compete six times in the Winter Games.

- The women's slalom is staged in two runs for the first time at the Games, and Hanni Wenzel picks up Liechtenstein's first Olympic gold.

- American Phil Mahre slips into second place in the slalom, despite a lot of hardware em-

20

bedded in his ankle thanks to an early season accident.

- Soviet cross-country ski racer Nikolai Zimyatov three times poles to gold (capturing yet another in 1984, for the 30km), while teammate Aleksandr Tikhonov captures his fourth consecutive biathlon relay gold.

Sarajevo

The Fourteenth Olympic Winter Games

cold facts: Attendance: 49 countries
Guys: 1127
Gals: 283
Most Medaled Country: USSR (25)
Uncle Sam's rank: tied for 5th
TV Rights: ABC/ $91.5 mil/ 63 hrs

At the Games' start, Yuri Andropov is dead, there is chaos in Beirut, and the Olympic venue is best known for having been the site of the assassination that led to World War I. Two years' work, with the assistance of the military, readies the Yugoslavian village with TV cables, new bobsled and luge runs, and ski lifts and trails. Succumbing to the perennial Winter Games fear of snowlessness, the Sarajevans invest in enough Swiss snow-making equipment to cover the cross-country loop, but not the downhill race courses. The US arrives with no squad of greenhorns: the stars-and-stripes team includes seven current or recent world title holders. A record 49 countries participate in the first Winter Games to be held in Eastern Europe. Accused again of verbal backflips, the IOC disqualifies two skiers because of "professionalism." A decade later, aggression in Bosnia has decimated most of the Olympic venues in the Bosnian capital.

- Dubbed "the GDR's Brooke Shields," Katarina Witt garners a figure skating gold by a narrow margin.

- All-American boy Scott Hamilton handily skates away with the men's gold, while Canadi-an Brian Orser figures for silver.

- Jayne Torvill and Christopher Dean's innovative Bolero routine points ice dancing in a new direction.

- American sprinter Dan Jansen

21

makes his first Olympic appearance, placing fourth in speedskating's 500m.

- East German speedskater Karin Enke—a.k.a. "monster woman"—outlegs the competition, setting Olympic records in the 1000m and 1500m.

- American skiers have a vintage year, as Bill Johnson wins the men's downhill and the brothers Mahre grab the top two spots in the men's slalom. In the women's events, Debbie Armstrong and Christin Cooper place one–two in the giant slalom.

- Finn Marja-Liisa Hamalainen is 1984's first double-gold-medalist, winning the women's 5km and 10km cross-country ski races.

Calgary

The Fifteenth Olympic Winter Games

cold facts: Attendance: 57 countries
Guys: 1270
Gals: 364
Most Medaled Country:
USSR (29)
Uncle Sam's rank: tied
for 8th
TV Rights: ABC/ $309 mil/
95 hrs

Barely past its centennial year, Canada's energy capital hosts a cowboy version of the Games. Calgary mayor Ralph Klein avers, "The Olympics should be the best big party any of us has ever been to. If it's not, we may have missed the point." At Calgary, no one misses the point. Olympic mascots Howdy and Hidy greet stampedes of urban cowpersons, cowgirl crooner k.d. lang cavorts on stage, and the grandstands are a blur of stetsons and blue denim.

Weather again takes center stage, as Chinook winds produce plenty of sound and fury: 70mph gusts of wind huff and puff and blow snow where it's not supposed to go, forcing many of the refrigerated sports events to be cancelled. The second largest city to host the Winter Games, Calgary is rife with logistical problems: situated some 90 kilometers from the other venues, the alpine and nordic events incite much Olympic grousing.

Under the tutelage of oilman-Olympic committee president Frank King—known as the Man Who Would Be Ueberroth—the Games strike it big in commercial revenues, netting profits of Olympic proportions. Television rights alone garner three times the tag for the Sarajevo Games' rights.

- France's World Cup-less Franck Piccard underdogs the competition—who fall and fly off the icy downhill course—to pick up the gold for the men's super-G and bronze for the downhill.

- Italian Stallion Alberto Tomba—seasoned with seven World Cup victories—finds gold in the gates, capturing the men's slalom and giant slalom titles.

- American speedskater Bonnie Blair takes back the world record from East German Christa Rothenburger—whose tenure lasted two months—crossing the 500m finish a skate's length ahead.

- US hopes for a men's speed-skating medal are shattered when sprinter Dan Jansen—who receives the news of his sister's death during the Games—catches an edge and slides into the wall on hands-and-knees.

- Short track speedskating—dubbed "kung fu war on ice"—debuts as a demonstration sport.

- The press dubs the men's figure skating competition "dueling Brians." American Brian Boitano—the "technical one"—goes for gold, while Canadian Brian Orser silvers.

- American Debi Thomas's disappointing third-place finish allows Canadian figure skater Elizabeth Manley a surprise silver.

- Actress-aspiring Katarina Witt is the first to twice don the gold necklace in figure skating since Sonja Henie.

- The US hockey team, skating on thin ice, finishes seventh and is jeered by the IOC President.

- Three-time Soviet ice-dancing champions Natalia Bestemianova and Andrei Bukin—a.k.a. "B and B"—score perfect sixes, despite whispers of "vulgarity."

Albertville

The Sixteenth Olympic Winter Games

cold facts: Attendance: 64 countries
Guys: 1318
Gals: 490
Most Medaled Country:
Germany (26)
Uncle Sam's rank: 6th
TV Rights: CBS/ $243 mil/
116 hrs

Back in the Savoie again, the Games flaunt a Gallic flare for extravagance while sometimes flouting tradition. Thrice-gilded homeboy Jean-Claude Killy, co-president of the billion-dollar budgeted Olympic Organizing Committee, promises to send spectators home "feeling that they spent a fortnight on another planet." A zanier-than-thou Opening Ceremony features lugers in teeter-totters and a yo-yo ballet of bungee-corded dancers. Traditionalists liken the new wave extravaganza to a performance-artsy interpretation of Dr. Seuss on acid.

A pre-Games avalanche gives organizers visions of snow-buried spectators, but February's snow is neither too little nor too much: only one event is postponed due to weather, and nary an ersatz flake hits the slopes.

The last of the quadrennial Games, Albertville marks a number of firsts. The erstwhile Soviet Union competes as a five-state alliance, while the two Germanies march to the beat of a single drummer for the first time since 1964. The Baltic states of Estonia, Latvia, and Lithuania fly their own colors, while the 192-member Unified Team—a patchwork of athletes from Russia, Ukraine, Byelorussia, Kazakhstan, and Uzbekistan—flies the five-ringed Olympic banner and celebrates victory to the tune of Beethoven's "Ode to Joy." With neither flag nor anthem to call their own, and mourning the untimely demise of the Soviet State Committee for Physical Education and Sport, Team Beethoven doesn't sing the second-hand blues: only the newly-remarried but clearly-not-honeymooning German team attracts more precious metals. All but five of Germany's 26 medals go to athletes trained by the East German sports machine.

A post-Communism zeitgeist permeates the Games, ever-so-slightly tempering the Us-versus-Them jingoism that has tainted previous pageants. 1992 is a kinder, gentler year, at least in terms of brawling ice wars and other lapses in Olympic etiquette. Gravity is less kind, and the Winter of 1992 becomes the Year of the Fall: figure skating *faux pas* replace the compulsories, and the ski slopes are spattered with spectacular spills. Mogul skiing and short track speedskating debut as medal sports, and biathletic women take their first shot at Olympic medals. While ski ballet, speed skiing, and curling figure in the Olympic roster as non-medal events, demonstration sports sing their swan song in Savoie.

Back in the saddle again, CBS hosts the Games for the first time in thirty-two years, shelling out a tidy $243 million for the rights to televise Albertville, and another $100 million to make the prime-time party something to write home about. The 15-night media extravaganza scores ratings 10 percent higher than network executives' highest hopes. German TV's 180-hour coverage, however, gets the cold shoulder.

In all, 2,174 athletes—some of them born-again amateurs—test their mettle and *savoire-faire*. A Winter Games record of 64 nations compete, and a record-setting 20 countries medal. The spoils: Lalique crystal medallions, encircled by gold, silver, or bronze. Among the alumnae of the class of '92 are the most-medaled athlete and both the oldest and the youngest gold medalists in Winter Games history. At home and abroad it's the year of the woman: American women out-medal the men nine to two. Albertville takes the shape of Games to come, with numerous athletes' villages and temporary bleachers and stands. The 131 competitions take place in 10 different towns, scattered over 640-square savoyard miles, where French athletes, on home turf, turn in their best performance since Grenoble, 1968, *anno* Killy.

Albertville
(figure skating, ice dancing, and speedskating)

A new stadium, with a seating capacity twice the population of Albertville, holds the opening and closing ceremonies. Figure skaters and ice dancers perform in their own arena on ice to be envied. Albertville's outdoor ice track, however, is built only to last the Games and is exposed to temperature fluctuations. Far from Calgary-caliber, Albertville's speedskating ice is not the stuff that records are made of, and records stand unchallenged. Short-track speedskating events are held indoors in a traditional skating rink on a 111.12m circuit, with 28.85m straightaways.

- Figure skating's yawn-inspiring compulsories are 86'd from the Games.

- Even without a triple axel, American Kristi Yamaguchi cinches the women's figs gold while Japanese Midori Ito—whose triple axel makes her a triple threat—settles for silver.

- Smart-money Canadian skater Kurt Browning takes a tumble and falls from the running.

- Ukrainian Viktor Petrenko gets the jump on his costumed competition, earning the first-ever "Soviet"—for lack of a better term—figure-skating gold, in either the men's or the women's event.

- American Paul Wylie breaks a choking habit to garner silver and the evening's only standing ovation.

- Czech bronze medalist Petr

Barna lands the first Olympic quadruple jump.

- The Unified Team's Natalia Mishkutenok and Artur Dmitriev's artistic acumen earns them 4 1/2 minutes of golden fame in figure skating pairs.

- Sentimental American favorites Calla Urbanski and Rocky Marval—"The Waitress and the Truckdriver"—finish an unsentimental tenth in pairs.

- Champaign's favorite speeder Bonnie Blair does the vini-vidi-vici at Albertville, netting both the 500m and the 1000m speedskating gold. The B-woman's three-Winter gold haul makes her the goldenest of the Winter girls, and she's the first American woman to be gilded in consecutive Games.

- Ye Qiaobo sews up silver in the 500m—an infinitesimal two hundredths of a second shy of gold—to become the first Chinese athlete ever to win a Winter medal.

- "Roller derby on ice" debuts as a medal sport, and American Cathy Turner ices the pack in women's short track.

- German Jens-Uwe Mey stages a repeat performance in the men's 500m, dashing Heartbreak Kid Jansen's chance to medal. Jansen places fourth with a sluggish 500m time, more than a second off the world record time he posted three weeks earlier.

Val d'Isere
(men's alpine)

Killy sets out to make too-tame Olympic downhill courses a legacy of Games past, hiring erstwhile Olympian Bernhard Russi (1972 gold medalist and technician extraordinaire) to come up with a course designed for thrills and spills. Russi's course puts the adrenaline back in downhill, with a final "bump" that treats skiers to 200 feet of big air. The passwords for '92: tough, tight, and très technical. Val d'Isere, by the way, is the hometown of don of downhill Killy.

- First one down the hill, Austrian Patrick Ortlieb holds on to victory as the 55 other skiers take their runs.

- Calgary bronze medalist and Savoyard native Franck Piccard settles for silver, just five hundredths of a second from gold.

- All the polyvalent favorites in the men's combined event biff in a big way.

- 47 countries compete in the ski events. Snowless-country entrants include two Senegalese downhillers and a one-man Filipino team.

Les Menuires
(men's slalom)

Frowned upon by environmentalists for its environmental insensitivity, Les Menuires has quite the reputation as a très *moderne—some say* très *ugly—gallic playground. Gates sit a scant 50 feet from the finish.*

- The self-annointed "messiah of skiing" slaloms with the giants, making Alberto Tomba the first Olympic skier to defend a GS title. Albertville goes down in history as "Alberto-ville."

- Norwegian Finn Christian Jagge robs cappuccino-quaffing Tomba of slalom gold by .28 seconds.

- Born-again Luxemberger Marc Girardelli breaks his Olympic jinx, twice silvering in slalom.

- 20-year-old Norwegian *wunderkind* Kjetil Andre Aamodt—in his third year of World Cup competition—posts the fastest time in the super-G.

Meribel
(women's alpine and ice hockey)

The Russi-designed women's downhill run boasts a 2,717-foot vertical drop thanks to a special FIS dispensation to exceed international regulations. The "Face du Roc de Fer" soon gets a rep as the steepest and fastest women's downhill in the world, and a mid-course bump is dubbed "the noodle." Indoors, the 7,000-seat hockey arena has an almost intimate feel, and spectators sit as close as it gets to the action.

- Salzburg super slalomist Petra Kronberger garners her second slalom gold at the Games.

- Deborah "Tombanogni" Compagnoni is super-G's golden girl, despite two pre-season knee operations.

- New Zealand reaps its first Winter Games medal as Annelise Coberger captures slalom silver.

- Pernilla Wiberg puts Sweden back on the marquee, taking the country's first alpine gold since 1980.

- Four-time Olympic also-ran Blanca Fernández Ochoa—whose brother Francisco championed the slalom at Sapporo—reigns in Spain as slalom bronze medalist.

- Alaskan Hilary Lindh captures the first US women's downhill medal since 1976, while fourth-finishing US slalomist Julie Parisien finishes .05 seconds away from the medals podium.

- Team USA goalie Ray LeBlanc, on loan from the Chicago Black Hawks' farm team, posts the first Olympic shutout by an American goalie since 1964.

- The Unified Team's Big Red Machine lays to rest Canada's golden aspirations just hours before the Closing Ceremonies.

- The third place-winning Czech team's precision shooting checks top-seeded Sweden's hopes to medal.

- NHL alumnae enroll in the Games, although an NHL Dream Team is still an American dream that has yet to come true.

Tignes
(freestyle skiing)

Named after an old berg submerged in a hydroelectric power project in the 1950s, Tignes—the site of the first freestyle world championships—boasts a football-length field full-o-bumps the size of volkswagens. Freestyle skiing debuts as a medal sport.

- Heavily favored Jersey girl finds gold in them there hills: prima Donna Weinbrecht takes the first-ever women's mogul gold.

- Frenchman "Crazy Eddy" Grospiron, dubbed the "bad boy of the bumps," out-zud-niks the competition for the men's freestyle gold.

Courchevel
(ski jumping and nordic combined)

Courchevel, the so-called "Rodeo Drive in the snow," boasts the second most catastrophically expensive construction project of the Games. The earth under the ski jump moves during the winter prior to the Games, and organizers move heaven and earth to get a jump on the problem.

- Scissors-footed Finn Toni Nieminen becomes the youngest medalist ever in the Games, winning the 70m bronze. At the age of 16 years and 259 days, the flying Finn also becomes the youngest gold medalist ever in the Games by leaping past the competition in the 90m.

- "Eddie the Eagle" Edwards is offed from the English team due, he says, to politics.

- Thirteenth-finishing Jim Holland turns in the best US trans-Atlantic flight.
- More than half of the 58 jumpers fly in V-formation, while all top four finishers veto the classical style.
- Fabrice Guy and Sylvain Guillaume treat France to a double dip of nordic combined medals.
- Winning the team jump, Japan attracts its first Winter gold since Sapporo.

Les Arcs
(speed skiing)

The longtime host of speed skiing's World Cup, Les Arcs boasts a 40-degree track that earns the resort a reputation as the speed skier's mecca.

- Savoyard doctor Michel Prufer smashes his own world record by 5.558 km/h, easily turning in the demonstration sport's best Games time.
- Kamikaze skier Jeffrey Hamilton earns a third-place finish for the stars and stripes.
- Finnish Tarja Mulari's winning time breaks the previous women's world record.
- A practice run claims the life of 27-year-old Swiss skier Nicholas Bochatay the day before closing ceremonies.

Les Saisies
(cross-country and biathlon)

The snowiest of the Savoie venues, Les Saisies' cross-country course is carved in the forest in the shape of the five Olympic rings. The biathlon course, with its shooting range near the start and finish, helps spectators keep an eye on the competition.

- Norway does a broom job on men's cross-country events, sweeping all five of the men's golds. Teammates Vegard "The Viking" Ulvang and Bjorn Daehlie clean up three golds and a silver each.
- The Unified Team's Lyubov Egorova runs away with three golds and two silvers to become the most successful female athlete in a single Winter Games. At the age of 39 years and 352 days, she's the oldest woman to win a Winter gold.
- Teammate Elena Valbe stockpiles more precious metals, mounting the podium five times to collect one gold and four bronze medals.

- Women compete in the biathlon for the first time in Games history. Of the nine women's medals, the Unified Team's dudettes-in-arms grab four, while the German frauleins shoot for three.

- Biathlete Uro Velepec shoots and skis for Slovenia, eight months after having served as a sniper to protect government officials.

La Plagne
(bobsled and luge)

Built on an outcropping of schist, an unstable base for construction, the bobsled course turns into a winter's tale of woe when ammonia leaks from the refrigeration system. The tab: a whopping $20 million beyond the $22 million already spent. And that's not all: the banked turns melt during certain periods of the day. Plunging 1800 meters through 19 turns, the bob run at La Plagne favors the most skillful drivers. Luge events are held on the bob run, but starts are lower down the track.

- The celebrated former Soviet bobsled team competes for Latvia, six months into its newfound state of independence.

- NFL running-back-turned-bobsledder Herschel Walker is benched from the podium as the sled fails to break a 36-year losing streak.

- The first-ever Irish bob squad enters the Games, hobbin' and bobbin' to 32nd place.

- A royal disappointment in bobsled competition, Monaco's Prince Albert decides to keep his day job, finishing 43rd out of 46.

- Tattooed US slider Duncan Kennedy's tenth-place finish is a no-win luge time.

- Germany is still a big-time luger, sweeping the men's golds in both singles and the two-man.

- Sisters Doris and Angelika Neuner share the spoils, earning Austria's first women's luge necklaces.

- Reigning world champion Susi Erdmann slides to third place, adding to Germany's four-medal haul.

Pralognan
(curling)

Practiced in 25 countries, curling fails to attract a full crowd of spectators at Albertville, and journalists are less than smitten by the demonstration sport's sweep.

- Calgary *redux* in reverse, the Swiss men sweep gold away from the 1988-champion Norwegians.

- Tidy German women clean up with brooms while the Norwegian and Canadian teams ride sweep.

Multi-colored balloons fill McMahon Stadium during the Calgary Winter Olympics opening ceremonies.

From Albertville to Lillehammer: Olympic Milestones to Remember

▼

February

- Due to the shortened preparation period leading up to the Lillehammer Games, the USOC announces a special grant program called "Team '94" and approves $2 million to help fund seven winter sport national governing bodies.

- Tommy Williams, the youngest member of the 1960 gold-medaling US hockey team and US Hockey Hall of Famer, dies at the age of 51.

March

- Austrian skier Petra Kronberger bags her third consecutive women's overall World Cup title.

- Paul Accola nudges out Tomba to win the men's overall World Cup title.

- Kristi Yamaguchi is the first American woman since Peggy Fleming to defend her World Figure Skating Championships title; Ukrainian Viktor Petrenko garners the men's title.

- China's Ye Qiaobo makes up for her second place Olympic finish in the 500m speedskating event, winning the event at the World All-Around Championships in Calgary. German Peter Adeberg wins the men's 500m.

- Douglas Roby, former USOC president and IOC member, dies at the age of 94. During his tenure as USOC president, Roby suspended Tommie Smith (Olympic 200m gold medalist) and John Carlos (Olympic 200m bronze medalist) for staging the Black Power salute on the victory stand at Mexico City.

33

May

- Robert Kane, former president of the USOC and athletic director at Cornell, dies at the age of 81. The US Olympic team did not attend the 1980 Moscow Summer Games during Kane's tenure.

July

- The IOC approves a UN plan to allow Yugoslavs to compete individually at the Games. Yugoslav Olympic officials agree to the plan, even though it excludes Yugoslav national teams.

- A *USA Today* survey of US Olympic Team members reports that 68 percent believe that USOC support is better than it was four years earlier.

October

- LeRoy Walker is unanimously elected the 23rd president of the United States Olympic Committee, the USOC's first African-American president in its 92-year history. Walker's tenure carries through the 1996 Atlanta Games.

November

- Robert McCall, the Canadian figure skater who captured ice dancing bronze with partner Tracy Wilson, dies at the age of 33.

January

- The USOC selects figure skater Nancy Kerrigan as athlete of the month.

- Herb Brooks, erstwhile coach of the 1980 Team USA and pioneer of hybrid hockey, takes the helm of the New Jersey Devils. Brooks's post-Games resume includes being fired by the New York Rangers and by the Minnesota North Stars.

February

- The NHL announces it won't make professionals available to play at Lillehammer.

- The USA's 15-medal haul at the Winter World University Games in Zakopane, Poland—for alpine skiing, figure skating, and speedskating—is the team's best catch ever at the WWUG. The next WWUG will be held in Jaca, Spain in 1995.

- US skaters post their worst performance since 1964 at the 1993 World Figure Skating Championships in Prague. Taking no medals, the US earned a small berth of only two men's and two women's singles, three pairs, and one dance couple, making Lillehammer the smallest total US entry since 1976. Ukrainian *wunderkind* Oksana Baiul gives a stunning first-place performance, becoming the youngest world champion since Sonja Henie.

- Lillehammer hosts the 1993 World Cup Luge Teams competition. US slider Duncan Kennedy leads the US team to a fourth place finish on the Olympic Hunderfossen track; 1992 Games singles gold medalist Georg Hackl (Germany) slides on the winning team.

- Luger Wendel Suckow becomes the first US world titlist in Calgary, edging out Germany's favored Georg Hackl. In the sport's 29-year history of world championships, no American had ever medaled. Suckow is named USOC athlete of the month.

- German and Unified biathletes overachieve at the World Biathlon Championships at Borovets, Bulgaria and the World Cup in Lillehammer (in March).

- '92 Olympian Brian Shimer sets the course record at the four-man event of the bobsled World Championships in Igls,

Austria, capturing the bronze. Shimer pilots a test ride of the US's two-man Lillehammer prototype sled at Lake Placid.

- The Olympic Hall in Hamar, to the south of Lillehammer, receives its first big-league try-out during the 1993 World All-Around Speedskating Championships.

- Morioka, Japan hosts World Alpine Ski Championships and Falun, Sweden hosts World Nordic Ski Championships.

- 1984 Team USA hockey player Al Iafrate wins the All-Star hardest shot competition clocking in with a scorching 105.2 mph.

- Gretchen Fraser, a.k.a. "Gret-chen of the flying pigtails," receives a package with no return address. The contents: Fraser's 1948 gold and silver Olympic alpine medals, which had been stolen from a Sun Valley Lodge display.

- Host of future Games Greg Gumbel sneaks a peek at Lillehammer to prepare for his role as CBS Olympic anchor for the '94 Games.

- The Lillehammer townsfolk gather 'round Main Street to kick off the 365-day count-down to the 1994 Games. Every day thereafter, the town auctions a t-shirt bearing the countdown number, garnering more than 3000 big ones for the choicest threads.

March

- Figure skater Kristi Yamaguchi claims "discussions are taking place" with CBS regarding guest commentatorship at the 1994 Games.

- Lake Placid's luge track hosts US National Championship followed by Olympic Team Trials Middle Stage.

- Many top female downhillers boycott the final day of train-ing for a World Cup race on Hafjel mountain in Lillehammer to protest the choice of hills for the women's downhill course at the 1994 Games. Hosting the Games on Hafjel is com-pared to hosting the Masters golf tournament on a three-par course.

- Sun Valley girl Picabo Street silvers in the downhill at the Hafjel World Cup race, and the US team declines to partic-ipate in the Olympic protest.

- Altenmarkt, Austria hosts World Freestyle Ski Champi-onships.

April

- Sweden eliminates Team USA in the quarterfinals of the World Hockey Championships in Munich. Team USA's 2-2-2 finish has them seeded sixth in the 1994 Games.

- US figure skater Mark Mitchell, considered by many to be the US's best bona fide amateur, leaves longtime coach Ronna Gladstone to spend the summer under the tutelage of Carlo Fassi.

- NBC's Barcelona host Bob Costas is the golden boy of the 14th annual Sports Emmys in New York.

- Arkady Chernyshev, former coach of four gold-medaled Soviet Olympic hockey teams (1956-72), dies at the age of 78.

May

- The US Olympic Committee proposes designating $7.6 million from its 1993-96 budget to expand its Operation Gold program to raise bonuses for top athletes.

- The US Figure Skating Association approves eliminating athlete trust funds. Under the old trust fund system, the USFSA held skater's earnings in trust until he or she turned pro.

- The Istanbul, Turkey, Olympic Bid Committee matches offers from Sydney, Australia, and Beijing, China, in its bid for the 2000 Games. The committee pledges to pay travel costs for all athletes, officials, coaches, and referees, to the tune of $20 million for 15,000 participants.

- Organizers announce that the 1994 Goodwill Games in St. Petersburg, Russia will feature 24 sports, including short track speedskating.

- Team USA Olympic hockey coach Tim Taylor tools up for team selection, holding tryouts for collegians in Lake Placid, with a second tryout in June.

- Stepping out of a Ferrari 348, Alberto Tomba tells reporters at Misano Autodom in Italy that he might forsake skiing for auto racing "within two or three years."

- Herb Brooks, former Team USA coach, resigns as coach of the New Jersey Devils.

June

- 100th IOC session.
- The Lillehammer Olympic Organizing Committee acquiesces to protesters' demands to move the 1994 women's downhill course from straightforward Hafjell mountain to the more difficult men's course on Kvitfjell.
- The USOC Executive Committee approves the bonus formula for Operation Gold's $7.6 million program to reward athletic performance.
- ISU approves Brian Boitano's return to amateurism. Other born-again amateurs include Christopher Bowman, Scott Hamilton, and Annet Pötzsch.
- USOC approves Children's Defense Fund founder Marian Wright Edelman's nomination to USOC Board of Directors.
- Miller Lite advertisements—featuring luge bowling—offend luge officials, who claim, "It's easy to confuse people about the sport."
- Iran threatens to boycott the 1996 Summer Games, even though they haven't been invited to attend.
- Bobsledder Brian Shimer auctions a Lexus automobile to raise money for the US team.
- Temperatures rise in Washington as politicians talk of Senate and House resolutions against Beijing's bid for the 2000 Games.
- Lausanne, Switzerland, opens the new Olympic Museum, with a second-floor gallery highlighting the Winter and Summer Games.

July

- San Antonio hosts the US Olympic Festival July 23 through August 1. The $186.3 million 650,000-seat Almodome holds speedskating, ice hockey, and figure skating events.
- US television rights for the 1996 Games go on the block; NBC's winning bid of $456 million surpasses the $401 million the network shelled out for the Barcelona Games.

August

- The US Olympic hockey camp is expected to produce the pre-Olympic exhibition squad. Team USA promises to be the youngest to play hockey at Lillehammer.

- David Ogrean becomes USA Hockey's fourth executive director in 56 years.

- USA Boxing Executive Director James Fox announces his resignation to become the USOC's director of broadcast marketing, replacing Ogrean.

September

- Monte Carlo, Monaco hosts the 101st IOC session. Members vote on the host city for the 2000 Games. Bidding cities include Sydney, Australia; Beijing, China; Berlin, Germany; Manchester, Great Britain; Milan, Italy; and Istanbul, Turkey.

- Athletes compete in the Pan American Winter Games (September 6–13).

October

- New York City hosts the United States Olympic Congress.

- Brian Boitano competes in Skate America to mark his official return to the ranks of amateurs.

December

- Ukrainian child star Oksana Baiul shoots to win figure skating national championship en route to Lillehammer.

- US biathletes are selected at the Olympic trails in Anchorage, Alaska, and Olympic luge athletes are named after the World Cup Series concludes.

January

- US trials are held at Kincaid Park in Anchorage to select the US cross country ski team. US freestyle and nordic combined skiers are also named following competitions this month.

- The 1994 US championships at Joe Louis Arena in Detroit serve as figure skating's Olympic trials.

February

- Atlanta Centennial Olympic Properties (ACOP) inaugurates its Cultural Olympiad with "Olympic Winterland: Encounters with Norwegian Cultures," a 30-event celebration of Norwegian artists.

- Four sled-dog teams comprised of 60 dogs and eight sledders leave Lillehammer during the closing ceremonies to travel 10,000 miles across Siberia. After boarding a sailboat to cross the Bering Strait, they are scheduled to arrive at Nagano, Japan in the autumn of 1995. The purpose of the canine trek: to urge other Olympic venues to be considerate of Mother Nature when preparing to host the Games.

Amateurism in Winter's Wonderland

▼

DAVID YNTEMA

When should the Olympics remind you of *Alice in Wonderland*? Whenever the poohbahs that run the Olympics and the international sports federations say anything about amateurism. The Olympics are an upside-down world where a professional can be an amateur and amateurs earn more than professionals. As professional baseball's Yogi Berra might have said, if Pierre de Coubertin were alive today, he'd be a-rolling over in his grave.

The Olympic Games that Baron de Coubertin helped revive for gentlemen from around the world have become big business. Today they are the plaything not of gentlemen but of corporations; the playground not of amateurs but of professionals. Competitors are no longer restricted to gentlemen of property and standing but include *bona fide* members of the working class. A waitress and a truck driver, Carla Urbanski and Rocky Marval, were among America's skating pairs at the Games in Albertville. Some of today's finest American ice skaters— Nancy Kerrigan, Tonya Harding, and Todd Eldredge—also emerged from working-class backgrounds. Similarly, almost anyone can play these days. Katarina Witt and Brian Boitano, 1988 Olympic gold medal winners who have since turned professional, are once again called amateurs—and not just because their careers may be dimming due to comparatively weak technical skills or serious knee injuries.

How can Witt and Boitano become eligible for the Games again after having skated professionally? Once, in a far-off time, when an Olympic athlete turned professional the decision was considered permanent. In those days you couldn't retrieve lost status. Today it's a whole new set of Olympic Games. You *can* go home again, easily.

The confusion over what makes an amateur an amateur and a professional a pro is hardly new. But in recent years, especially in the context of cold war politics, it has been hard to tell the amateurs from the pros without a scorecard. Aren't all Western athletes amateurs? Even if, as some suggest, they may have been paid by Adidas or other manufacturers? What about East European and Soviet athletes prior to the 1990s? They didn't join professional tours, but they "earned" apartments and other luxuries. They sure looked like professionals. The different views of amateurism in the East and West point not only to the cultural specificity of the concept, but to the confusing nature of amateurism itself.

The history of the idea of amateurism shows just how confounding the concept has been, and why it's tough to pin down. It also suggests reasons for amateurism's long hold on the Olympics. Now that the days of amateur athletes in the Olympics are numbered, especially in high-profile sports like figure skating, alpine skiing, and ice hockey, it is easier to see why the problem has been so vexing for so many for so long.

Tim Taylor, hockey coach at Yale University and coach for the 1994 United States Olympic Hockey team, declared in an interview with the *New York Times* that "the whole amateur–professional issue is pretty muddled and pretty much a thing of the past." That's what another college coach might have said about a century ago, the first time the issue seemed settled. In the 1870s many athletic male American collegians enjoyed a happy existence, taking in course work, earning gentlemanly grades in the classics and moral philosophy, and (like some recent college athletes) routinely making a lot of dough by playing sports. The stakes for collegiate sporting events got to be so high, however, that the public clamored for reform. Public outrage over prize money forced American universities and colleges to embrace the amateur ideal. In 1885 the National Association of Amateur Athletics defined sports amateurism for Americans. From then on college athletes were barred from accepting money for winning athletic contests. At least in theory.

Victorian England, generally good at inventing traditions for itself and others, created the idea of amateur athletics. Amateurs were gentlemen; professionals were workers. London's Amateur Athletic Club, founded in 1866, was the first athletic club strictly for amateurs. It prohibited members from profiting from athletic events and excluded from its rolls as "professional" anyone who was a "mechanic, artisan, or labourer." In short, amateurism was limited to the upper class. Because it was associated with Britain's rigid class system, this brand of amateurism was difficult to translate for athletes in other cultures. Even the English-speaking United States originally rejected the elitist idea; it just didn't fit in with America's more fluid class structure.

Good sportsmanship and fair play were other values associated with amateurism. But the real value for the British originators was that by playing among themselves, the gentlemen finally had a chance to win. Most of the gentry lost when they competed against the "professional" working class, so they picked up their games and went away. Suddenly money became a tawdry subject, something for the lower classes to worry about. True sport was above all that, thank you very much.

Like other Victorians, the inventors of modern sports amateurism looked to the ancient past to validate their beliefs. Scholar David C. Young has shown that by relying on bad historians of antiquity, the revivers of the Olympics claimed modern amateurism as a rebirth of an ancient Olympic tradition. They were wrong. Young notes a lack of evidence for amateurism or elitism in the ancient

42

Games. In fact, prize money inspired those athletes from the get-go. Worse for the revisionist Victorians and their followers in the Olympic movement, many successful Greek athletes were ordinary laborers.

Gambling may have caused some of the late 19th-century fear of professionals. While Olympic athletes have never been much associated with gambling, professional athletes and sporting contests were linked to gambling during most of the nineteenth century. Betting on sports like horse racing, track, and boxing was widespread both in Europe and North America. Americans at the turn of the century tried to clean up sports and clamp down on gambling. Amateurs were thought to cheat less and gamble less; they could be trusted while professionals might throw the game. The Chicago Black Sox scandal in 1919 only renewed suspicions that professional athletes were in cahoots with gamblers. The anti-gambling crusade of the Progressive Era lent credence to the idea that amateur sports were somehow purer.

American athlete Avery Brundage, long an official with the International Olympic Committee (IOC) and eventually its chief, was a competitor at the Games held in 1912. During those Games the Olympic law-givers created a stricter definition of amateurism, redefining it in terms of individual action. Did the athlete ever get money for playing a sport? Even a different sport from the one he wanted to compete in? That, as Jim Thorpe found out, was enough to warrant disqualification, even retroactively. Thorpe's is the best-known case of an athlete whose medals were taken away because of amateurism rules. He won gold medals for the decathlon and pentathlon in 1912. After the Games ended and the new rules were put in place, it was discovered that he had earned $15 a week playing semi-pro ball while attending the Carlisle Indian School in Pennsylvania a few years earlier. Boom. The world's greatest athlete was stripped of his medals and his name was erased from the record books. But stay tuned for more on that story.

Olympic rule makers redefined amateurism yet again in 1925. Now it meant that an athlete could not derive his livelihood from sports, even indirectly. He could, however, gain up to fifteen days reimbursement for playing in the Games. The Olympic Congress also redefined "professional," this time as someone whose living derived even in part from athletics. Thus in 1932 Finnish runner Paavo Nurmi, a three-time Olympian and frequent winner of men's racing events, was barred from the Los Angeles Games based on allegations that he had taken money.

Olympic Rule 26, which defines amateurism, was broken as routinely as it was redefined. By the 1950s many athletes received payments for the time that their sport took them away from their jobs. During the 1960s more than a few athletes—most notably alpine skiers—were taking money under, over, and around the table. American athletes were rewarded with college scholarships. Jean-Claude Killy, French skiing star of the 1968 Winter Games, was notorious for violating the rules but was not penalized. Four years later, in the Winter Games at Sapporo, Austrian skier Karl Schranz was booted from the Games for having represented an equipment maker. His spirited (and accurate) defense that others did the same failed to persuade Olympic officials, but it helped make him a hero at home. The subsequent intensified crackdown on violators of the rule was tied in part to an increasing commercialization of the Games. Avery Brundage, still in charge, opposed relaxing the rules governing amateur participation even as Olympic organizers took ever more money from television networks.

During the 1970s and early 1980s the dishonest amateur took cash payments under the table. Honest amateurs took their opportunities to promote sports clothing and equipment. They remained amateurs by turning the money over to a third party that laundered the money back as allowances for food, clothing, shelter, and candy.

In the 1970s Lord Killanin, Avery Brundage's successor as head of the International Olympic Committee, allowed athletes to receive payments for endorsements. Professionals, however, were still banned from the Games, and by the 1980s the term "amateur" was transformed to "non-professional." In 1983 the IOC reinstated Jim Thorpe, putting his name back in the record books and giving reproduction medals to his family. Killanin also effectively passed the buck of defining amateurism by deferring to the international federations governing each sport. The federations began to set the rules for eligibility in each event. Generally the federations, with the IOC's blessing, gave athletes wide latitude in gaining income from endorsements and other indirect payments for their athletic performances.

This cooperation marked a change in relations between the IOC and the federations, as the IOC and some federations had long quibbled. For instance, the International Ski Federation argued during the 1930s and 1940s that ski instructors should be allowed to participate in the Olympics. They were finally admitted in time for the 1948 Games, but only on the condition that they quit teaching by the previous October. The ski federation sought eligibility allowances again in 1951, asking that ski instructors again be permitted to move from professional to amateur status. Thus skaters Witt and Boitano are not the first to regain eligibility. And 1998 will be far from the first time professional hockey players get in the Games. According to historian Allen Guttman, pro hockey players competed "unofficially" at the 1948 games. That Olympiad's Swiss organizers wanted the pro players, figuring that they were more likely to bring fans into the stadiums.

Sacrificing amateurism for the sake of bringing in more fans, especially in front of television sets, is at the heart of today's move toward an open Olympics. To paraphrase writer Mark Twain's view of another age, the chief end of today's Olympics is to make money, through television if possible, sponsorships if necessary. Today's Olympic Games depend on American TV networks and corporate sponsors like Coca-Cola for their financing. The networks sell their audience to advertisers like Coke. Together the IOC, TV networks, and corporate interests hope and pray more of us will watch the Games if the best athletes, and that means professionals, participate.

The contradiction between the Olympic ideals of pure amateurism and improving performance has become clear. The performance ideal is expressed in the Olympic motto, *citius, altius, fortius* ("faster, higher, stronger"), but achieving ever higher levels of performance requires more specialization and professionalization. It also demands better and more expensive high-tech equipment and training facilities. Bobsled teams' training on computer-simulated bobsled runs before they even get to Lillehammer is not cheap.

This year the US Olympic Committee is returning to the Games' ancient roots, when to the victors went the prize money. They are giving bonuses to American medal winners. Even so, the committees will watch how the money is distributed, looking for an unmarked line between professionals and para-professionals. (Winning lugers get to keep their money, NHL stars are "expected" to direct theirs to worthy causes.)

Spectators may be tempted to think too harshly of the new Olympic world and too fondly of the less commercial days. The fact is that the old Games were more elitist and hypocritical. Today extraordinary waitresses and truck drivers can compete with the world's best athletes, but only if they are given appropriate financial and technical support. While amateurism, like nostalgia, isn't what it used to be, neither is the expensive high-tech world of the Olympics.

OLYMPICS TELEVISION SCHEDULE

CBS OLYMPICS BROADCAST SCHEDULE
Lillehammer, Norway
February 12–27, 1994
Note that all times are Eastern Standard,
and subject to change

Saturday, February 12
8–11 p.m.—Opening Ceremony
11:30 p.m.–12:30 a.m.

Sunday, February 13
9 a.m.–12 noon
2–6 p.m.
8–11 p.m.
11:30 p.m.–12:30 a.m.

Monday, February 14
7–9 a.m.
8–11 p.m.
11:30 p.m.–12:30 a.m.

Tuesday, February 15
7–9 a.m.
8–11:30 p.m.
12 midnight–1 a.m.

Wednesday, February 16
7–9 a.m.
8–11 p.m.
11:30 p.m.–12:30 a.m.

Thursday, February 17
7–9 a.m.
8–11 p.m.
11:30 p.m.–12:30 a.m.

Friday, February 18
7–9 a.m.
8–11 p.m.
11:30 p.m.–12:30 a.m.

Saturday, February 19
1–6 p.m.
7–11 p.m.
11:30 p.m.–12:30 a.m.

Sunday, February 20
9 a.m.–12 noon
3:30–6 p.m.
8–11 p.m.
11:30 p.m.–12:30 a.m.

Monday, February 21
7–9 a.m.
1–6 p.m.
8–11:30 p.m.
12 midnight–1 a.m.

Tuesday, February 22
7–9 a.m.
8–11 p.m.
11:30 p.m.–12:30 a.m.

Wednesday, February 23
7–9 a.m.
8–11 p.m.
11:30 p.m.–12:30 a.m.

Thursday, February 24
7–9 a.m.

8–11 p.m.
11:30 p.m.–12:30 a.m.

Friday, February 25
7–9 a.m.
8–11:30 p.m.
12 midnight–1 a.m.

Saturday, February 26
1–6 p.m.

7–11 p.m.
11:30 p.m.–12:30 a.m.

Sunday, February 27
9 a.m.–12 noon
4–6 p.m.
8–11 p.m.—Closing Ceremony
11:30 p.m.–12:30 a.m.

WINTER GAMES

▼

Green Games in Snowy Scandinavia

▼

GEORGE CANTOR

I f it is still possible to conceive of an Olympics as being "intimate," the 1994 Winter Games at Lillehammer, Norway will probably be as close as it gets. Cozy. Compact. Comfortable. Green, in the environmental sense (not, its organizers hope, in the snowy sense).

And very Norwegian. The heritage and sensibilities of this lovely Scandinavian land will permeate every aspect of the Games, from their mascots to their architecture to their pace. Hosting its first Olympics since the Oslo Winter Games of 1952, Norway hopes to reintroduce itself to international tourism.

This is an expensive country, with prices reflecting its high salaries and broad network of state-run social services. It is a bit out of the way. You don't pass through Norway en route to somewhere else. You go there because it is your destination. The weather is also somewhat uncooperative.

It is not a nation with a heavy tourism infrastructure. The luxurious resort, the chic shops, the *après*-ski party-down atmosphere—that is not the Norwegian way. Outside of Oslo, hotels tend to be very small and family-run. Most Norwegians choose to stay in a cabin, either their own or one lent by a friend, for their winter vacation. The Norwegian drinking laws are among the most serious in the world. Liquor is strictly controlled and heavily taxed, and there are stories told of drivers given jail terms after consuming one beer and backing out of their own driveway.

So in many regards, Lillehammer is an even less likely choice for the Winter Games than was Albertville, France, in 1992. While that town was a fairly nondescript rail crossing, it was close to some of the most glamorous resorts in the French Alps. Courchevel. Val d'Isere. Meribel.

Lillehammer, on the other hand, is close to Hunderfossen. And Gjovik. And a few other places whose names mean absolutely nothing to the world's travelers and sports community. But they will. Because in February, 1994, some of the most spectacular athletic venues ever built—including an arena in the shape of the capsized hull of a Viking ship and another tucked into the hollow of a mountain cave—will make these Games especially memorable.

51

Lillehammer is a lovely city of 25,000 people, on a lake, about 110 miles north of Oslo. Previously, it was known as something of a rural cultural center, the home of some interesting museums and noted literary figures. The great playwright Henrik Ibsen stayed on a nearby farm and set his stories of *Peer Gynt* in the hills near Lillehammer. And, of course, it was the hometown of Thor Bjorklund, who, in 1925, invented the cheese slicer.

Its inhabitants affectionately call it "Trolltown," a tribute to its storybook quality and the folklore of the surrounding land. Its narrow, pedestrian-only commercial streets and its pastel houses, brightly colored to ward off the gloom of the long northern winter, give the place an almost Disney-like appearance, too cute to be real. It has both summer and winter tourist seasons. To be seriously considered as a site of the Olympics, though, seemed as unlikely a tale as those told about Peer Gynt.

But the Gudbrandsdalen—the scenic valley in which Lillehammer is located—was in an economic slump in the 1980s. It was not sharing in the prosperity that offshore oil was bringing to much of the country. Nordic skiing, a sport that brought so many Danes into this region that it was called Denmark's northernmost province, was slipping in popularity, replaced by the alpine version of the sport. Almost in desperation, Norway's Olympic committee decided to get behind a bid for Lillehammer as a way to rejuvenate the entire region. When that decision was announced, most Norwegians, including the crown prince, Harald, thought the idea was bizarre.

"Things were bad here and people were leaving," says Gerhard Heiberg, the local industrialist who heads the Lillehammer Olympic Committee. "There was a lot of unemployment and a lot of pessimism. We went for the Olympic Games, not as a goal, but as a means of achieving something else—to attract tourism and help industry. Norway is the best-kept secret in Europe."

But Norway made its pitch at the right time. Weary of sites that were too urban or too widely spread out, the international committee was receptive to the idea of an intimate Games. To the utter astonishment of just about everyone, Lillehammer won the 1988 balloting. These Winter Games are the first to be held under the new Olympics schedule, which cut two years off the usual preparation time. But with customary Norwegian doggedness, Lillehammer set about its business. The last Olympics venue was finished a full nine months before the start of the games, which will be opened by the formerly skeptical crown prince, now King Harald V.

Norway's ties to winter sports go back to its very foundation. The words "ski" and "slalom" are derived, in fact, from the Norwegian language. The official symbols and mascots of the '94 Games, stick-figure kids named Hakkon and Kristin, are based on 4,000-year-old pictographs found carved on an Arctic rock, the world's oldest known depiction of skiers. Lillehammer even has a skier in its coat of arms. The civic emblem commemorates the "Birkebeiners" (birch skiers), who tied tree branches to their legs and skied across the mountains to rescue the infant heir to the Norwegian throne in the Christmas season of 1205.

Each year, about 5,000 skiers retrace their route in the annual Birkebeiner Race, which starts in Lillehammer. It was, by far, the town's biggest sporting event—until now.

Those words, "until now," figure in virtually every discussion of these Games. There were distinct fears that Lillehammer would lose a part of its character and its soul under the crush of the crowds and the changes the Olympics would bring. The Games were not an easy sell, although by 1993 about 80 percent of a poll of its residents conceded they would be a good thing. More than anything else, that is a tribute to the environmental constraints placed on these Games, standards its organizers hope will serve as a guide for future Olympics.

When one of the major arenas was determined to be located too close to a wetlands, used as a sanctuary by migrating Arctic birds, the site was moved 55 yards away, its entrance switched to the opposite side of the structure, and trees planted to absorb the noise. Blue anemones that had to be removed from one ski jump were carefully replanted nearby. Other trees were color coded with tape, indicating the amount of fines the construction company that disturbed them would have to pay. The bobsled run was so carefully blended into the forest that it is almost invisible through the snow. Coca-Cola products were blamed for most of the litter at Albertville, so the company agreed to produce only recyclable cups and bottles here. Even bullets used in the biathlon will be retrieved from the forest.

The plan to hold every event within Lillehammer and its environs, however, did not hold up. When neighboring localities heard about the billion-dollar budget allocated for the Games, they began demanding their share. It was politically impossible to ignore them, so many major events—particularly hockey and figure skating—will be held in nearby towns. None of them are more than 35 miles from Lillehammer. Moreover, the access roads are flat, valley highways; not the winding, mountainous tracks that made commutes between the sites of the '92 Games so tortuous. There will also be an extensive system of shuttle buses and trains, because private cars will be completely barred from the streets of Lillehammer. They will be permitted, however, in the towns of Gjovik and Hamar, sites of the hockey and figure skating competitions.

Lillehammer has only a few thousand hotel rooms, not even close to the capacity required for an Olympics invasion. The Norwegian government was reluctant to build many new ones because the experience in past Olympics was that they never could be run profitably and became costly white elephants. Lillehammer, more remote than most sites, could not afford that sort of profligate construction. Nor did it want to disturb any more of its setting than it absolutely had to. So it is relying on private households to take up the accommodations slack. When the Japanese Olympic committee expressed concern over the lack of housing at the downhill ski site at Kvitfjell, it was politely informed that if this seemed to be a problem Japan was welcome to build a hotel there itself.

Rooms in the immediate Lillehammer area were snapped up long ago by dignitaries and Olympics officials. Most people will stay in Oslo and make the 95-minute daily trip for the events. Special trains and buses will leave every 10 minutes from the capital's central station. The Olympic village built for the athletes will be converted to university housing, and the media facilities will be transported to a nearby town and used for private housing.

Events will be held in six locations. Besides Lillehammer and its suburb of Hunderfossen, there will be major downhill ski attractions at Hafjell and Kvitfjell, about nine and 21 miles respectively up the valley. There will be hockey at Gjovik, on the opposite side of Lake Mjosa, about 27 miles from Lillehammer and 76 miles from Oslo. Figure skating and speedskating will go on at Hamar, the furthest venue from Lillehammer, at 35 miles, and about 74 miles from Oslo.

This is how the events and sites will break down:

Lillehammer Olympic Park
(Opening and closing ceremonies, ski jumping, freestyle skiing, nordic combined skiing, cross-country skiing, biathlon, ice hockey)

This may be the most dramatic setting ever devised for the Olympic ceremonies, which would be moving enough if held in an alley. Lillehammer has built its $17 million stadium on a hill overlooking the town and Lake Mjosa, the largest in Norway. Two parallel ski jumps will send athletes plummeting into the midst of the viewing area, which forms an amphitheater that can hold 50,000 spectators. According to preliminary plans, the jumps will be theatrically incorporated into the opening ceremonies, which will certainly get the Games off to one of their most energetic starts ever. The stadium will also be the site of the jump competition.

Adjacent to the amphitheater is the Kanthaugen Freestyle Arena, which is where the moguls and aerials for both men and women will take place. It holds about 15,000 spectators.

A bit further along in this park area is the Birkebeineren Ski Stadium, carefully hidden in the Norwegian woods as to be almost invisible from the other sites. This will be the busiest arena in Lillehammer, with all cross-country and nordic combined events, as well as the biathlon, being held here—a total of 18 competitions. The tracks loop through the nearby woodlands and finish back in the stadium. In most Olympics, these events are tucked off in a more distant corner of the ground plan. But these events also happen to be the ones in which Norway excels, so they were placed front and center in Lillehammer, with room for 25,000 spectators. While the events usually hold little interest for Americans, tickets to them are among the hardest to come by in Norway.

The final component of the Olympic Park is Hakon Hall, one of the two hockey sites. Thirty of the 46 matches will take place here, including the finals, because its 10,500-spectator capacity is almost twice the size of the arena in Gjovik. This is a massive, six-story structure, which houses television studios, restaurants, squash courts, eight bowling alleys, and a climbing wall, besides the hockey arena. It is also something of an environmental showcase, with its heating system using water recycled from the showers, an important energy savings in the Norwegian climate.

Lillehammer describes all these venues as being "within walking distance" of each other. You should be warned, however, that the Norwegian definition of walking distance can differ dramatically from the American concept. This is a nation of outdoor activities, in which a few miles is regarded as a short stroll. If you don't relish the thought of that sort of a cold-weather ramble, check out the shuttle bus schedule.

Hunderfossen
(Bobsled and luge)

This track has been built flush with the natural terrain, which makes it close to ideal from both an environmental and spectator's viewpoint. No structural impediments will mar the landscape and block the sightlines. In addition, the track is the first in the world to have its own sealed refrigeration system, which insures a uniform ice surface and the possibility of enhanced speed. About 10,000 spectators will be able to attend events here, about eight miles from the Olympic Park.

Hafjell
(Slalom and giant slalom)

If there was a venue in these Games that prompted a less-than-enthusiastic initial response, it was this course, which was originally designated the site of the women's downhill events, as well as all slalom events. Twelve of the top 15 women skiers in the world boycotted training sessions here in 1993. Their complaint? The course was too easy. Said World Cup champion Katja Seizinger, of Germany: "If people see this downhill on television, they will say: 'I might as well go to the library.'"

Norwegian media jumped all over the organizers, with big headlines blaring "SKANDALE" in the country's largest newspaper. Officials immediately set about to ensure that the event would not send bored viewers into the book stacks. But the five-year-old, intermediate-rated course, upgraded at a cost of $2 million as part of the plan to scatter the events and benefit as many localities as possible, did not satisfy the competitors or the International Ski Federation, which appealed to Lillehammer organizers to relocate the women's race to the steeper men's course at Kvitfjell. Finally, in June of 1993, Lillehammer's Olympic Organizing Committee relented, and the women, in turn, agreed to reduce their training days from three to two and to race the same day as the men in case of bad weather.

Kvitfjell
(Downhill skiing and super-G)

By contrast, this run, designed by Bernhard Russi, who fashioned the Albertville course, got rave reviews from the athletes in 1993. Russi's course for the '92 Games was the most controversial element of those Olympics. Many skiers admitted it scared the daylights out of them. But they adjusted, and Russi is now regarded as the master builder of challenging downhill runs. A.J. Kitt, the top American downhill racer, compared Kvitfjell favorably to Kitzbuhel, Austria, which has been described as the "Augusta National of downhill." "It is not really dangerous and a good test of skiing," said Kitt.

This is the mountain that inspired Ibsen, and parts of the course are named after his characters in *Peer Gynt*—in the hope, perhaps, that it will also inspire great theater. The average gradient is 29 percent, and along the way there are two semi-terrifying 90-meter jumps. Spectator capacity is about 25,000 but, according to reports at the 1993 tests here, the skiers disappear from sight for long stretches in the wooded areas.

Gjovik
(Hockey)

This is the site that makes the concept of spreading out the Games look like sheer inspiration. The Hall of the Mountain King has been blasted out of bedrock to become the world's only arena located inside a cave. The sheer dramatic impact of the site hushed the spectators who attended opening ceremonies in early spring of 1993. A good thing too, because the closed-in rock walls should make this the noisiest arena in hockey. The cavern is 311 feet long, 78 feet high, and spans 200 feet. It will hold 5,500 spectators. After the Olympics, it will be used as a conference center.

Hamar
(Speedskating, figure skating)

There are two new arenas in this old Viking port city. The Amphitheater, just outside the town center, will be used for figure skating and short track speedskating. A round structure, it can hold 6,000 spectators.

But it is Hamar's Olympic Hall that seems destined to become the visual signature of these Games. Designed in the shape of a Viking long boat keel, with roof beams formed from 1,000 trees, the interior recalls the sense of soaring majesty one feels in a great cathedral. Early visitors were unanimous in praise of its design. The $33 million facility can hold 16,000 spectators for the speedskating events. But because these are events at which the Norwegian teams excel, tickets to the hall are expected to be extremely difficult to obtain.

In addition to all the athletic construction, Lillehammer has rebuilt its Art Museum in an especially striking manner. Nicknamed the Grand Piano because of its shape, the addition to the museum displeased traditionalists who felt it contrasted jarringly with the architectural style of the old town. But Queen Sonja described it as "a pearl in the Norwegian cultural necklace," and enthusiastic crowds have poured in since its reopening in early 1993. The museum houses one of the world's most important collection of Edvard Munch paintings.

The other major museum in the city is called the Maihaugen. An open-air facility, it is a collection of historic structures from this part of Norway, assembled in a townlike setting on a hill, something like a Scandinavian Greenfield Village. The museum was the personal project of Anders Sandvik. A dentist who roamed the Gudbrandsdalen, he accepted gifts of property from patients who could not pay him in cash. Eventually, he was given entire buildings and arranged to have them moved here. Sandvik's fear was that the area's history was in danger of being obliterated by the forces of modernity. This was in 1887, when the museum first opened. So, as you can see, Lillehammer's determination to protect its heritage goes back a lot further than these Olympics.

Tickets and Rooms

The US agent for tickets and package tours to the Lillehammer Olympics is Cartan Tours. Offices for the Olympics Division are at 1334 Park Ave., Suite 210, Manhattan Beach, California 90266. The toll-free phone number is (800) 841-1994. Cartan is the sole ticket agency in this country.

There are usually last-minute room cancellations at any Olympics, and in Lillehammer the accommodations number to check is (011) 47-61-26-4200. Fax is (011) 47-61-26-9250. No tickets to the events can be obtained here. The Tourist Information and Reservation Center at Oslo's Central Train Station will be handling hotel and home accommodations in that city. The phone number is (011) 47-62-59-299 and fax is (011) 47-62-69-655.

BIATHLON

WARM-UP

Although not a Winter Olympic sport until 1960, biathlon, a grueling sport that combines furious cross-country skiing with expert marksmanship, has its origins in ancient Scandinavian society. Early Scandinavians, after inventing skis for transportation across the snowy terrain, soon discovered that stalking prey was easier on skis than afoot.

Later, when survival became less of a day-to-day struggle, the combination of skiing and shooting was included in the training of infantry soldiers, particularly in Finland. This led to the military ski patrol race, which began early this century among European armies.

fact: Victor Arbez, 1960's fastest-skiing biathlete, missed 18 out of 20 targets. A racing heart isn't the only thing that can skew a biathlete's aim: wind, bad ammo, and cold weather's effect on the rifle can cause a biathlete to miss the 11.5-centimeter target.

In 1958, the first world biathlon championship was held in Austria. The 20km biathlon was added to the Olympic program in 1960; in 1968, the 30km relay was added. The 10km race made its Olympic debut in 1980. Olympic biathlon had been an all-male preserve, but in 1992 women made their skiing and shooting debut in three events: the 7.5km, 15km, and a relay (3 x 7.5km).

SPECTATOR'S GUIDE

Combine cross-country skiing with riflery and what do you get? A sport that few in the US seem to understand. Biathlon is something of an unknown competition in America, with fewer than 1,000 Americans participating. It is as much a test of composure as it is a race against the clock. While much of the skiing occurs out of sight of the spectators (and the television audience as well), the start, finish, shooting range, and penalty loops are within the stadium and camera range.

fact: A biathlete has about twenty seconds to prepare to shoot at a target stop. That means she's got less than half a minute to load her rifle and calm her heart rate.

At the start of the race, biathletes leave from a starting gate just in front of the stands, one at a time, one minute apart. Each competitor skis a set distance along the course, the .22 caliber rifle (which weighs as much as 11 pounds) slung over a shoulder. Then, with heart racing at 160 to 180 beats per minute, heaving breath, and no time to spare, the racer comes to a complete stop, aims, and shoots, from alternating prone and standing positions, at a configuration of five black dots 50 meters away. If a competitor skis too quickly, she will be unable to slow her breathing and heartbeat as she approaches the range. The best biathletes are able to come down from 180 to 120 beats when they're shooting, squeezing the trigger in that millisecond of relative stillness between heartbeats.

Concentration is, of course, essential. Those dots they're aiming at have diameters of 115 millimeters (4.76 inches) for the more difficult standing shots, 45 millimeters (1.76 inches) for prone shots. Each miss in the men's 20km and women's 15km race adds one minute to the competitor's final time; each miss in the men's 10km and women's 7.5km and both relay events means the competitor must ski a 150-meter penalty loop.

fact: Much of a biathlete's training time is spent on a treadmill. During a treadmill workout, the athlete's blood is drawn and computer-analyzed to determine its lactic acid content. When blood lactate is high, an athlete's performance suffers. Treadmill workouts train a biathlete to know how to avoid lactic acid-producing overexertion.

In the men's 20km, which covers about 12.5 miles, the competitors return four times to shoot five shots at five targets 50 meters away. The women's 15km follows similar rules. The 10km and 7.5km sprints require only two shooting stops.

France's Anne Briand (number 3) and Germany's Petra Schaaf shoot it out on the final leg of the 3 x 7.5km relay at the 1992 Games. Briand went on to win the race for France.

The men's and women's relay teams each comprise four racers, each skiing 7.5 kilometers (4.5 miles). Each member stops twice to shoot up to eight rounds at five metal targets. The three extra rounds are loaded as single shots, meaning the competitor must open the bolt of the rifle for each extra shot required, take out a round, and insert a round. About 10 seconds are needed for reloading, and a penalty loops tags on some 40 seconds to a contestant's time, depending on snow conditions.

quote: "It would take a talented skier about three years to learn the shooting skills" to become a competitive biathlete, according to US Biathlon executive director Jed Williamson. "We've never yet made a skier out of a shooter."

Unlike the individual races, the relays feature a mass start. They do not feature a baton exchange. The passover zone in the relay is a 20-meter length of track wherein the person completing his or her leg must physically touch a teammate's body with his or her hand. A hand-to-hand tag is not permitted.

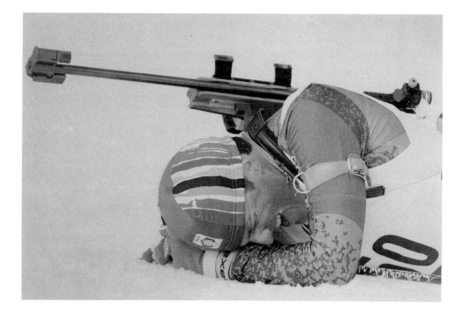

Italy's Andreas Zingerle tries to catch his breath after finishing the 10km event at the Albertville Games. Zingerle finished seventh in the competition.

HOPEFULS

A word to the wise.

"The thing you've got to remember about the biathlon is that it is an incredibly turbulent sport," says Max Cobb, program director for the US Biathlon Association. "Someone who's 25th one day can be first the next day. That's very common in the biathlon."

Still, the 1994 Games will include a passel of strong favorites on both the men's and women's side.

And when you begin talking about whom to watch, the list of names in the men's competitions begins with Mark Kirchner's.

Kirchner, of Germany, won the gold medal in the 10km men's event at Albertville, and the silver medal in the 20km race. He's supported by teammate Sven Fischer, a mere babe at 20, who won the 1993 overall World Cup 10km title in his first year on the circuit.

Mikael Lofgren, of Sweden, another serious challenger, was the overall 1993 World Cup winner.

Other names to track are Andreas Zingerle, Wilfried Pallhuber, and Pier-Alberta Carrara, of the strong, experienced Italian team; Patrice Bailly-Salins, of France, and Josh Thompson, the main US contender.

The 1992 women's 3 x 7.5km relay starts with a flurry of poles in Les Saisies, France. The French team seized the gold, followed by Germany and the Unified Team.

The dark horse in the 20km event? Expect Valeri Medvedtsev, of Russia, to be back. Medvedcev won the gold medal in Calgary in 1988 but didn't compete in the 20km in Albertville because of poor time trials.

In the 10km, keep one eye on the German duo of Fischer and Kirchner, and another on Ludwig Gredler, of Austria, one of the fastest skiers on the World Cup circuit.

The 10km dark horse? Try Eirik Kvalfoss, of Norway. Like Medvedtsev of Russia, Kvalfoss is attempting something of a comeback—from *way* back. Kvalfoss won the 10km gold medal a decade ago. He could have something of a home-field advantage going for him in Lillehammer.

On the women's side, Anfisa Restsova, of Russia, has proven herself the fastest woman on the circuit by far, winning six World Cup events in 1993. That's no surprise, really. Restsova won the 7.5km gold medal at Albertville.

Another German skier is a good bet here, too. Antje Misersky won a gold medal and two silvers at Albertville.

Others to watch include Myriam Bedard, Canada's best-ever biathlete and a bronze-medal winner at Albertville; Anne Briand, of France; and a pair of Joans, Guetschow and Smith, of the US.

The dark horse on the women's side? Annette Sikveland, of Norway, the junior World Cup champ in 1992.

Silver medalist Mark Kirchner of Germany, gold medalist Evgeni Redkine of the Unified Team, and bronze medalist Mikael Lofgren of Sweden display their 20km awards.

Myriam Bedard

Myriam Bedard abandoned the sequins and frills of figure skating as a youth because of the expense.

Then, she picked up a rifle.

The rest is Canadian Olympics history.

Bedard, 25, of Quebec City, is the best biathlete in Canadian history, and its only Olympic medal-winner in the event. She won the bronze medal in the 15km race in Albertville in 1992, and she'll be a strong contender for the gold at Lillehammer in 1994.

That's quite a stretch from firing her first shot with the Canadian Army Cadets as a 15 year old in 1984, then renting a pair of ski boots, stuffing tissue in the toes so the boots would fit, and winning the first biathlon she entered.

And the march has continued. Last February, Bedard gave Canada its first-ever international biathlon victory by winning the women's 7.5km sprint at the world championships in Borovets, Bulgaria. She also won a silver medal in the 15km event.

"It's fun that at such a young age I can win these big titles," Bedard told the *Canadian Press*. 'What's interesting is I'm improving all the time. I hope this continues because I have plenty of time to win some more races."

Indeed. Biathletes generally don't peak until age 28-30. The giddiest of questions could be: Do the competitors have enough time to catch her?

At Borovets, Bedard finished a whopping 16.6 seconds ahead of silver medalist Nadezhda Talanova of Russia.

"Many people don't agree with a sport with a rifle," she told Mary Jollimore of the *Globe and Mail*. "Many people think it's not a sport for women, but they don't really say it."

It's turned out to be the perfect sport for Bedard. So perfect, in fact, that she recently won sponsorship for her training from the Metropolitan Life Insurance Company. She receives a salary, certain company benefits, performance bonuses, and a full-time job with the company when she retires.

This for an athlete who, a few years earlier, went begging for a car to local automobile garages—a *car!*—and didn't call it quits until someone loaned her a ride for the summer.

"Myriam has the values we cherish," Met Life executive Richard Painchaud told the *Globe and Mail*. "She's a real motivational person. We sought her out. We're there to help her go through the mine fields. She's the first athlete we've sponsored."

Bedard, 5-foot-3, 115 pounds, and with the looks of a model, may be the perfect spokesperson for the sport.

Part of it is the humility. Almost ten months after the '92 Olympics, Bedard said she was still getting requests to "present trophies, be part of fund raising events, be an honorary president."

"What I've learned," she told *Montreal Gazette* reporter Dave Stubbs, "is that winning an Olympic medal changes your life. I told my boyfriend that I wish I could have five days at home to watch a few videos at night, or to go for a quiet walk without looking at my watch.

"I've wanted to share my success and my medal with many people since I've been home, especially children. [But] I understand now why many artists try to have a home somewhere away from everything, without a telephone. I'm the kind of person who has always been alone, trained alone, with no attention."

Still, there is the upside. And Bedard acknowledges that, too.

"In the past, before the Olympic medal, one out of 100 people maybe knew about the biathlon. Now, only one out of one hundred *don't* know." —*E.K.*

Joan Guetschow

Joan Guetschow, of Minnetonka, Minnesota, isn't your typical homecoming queen.

Nor, for that matter, your regular National Honor Society member.

Guetschow spends most of her time these days carting around a nine-and-a-half pound, .22 caliber rifle.

"Ah, yes," says her mother, Jan, with a smile, "the Christmas she came home with a rifle."

That was five or six years ago, when Joan, a collegiate champion cross-country skier, caught the biathlon bug.

Back then, of course, she was a long shot—if that—to succeed.

No more.

Today, Guetschow, a competitive swimmer and champion triathlete who joined her high school ski team in suburban Minneapolis to keep in shape for track, is one of the headliners on the US women's biathlon team.

Geutschow, who was born September 9, 1966, won 12 letters in high school in swimming, track, and cross-country skiing, was an All American honorable mention in swimming, and was team MVP in all three of her sports. In college at the University of Minnesota and Central Oregon Community College, she was an All-American skier, and in 1988 was the 10km college champ.

But her real claim to fame was winning the Olympic trials in Lake Placid in 1990, finishing first in the 7.5km event and second in the 15km competition, and taking part in the '92 Games in Albertville, France, where the women's biathlon became a medal sport for the first time.

Now, she has her sight set on Lillehammer.

It hasn't all been a joy ride. Since dedicating herself first to skiing, then to the biathlon, Guetschow has changed residences 18 times and has had 13 different jobs.

"I've had some bad luck, too," she told Jay Weiner of the *Minneapolis Star Tribune*, in something of a whopper of an understatement. Guetschow, who speaks fluent Finnish, broke her left hand in 1990, her right arm in 1991, and suffered a serious leg and shoulder bruise in a roller skiing accident. In 1989, she cut off the tips of two toes while mowing her lawn. She also skis with medication to control an irregular heartbeat.

No wonder pain-killer company Nuprin nominated her for a comeback award in 1992.

In addition to winning the trials in 1992, Guetschow also took first place in the North American Biathlon Championships in Alaska, first in the US Biathlon Nationals, and was selected US Biathlon Association Woman Biathlete of the Year.

She almost didn't get there.

"My first thought (after the mowing incident) was I was going to go back to swimming," Guetschow said. "I thought the injury would really mess my balance up. But the doctors made a special insole for my foot, and I worked extra hard on balancing on that foot, so I don't notice it now."

Now, she's planning on hanging around for awhile.

"Skiing is a good long-term sport," she says. "You can train for it in a variety of ways, whereas about all you can do to train for swimming is swim more. Also, women skiers peak later, usually in their 30s, whereas anything much above 20 is getting old for a swimmer."

Which means Guetschow could be around for a while. —*E.K.*

The tentative biathlon schedule is as follows:

Friday, February 18
15km, women

Sunday, February 20
20km, men

Wednesday, February 23
7.5km, women
10km, men

Friday, February 25
4 x 7.5km relay, women

Saturday, February 26
4 x 7.5km relay, men

Biathlon

▼

HIGHLIGHTS

Biathlon competition was not part of the Winter Games until 1960, when the 20km event made its appearance. The 4 x 7.5km relay event debuted at the 1968 Games in Grenoble, the 10km event was inaugurated in 1980 at Lake Placid, and women first competed in 1992. The Scandinavians, East Germans, and Soviets have long dominated the sport.

Soviet biathlete Alexandr Privalov captured the bronze in the 20km race in 1960 and a silver in 1964, while contenders from Sweden, Finland, Norway, and the Soviet Union rounded out the medalists those first two years. A French biathlete, Victor Arbez, was the fastest skier in 1960, but proved to be a dismal marksman, missing 18 of his 20 targets. Norway's Magnar Solberg took the gold in the 20km with a perfect shooting score in 1968 and captured the gold again in 1972, at the age of 35. Finland's Heikki Ikola was favored to win the 20km in 1976, but had to settle for silver behind Nikolai Kruglov, a Russian Army lieutenant. The Scandinavians were completely shut out at Lake Placid, where West Germany managed to capture a bronze in the relay, the only medal not won by East Germany or the USSR. The 1980 champion in the 20km event was Russian Anatoli Aljabiev, the only man to hit all his targets; he also took the bronze in the 10km event. East German Frank Ullrich won two medals in 1980. Alexander Tikhonov won his record fourth gold in Lake Placid as a member of the Soviet relay team.

US biathlete Lyle Nelson was 34 when he competed in his third Olympics at Sarajevo in 1984. That year Eirik Kvalfoss of Norway took the gold in the 10km ahead of West German Peter Angerer and East German Matthias Jacob. Angerer captured the 20km gold ahead of 19-year-old East German Frank-Peter Roetsch and bronze medalist Kvalfoss. The relay was again won by the Soviet Union, with

Norway claiming the silver and East Germany the bronze; the US team placed eighth.

For the 1988 Games Josh Thompson, the first US medal contender in biathlon, toted a new, lighter but stronger rifle stock designed by US biathlete Glen Eberle. But the Calgary Games belonged to East German biathlete Frank-Peter Roetsch, the first ever to capture both the 10km and the 20km biathlons; he had been silver medalist in the 20km event in 1984. Three Soviets also medaled in the 10km and 20km events in 1988, while Italian Johann Passler took the bronze in the 20km. In Calgary the Soviet Union continued its stranglehold on the relay, winning its sixth gold out of six times this event had been held at the Winter Games. Italy took a surprise bronze in the relay, behind West Germany.

Albertville Highlights: Women Debut

The Olympic course at Les Saisies was no cake-walk: four of the five ski loops concluded with a heart-taxing uphill en route to the shooting range. The US team entered the Games with no Olympic medals to their credit, and bid adieu to the Alps none the richer. Germany and the Unified Team, to no one's surprise, were Albertville's big winners, in both the men's and women's competitions.

fact: American biathletes enjoyed banner crowds of thirty spectators at the pre-Albertville trials in Lake Placid; at about the same time, a biathlon championship in Minsk, Belarus, drew 50,000 people.

In the men's competition, Mark Kirchner and Ricco Gross shared Germany's spoils: Kirchner captured the 10km gold and 20km silver, Gross silvered in the 10km, and both shared in the relay gold. The title-holding Unified Team—led by 1988 10km silver medalist Valeri Medvedzev—settled for second place in the relay, while Yevgeny Redkine—the 1990 junior world champion—bested the competition in the 20km. The Swedish team, with a third-place relay finish, earned the most improved performance, having placed seventh in the event in Calgary.

Women debuted in the biathlon at Albertville, with teams drawn primarily from the ranks of cross-country athletes. Only France and Canada took medals away from the German and Unified teams; by avoiding penalty loops, the straight-shooting French *filles* wrested the relay gold. The Unified Team's Anfissa Restzova—Calgary's 20km silver medalist and 4 x 5km gold medalist—became the first Olympic women's biathlon champion, adequate consolation for having failed, as a new mother, to regain her berth on the cross-country team.

fact: Much-injured fourth-year US team member Joan Guetschow (fluent in Finnish and an accomplished triathlete) was nominated for the Nuprin comeback from injury award in 1992.

Overcoming a one-minute penalty for a missed target with some speedy skiing, Germany's Antje Misersky garnered the 15km gold. The Unified Team's Svetlana Pecherskaia—1990 world champion and 1991 world cup titlist (under her maiden name, Davidova)—settled for silver, having missed a target on her second round. And Myriam Bedard, who missed targets in both the second and third rounds of shooting, still managed to earn Canada a spot on the podium.

Medalists

Biathlon—Men's 10 Kilometers

1992
1. Mark Kirchner, Germany, 26:02.3
2. Ricco Gross, Germany, 26:18.0
3. Harri Eloranta, Finland, 26:26.6

1988
1. Frank-Peter Roetsch, East Germany, 25:08.1
2. Valeri Medvedtsev, Soviet Union, 25:23.7
3. Sergei Tchepikov, Soviet Union, 25:29.4

1984
1. Eirik Kvalfoss, Norway, 30:53.8
2. Peter Angerer, West Germany, 31:02.4
3. Matthias Jacob, East Germany, 31:10.5

1980
1. Frank Ullrich, East Germany, 32:10.69
2. Vladimir Alikin, Soviet Union, 32:53.10
3. Anatoli Alyabiev, Soviet Union, 33:09.16

Biathlon—Men's 20 Kilometers

1992
1. Yevgeny Redkine, Unified Team, 57:34.4
2. Mark Kirchner, Germany, 57:40.8
3. Mikael Lofgren, Sweden, 57:59.4

1988
1. Frank-Peter Roetsch, East Germany, 56:33.3
2. Valeri Medvedtsev, Soviet Union, 56:54.6
3. Johann Passler, Italy, 57:10.1

1984
1. Peter Angerer, West Germany, 1:11:52.7
2. Frank-Peter Roetsch, East Germany, 1:13:21.4
3. Eirik Kvalfoss, Norway, 1:14:02.4

1980
1. Anatoli Alyabiev, Soviet Union, 1:08:16.31
2. Frank Ullrich, East Germany, 1:08:27.79
3. Eberhard Rosch, East Germany, 1:11:11.73

1976
1. Nikolai Kruglov, Soviet Union, 1:14:12.26
2. Heikki Ikola, Finland, 1:15:54.10
3. Aleksandr Elizarov, Soviet Union, 1:16:05.57

1972
1. Magnar Solberg, Norway, 1:15:55.50
2. Hans-Jorg Knauthe, East Germany, 1:16:07.60
3. Lars-Goran Arwidson, Sweden, 1:16:27.03

1968
1. Magnar Solberg, Norway, 1:13:45.9
2. Aleksandr Tikhonov, Soviet Union, 1:14:40.4
3. Vladimir Gundartsev, Soviet Union, 1:18:27.4

1964
1. Vladimir Melanin, Soviet Union, 1:20:26.8
2. Aleksandr Privalov, Soviet Union, 1:23:42.5
3. Olav Jordet, Norway, 1:24:38.8

1960
1. Klas Lestander, Sweden, 1:33:21.6
2. Antti Tyrvainen, Finland, 1:33:57.7
3. Aleksandr Privalov, Soviet Union, 1:34:54.2

1924-1956 Not held

Biathlon—Men's 4 x 7.5km Relay

1992
1. Germany, 1:24:43.5, Ricco Gross, Jens Steinigen, Mark Kirchner, Friderich Fischer
2. Unified Team, 1:25:06.3, Valeri Medvedtsev, Alexandre Popov, Valeri Kirienko, Sergei Tchepikov
3. Sweden, 1:25:38.2, Johansson, Andersson, Wiksten, Mikael Lofgren

1988
1. Soviet Union, 1:22:30.0, Dmitri Vassiliev, Sergei Tchepikov, Alexandre Popov, Valeri Medvedtsev

2. West Germany, 1:23:37.4, Ernst
Reiter, Stefan Hoeck, Peter Angerer,
Friderich Fischer
3. Italy, 1:23:51.5, Werner Kiem,
Gottlieb Taschler, Johann Passler,
Andreas Zingerle

1984 1. Soviet Union, 1:38:51.7, Dmitri
Vassiliev, Yuri Kachkarov, Alguimantas
Shalna, Serguey Bouliguin
2. Norway, 1:39:03.9, Odd Lirhus, Eirik
Kvalfoss, Rolf Storsveen, Kjell Soebak
3. West Germany, 1:39:05.1, Ernst
Reiter, Walter Pichler, Peter Angerer,
Fritz Fischer

1980 1. Soviet Union, 1:34:03.27, Vladimir
Alikin, Aleksandr Tikhonov, Vladimir
Barnashov, Anatoli Alyabiev
2. East Germany, 1:34:56.99, Mathias
Jung, Klaus Siebert, Frank Ullrich,
Eberhard Roesch
3. West Germany, 1:37:30.26, Franz
Bernreiter, Hans Estner, Peter Angerer,
Gerd Winkler

1976 1. Soviet Union, 1:57:55.64, Ivan Biakov,
Aleksandr Elizarov, Nikolai Kruglov,
Aleksandr Tikhonov
2. Finland, 2:01:45.58, Hendrik Flojt,
Esko Saira, Juhani Suutarinen, Heikki
Ikola
3. East Germany, 2:04:08.61, Karl-Heinz
Menz, Frank Ullrich, Manfred Beer,
Manfred Geyer

1972 1. Soviet Union, 1:51:44.92, Aleksandr
Tikhonov, Rinnat Safine, Ivan Biakov,
Viktor Mamatov
2. Finland, 1:54:37.25, Esko Saira, Juhani
Suutarinen, Heikki Ikola, Mauri
Roppanen

3. East Germany, 1:54:57.67, Hans-Jorg
Knauthe, Joachim Meischner, Dieter
Speer, Horst Koschka

1968 1. Soviet Union, 2:13:02.4, Aleksandr
Tikhonov, Nikolai Pusanov, Viktor
Mamatov, Vladimir Gundartsev
2. Norway, 2:14:50.2, Ola Waerhaug,
Olav Jordet, Magnar Solberg, Jon
Istad
3. Sweden, 2:17:26.3, Lars-Goran
Arwidson, Tore Eriksson, Olle
Petrusson, Holmfrid Olsson

**1924-
1964** **Not held**

Biathlon—Women's 7.5km

1992 1. Anfissa Restzova, Unified Team,
24:29.2
2. Antje Misersky, Germany, 24:45.1
3. Elena Belova, Unified Team, 24:50.8

Biathlon—Women's 15km

1992 1. Antje Misersky, Germany, 51:47.2
2. Svetlana Pecherskaia, Unified Team,
51:58.5
3. Myriam Bedard, Canada, 52:15.0

Biathlon—Women's 3 x 7.5km Relay

1992 1. France, 1:15:55.6, Corinne Niogret,
Veronique Claudel, Anne Briand
2. Germany, 1:16:18.4, Antje Misersky,
Petra Schaaf, Disl
3. Unified Team, 1:16:54.6, Elena
Belova, Anfissa Restzova, Melnikova

Trivia Quiz

1. The dots biathletes shoot at:

A) are of the same size for both the standing and prone shots. **B)** are of
different sizes, with the standing shots of smaller diameter than the prone
shots. **C)** are of different sizes, with the prone shots of smaller diameter than
the standing shots.

2. Biathlon relays are:

A) mass-start events in which teammates use hand-tags to complete a leg.
B) are individual-start events in which teammates pass a baton to complete a
leg. **C)** are mass-start events in which the athlete completing a leg must
physically touch his or her teammate's body.

3. Biathlon first appeared in the Winter Games:

A) at Squaw Valley in 1960, with the debut of the men's 20km. **B)** in the first
Winter Games, in 1924, where all distances except the relay were medal
events. **C)** as a demonstration sport at Innsbruck, in 1964.

4. Women have participated in the biathlon in the Winter Games:

A) ever since the sport was first introduced to the Games, for both men and women. **B)** only once, at Albertville in 1992, where they competed in both individual and relay events. **C)** since the Canadian hosts introduced the women's event in Calgary in 1988.

5. Each biathlete skis a set distance with:

A) a .22 caliber rifle weighing as much as 11 pounds slung over one shoulder. **B)** a specially designed graphite rifle weighing as little as 3.5 pounds. **C)** a pearl-handled .45 slung in a lycra hip pouch.

6. In between shooting stops, biathletes:

A) ski all-out to make it to the next stop as quickly as possible. **B)** don't ski all-out, knowing that a skyrocketing heart rate could shake their aim. **C)** frequently take cat-naps.

7. The men's relay has traditionally been dominated by:

A) the Norwegians, who have won every biathlon relay in the Games since 1964. **B)** the Italians, who usually fail to medal in the individual events. **C)** the Russians, who missed out only once on the relay gold since the event was first introduced.

8. The sport of biathlon:

A) is very popular in the US, with more than 25,000 participants. **B)** is not very popular in the US, with fewer than 1,000 Americans participating. **C)** is the official state sport of Hawaii.

9. Each miss in the men's 20km and women's 15km race:

A) adds one minute to the competitor's final time. **B)** adds 10 seconds to the competitor's lap time. **C)** robs the competitor of one shot in the next round.

10. Each miss in the men's 10km and women's 7.5km race:

A) means the competitor must ski a 150-meter penalty loop. **B)** adds 30 seconds to the competitor's final time. **C)** adds nothing to the final score provided the competitor makes up the shot with an extra round, loaded as a single shot.

Biathlon

Answers: 1-b, 2-c, 3-a, 4-b, 5-a, 6-b, 7-c, 8-b, 9-a, 10-a

71

BOBSLEDDING

WARM-UP

Using a strip of animal skin stretched between pieces of wood, humans first started sledding some 15,000 years ago as a means of transportation. During the heyday of the Roman Empire, one-man handsleds were used to carry supplies and mail, a practice that was also common among Native North American tribes. A giant step in winter navigation occurred when the Eskimos hitched dogs to their sleds.

During the 1870s, tobogganing became popular in Canada. Racing officially began in 1877 in Davos, Switzerland. In 1883, the British staged the first Davos international race. A year later the Grand National Toboggan Race attracted a field of 20 at St. Moritz.

fact: The first structured toboggan run was built in 1884 in St. Moritz, Switzerland.

St. Moritz and Davos both profess to be the birthplace of bobsledding. The first bobsled used for sport was brought to Davos in the winter of 1888–89 by Stephen Whitney, a tourist from New York. The bobsled consisted of two low "American" sleds bolted together.

fact: Bobsleds are named after the bobbing of crew members on straightaways to gain speed.

The American sleds had made their debut in 1887 and had proven their superiority over the local Davos sleds. To create the longer bobsled, the sleds were bolted together with a board. The front sled, used for steering, was connected to the long board by a round bolt so that it would be free to turn. It had a thick wooden rod running crossways through the front sled and extending 20 centimeters on either side to form handles. This new model was tested on the run, where it reached a considerable speed and was described as "a very dangerous machine to drive."

According to legend, the earliest of the sleds had no brakes, so the driver used a garden rake to stop. Primitive rope steering often permitted the sledders to veer successfully off course and into harm's way. Whitney and his bruised followers steered their one-man sleds lying down, head first, the better with which to run into snowbanks and trees. The problem of the erratic steering was solved to an extent by introducing heavier sleds; the first steel bobsled was a two-seater or multi-seater, used in the winter of 1889–90. The sleds were shortly thereafter named Bob, inspired by the "bobbing" of crew members on straightaways to increase speed. In 1896, the St. Moritz Bobsleigh Club was formed, and the sport began to grow. Other winter resorts took up the daredevil sport. By 1911, some sixty runs served sledders in Switzerland, although only a very few were more than ordinary streets with snow-reinforced curves. The first artificial bobsled run was built at St. Moritz in 1904.

fact: The East Germans are responsible for the sport's big innovations, including the two-part rear axle, the independent suspension system, and a better steering mechanism.

Austria was the site of the first national championship in 1908, followed two years later by Germany. The first European championships were staged in 1914. During the early racing years, when the sleds carried five people, the rules stipulated that two members of each team be women. But as bobsleds became slicker and faster and the danger increased, men were allowed to replace the women.

Until the 1920s, no equipment rules existed. Sporting attire for men consisted of thick woolen caps pulled down to expose only the eyes and nose to the cold, sweaters, elbow-length gloves, cuffs or leggings made of sailcloth or leather, and high hiking boots. At the outset, women always wore long winter coats over long skirts, high-topped boots, hoods, or the ever-present broad-brimmed hats tied by scarves; otherwise, the clothing was the same as that for skiing.

fact: Generally, there's an inverse relationship between a sport's technicality and the number of US medals. The more technical the sport, the fewer medals the US collects. Bobsled is no exception: the US hasn't medaled since 1956.

Safety was first addressed by simple protective devices, starting with seat cushions, runners with iron struts, and hand and belt loops that offered a grip.

Between 1920 and 1930, bobsledders started wearing protective helmets made of compressed cardboard, leather, plywood, and other materials; they became regulation items in the early 1930s.

In 1923, the International Federation of Bobsled and Tobogganing was organized, just in time to permit bobsledding to be included in the 1924 Winter Olympics, the sport's first recognized international race. In 1927, the first world championship was held at St. Moritz.

▼

SPECTATOR'S GUIDE

The Olympic program includes two bobsled races, the two-man and four-man. Four-man racing was part of the 1924 Olympic schedule, while two-man was added in 1932. Although women were among the pioneers of the sport, they have never competed in the Olympics.

The chief attractions of bobsledding are the speed of the sleds (approaching 90 miles per hour) and the danger to the crew (resting on a sled less than a foot above the ground while flying down a mile-long course containing a series of curves designed to control speed as well as increase it).

Bobsled speed is affected by three main factors: weight, air resistance, and friction. All things being equal, the heaviest sled/crew combination will run the fastest. Therefore, a maximum weight is set for each sled and crew combination. A four-man sled cannot exceed 630 kilograms (approximately 1,338 pounds), while two-man sleds cannot exceed 390 kilograms (859 pounds). Lighter crews can add weight to their sleds before a race. But heavier sleds can prove more difficult to start, a critical element to racers. Explosive starts result in fast finish times. Racers who beat a competitor's time by a second at the beginning of the race can finish up to three seconds faster at the bottom. Considering this, adding weight to a sled for competition can be more detrimental than helpful to a lighter bobsled team.

fact: Push time is the crucial factor—how long it takes the sledders to propel their craft and leap into it over the 50-meter starting run. A tenth of a second shaved off push time can earn a third of a second off the entire run.

Steering and the downhill line of the bobsled are also very critical elements. The sled's steering component is a rope pulley system. Drivers barely have to move the ropes to affect the direction of the sled. Therefore, less steering minimizes movement of the sled. Best results are when the crew stays as still as possible and the driver lets the sled do the work for him.

The downhill line of the sled should be as close to a straight line as possible. Sleds can lose tremendous amounts of speed at the top of the race by merely bumping into a wall. This translates into slower down times for the entire race. Drivers try to keep the sleds from rocking side to side when exiting curves, maintaining the straightest possible line down the course. A sled appearing to slingshot cleanly out of a curve is the sled that will post the faster finish time.

fact: The hardest part of launching a bob-sled is jumping into it without scratching your teammates with the hundreds of needles projecting from the soles of your sledding shoes; the needles grip the ice during push time.

The brakeman must be strong, and, since he is the last man to jump on the sled, must be the best pusher. He also is responsible for stopping the sled smoothly at the end of the run, using a lever attached to a saw-toothed brake bar that digs into the ice. The other two men on the four-man team follow the instructions of the brakeman, and the three of them will bob on signal from almost a lying position to a sitting position on the straightaways to help the sled jump forward. If the brake is applied before the finish line, the sled is disqualified.

For each event four heats are run, and the results are based on total time.

Each country is allowed a squad of 12, and competitors can be entered in both events. A country is permitted to enter two teams in each event. The starting lineups don't have to be selected until shortly before each event, and the draw to determine the starting order can be critical, since the early starters are likely to have a slower track.

The technical side of the bobsled is very specific. For example, the maximum distance from the front tip of the front runners to the rear tip of the rear runners is 270 centimeters for the two-man sled, 335 centimeters for the four-man sled.

Geoff Bodine's New American Bobsled

Race car driver Geoff Bodine became interested in bobsled racing while watching the 1992 Winter Olympics on television. He then went to the US team's training facility in Lake Placid, New York, to try the sport.

During that Lake Placid trip, Bodine rode as brakeman behind driver Bruce Rosselli on a one-mile course and piloted on two shorter runs. He called the experience hair-raising and compared it to flying an F-15 fighter jet.

Bodine is no stranger to speed. His turbo-charged Ford Thunderbird averages more than 100 miles per hour on NASCAR tracks. Yet after several

NASCAR racer Geoff Bodine, shown here at after a practice run for the Daytona 500, is developing a new sled for the 1994 American bobsledders.

trips down the icy runs in two- and four-man bobsleds, and after a minor collision with a snow bank, Bodine decided his future remains on auto-racing ovals.

Instead of abandoning his passion for the icy slides, though, he also decided to help the American team build a better bobsled. He provided money and organized an effort to construct an American-made sled with help from race car designers and university researchers.

American teams have traditionally used European sleds in competitions, and Bodine believes the Europeans, who now dominate the sport, keep the best sleds for themselves.

A bit of history: The first bobsleds consisted of animal skin stretched between wooden skis. Current models are sleek, aerodynamic, and heavy for better speed. Two-man models measure nine feet and must weigh under 850 pounds. The four-man is 12.5 feet and weighs about 1,388 pounds.

American-built sleds and American athletes ruled the sport until the late 1950s. Then Europeans came out with better sleds, and teams from Germany, Switzerland, and Austria began to win.

Good sleds cost $25,000 and up and are an important factor in a sport where a hundredth of a second decides races. Bodine provided $130,000 for his American sled project. Among those involved were Mont Hubbard, a University of California at Davis engineering professor; Chassis Dynamics, an Oxford, Connecticut, firm that builds race cars; and researchers from Washington University and the US Navy's Taylor Research Center.

Hubbard is an expert in sports biomechanics, having studied the engineering concepts involved in javelin-throwing, high jumping, and ski jumping. He also headed a team that developed the world's first bobsled simulator, which can be programmed to simulate any course in the world. The 1992 American Olympic team used the simulator for training. He also worked to improve sled runners and to lessen vibration.

Bodine unveiled the new two-man sled in January of 1993, saying he hoped it would lead Americans to a gold medal in Lillehammer, but the craft failed an inspection by the International Bobsled Federation two months later. The sport's governing body ruled the bobsled's body unacceptable.

The US team plans to revise the design and have new two- and four-man sleds ready for pre-Olympic trials and the Olympic Games.

At its unveiling, US bobsled driver Brian Shimer said the new model compares to his old sled like a Porsche compares to a Yugo. —B.L.

▼

HOPEFULS

German and Swiss teams have dominated the event for the last two decades, and many successful drivers, brakemen, and side pushers will be returning Olympians.

At the Albertville Games, for example, Switzerland won the gold in the two-man, followed by two German teams. In the four-man, Austria was first, with Germany second and Switzerland third.

German driver Wolfgang Hoppe is one of the world's most formidable bobsledders, with two Olympic gold medals (both won in 1984) and three silvers, one from 1992. He will be a favorite to win more medals.

Hoppe is not resting on past Olympic performances, however. His two-man sled was third at the 1992–93 World Championships at Igls, Austria, and his four-man sled finished fourth.

Swiss driver Gustav Weder also remains impressive. Weder piloted his four-man sled to a 1992–93 World Championships, and his two-man sled was second. Weder won gold and bronze medals in the 1992 Games.

Christoph Langen is another talented member of a talented German team. He won the bronze in the two-man sled in Albertville and was first again at the Igls World Championships.

The Austrians and Italians also are expected to remain competitive.

Hubert Schoesser was not aboard the four-man Austrian sled that won the gold in 1992, but he has come on strong since then. At Igls, Schoesser finished fourth in the two-man and second in the four-man. At a World Cup meet three weeks later at Lillehammer, Schoesser again finished fourth and second, in the two- and four-man, respectively.

Guenther Huber, an Italian, won three World Cup two-man competitions in 1992–93 and was fifth at the World Championships.

Among Americans, Brian Shimer is seen as having the best chance in Lillehammer. His four-man sled raced to third place at the World Championships.

American Bruce Roselli captured the North America's Cup Tour and improved steadily on the World Cup tour. Teammate Chuck Leonowicz scored several top-20 finishes on the World Cup circuit in two- and four-man sleds.

Briton Mark Trout finished seventh in a four-man sled at the Albertville Games and won a 1993 World Cup meet in Italy.

Watch, too, for representatives from warmer climes. Teams from Jamaica, Mexico, and the Virgin Islands won't win, but they know how to have fun in the snow.

Enjoy this year's competition. Rumor has it that Olympic organizers may discontinue bobsledding after Lillehammer.

Brian Shimer

Two-time Olympian Brian Shimer is probably the United States's best-known bobsledder, which means most Americans have never heard of him.

Shimer, a Florida native and former college football player, is also one of the world's best bobsledders. In the 1992 Olympics, he drove the two-man sled with pusher Herschel Walker that finished seventh. Since then, Shimer has compiled an impressive record on the World Cup circuit. The Shimer-piloted four-

American driver Brian Shimer and brakeman Herschel Walker push off to a seventh-place run at the Albertville Games.

man sled captured a bronze medal in the 1993 World Championships in Igls, Austria, the best US finish in 24 years.

Barring injury or mishap, Shimer's two- and four-man sleds should be strong contenders in Lillehammer.

While Shimer and his sled mates are well known on the European runs, it may take a medal at Lillehammer to cure their anonymity at home.

That lack of fame has made raising money difficult for the Americans. Shimer, 31, used his helmet to appeal for sponsors on a nationally televised competition last year. "Your sign here," his helmet said.

The only regulation bobsled facility in the United States is in Lake Placid, New York, not Shimer's sunny hometown of Naples, Florida. He was a state wrestling champion at Naples High School and a running back and wide receiver at Morehead (Kentucky) State University.

Shimer started bobsledding in 1985, after a recruiting drive by the US Bobsled Federation in which he tested well for strength and agility. He liked the sport's speed and danger. Shimer and his fellow drivers steer sleds hurtling down icy runs at 80 miles per hour, fighting gravitational force the whole way.

More recently, winning an Olympic medal has become his obsession.

Shimer was a brakeman on the US four-man sled in the 1988 Games. He left that team to pilot his own two-man sled. His seventh-place finish with Walker in the 1992 Games was a disappointment for the Americans.

Shimer's four-man team followed the Winter Games by capturing first place in the first three meets on the World Cup circuit. The team also grabbed two second places.

In addition to Shimer, the USA I World Cup four-man team comprises Randy Jones, brakeman, a Winston-Salem, North Carolina, native and Duke University football player and runner with a degree in mechanical engineering; Joe Sawyer, side push, a Denver, Colorado, native and former football linebacker who was a member of the 1992 Olympic team; Bryan Leturgez, side push, a Cedar Lake, Indiana, native who played football at Purdue University and ran track at Indiana University, and who replaced the injured Sawyer as the 1992 US Olympic team captain; and Karlos Kirby, side push, a Clive, Iowa, native and two-time collegiate track All-American who was a member of the 1992 US Olympic team.

Jones and Shimer are paired on a two-man sled that finished with two second-place finishes, one fourth, and one fifth on the 1992–93 World cup circuit. They should be contenders in Lillehammer. —*B.L.*

The tentative bobsledding schedule is as follows:

Saturday, February 19
Two-man

Sunday, February 20
Two-man

Saturday, February 26
Four-man

Sunday, February 27
Four-man

▼

HIGHLIGHTS

Bobsledding was one of the original sports at the first Winter Games in 1924. The US won five bobsledding gold medals during the 1920s, 1930s, and 1940s, garnering in all 14 Olympic medals by 1956, including five gold, four silver, and five bronze. Since then the East Germans and Swiss have dominated the sport. Of 24 total medals awarded in the Olympics from 1976 to 1988, East Germany won 13 and Switzerland 6.

Switzerland won the first four-man gold awarded in the 1924 Games, with England taking the silver and Belgium the bronze; the Swiss sled carried two brothers, Alfred and Heinrich Schläppi. In 1928 the competition was plagued by a heavy thaw; the US took the gold and the silver in the five-man event, the only Games in which that event was held. US pilot William Fiske was only 16 when he won the gold in the five-man, making him the youngest male Winter Games gold medalist ever; his teammate in the second-place sled, Thomas Doe, Jr., was only 15 years old.

The weather was so bad in 1932 that the bobsled competitions were held after the official closing of the Games. Again in 1932 the US teams took the gold and silver in an event, this time the four-man; the US also captured the gold in the two-man event, with a sled carrying brothers Hubert and Curtis Stevens. Heavy rains threatened to disrupt the competition in 1936, but the course eventually smoothed out. The US maintained its streak in 1936, winning the gold and bronze in the two-man event, but Switzerland won its second gold in the four-man that year.

fact: Spying on rival teams' equipment is a revered tradition among aficionados of bobsled technology.

At the next Games, in 1948, the US recaptured the four-man gold, and for the first time a non-US team won the gold in the two-man, earned by a Swiss team; a burst waterpipe flooded the course and halted competition in the middle of the second run. In 1952 German pilot Andreas Ostler became the first man to drive two gold medal winning sleds in the same Olympics. That year the US took the two silvers, and Switzerland the two bronzes.

Italy helped confirm the end of American bobsledding dominance in 1956, taking the gold and silver in the two-man event and the silver in the four-man; Switzerland won the two-man bronze and the four-man gold; the US had to settle for a bronze in the four-man. One of Italy's sledders in the two-man, Giacomo Conti, was 47 years old, the oldest gold medalist in the history of the Winter Games; Switzerland's gold medal winning pilot in the four-man, Franz Kapus, was 46 years old.

No bobsledding events were held in 1960, due to a lack of facilities at Squaw Valley; bobsled runs are expensive to construct and often see little use after the Olympic Games. In 1964 Canada won its first gold in the four-man, four bachelors from Montréal pulling off what was considered to be the biggest upset in bobsledding history; Britain took the two-man.

One of the most popular victories in the sport's history occurred in 1968, under threats of a dangerous thaw, when the fabled red-haired Italian, Eugenio Monti, led his country to a double victory in the two-man and four-man. In two previous Olympics, Monti had earned two silver medals and two bronze and, at the age of 40, he finally got his gold. West Germany garnered top honors in 1972, placing first and second in the two-man and taking the bronze in the four-man behind first-place Switzerland and second-place Italy; Switzerland also took the four-man bronze. That year the US failed for the first time to place a sled in the top ten.

fact: A common—though illegal—practice among bobsledders is to coat their runners with silicone.

The 1976 East German team came to Innsbruck with superb sleds and well-conditioned athletes; at these Games East German driver Meinhard Nehmer won the gold in the two-man and four-man bob. In so doing, he joined Ostler and Monti as the only drivers to pilot two sleds to the gold in the same Olympics. West Germany and Switzerland each took a silver and bronze at Innsbruck. In 1980 at Lake Placid East Germany took the gold and bronze in the four-man, with Nehmer again piloting the gold medal team, and silver and bronze—again with Nehmer medaling—in the two-man. Switzerland won the gold in the two-man and the four-man silver at Lake Placid.

In 1980 US team member Willie Davenport was attempting to equal the feat of Eddie Eagan, who became the first man to earn gold medals in both the Summer and Winter Games when he won a gold in the 1932 four-man bobsled to add to the boxing gold medal he'd won as a light heavyweight in 1920. Davenport competed in the 110m hurdles four times from 1964 to 1976, and was gold medalist in 1968 and bronze medalist in 1976. In 1980 Davenport and bobsled teammate Jeffrey Gadley were the first African Americans to compete in the Winter Games. A controversy between Davenport and his coach, Gary Sheffield, erupted over a racially inflected remark attributed to Davenport; shaken, the four-man sleds came in twelfth and thirteenth. The US team failed to garner a medal at Lake Placid, though placing fifth and sixth in the two-man was the team's best performance since 1956.

East German driver Wolfgang Hoppe earned the gold in both the two-man and four-man competitions in 1984, and two silvers in those events in 1988. With his 1984 victories he became the fourth driver to win two bobsled golds in the same Olympics.

fact: Because bobsled requires a lot of upper-body strength and foot speed, it's attracting cross-overs from football and track. Herschel Walker isn't the only crossover: Edwin Moses is also a serious bobsledophile.

The US team brought sleek new sleds to the 1988 Games, competing against the likes of the Puerto Rican team, made up of two New Yorkers, and Prince Albert Alexandre Louis Pierre of Monaco, the Marquis de Baux, who in 1988 was the youngest member of the IOC. Prince Albert's grandfather and uncle, the two Jack Kellys of Philadelphia, had also competed in the Games, the senior winning three gold medals in single and double sculls in 1920 and 1924, the junior winning a bronze in the single sculls in 1956. And then there was the underdog favorite, the 1988 Jamaican team, with only four months training behind them; they included a helicopter pilot, a reggae singer, and a sprint champion. Their team sponsor, a US business consultant, got the idea for a Jamaican bobsled team while watching the annual pushcart derby in Kingston in the summer of 1987.

Albertville Highlights: A Crossover Experiment

The 1992 bob run at La Plagne turned into a costly debacle when a leak in the refrigeration system added $20 million to the already stiff $22 million tab. That fixed, the banked turns—inclined to melt during certain periods of the day— added to organizers' worries. Technically, the course favored the more skillful drivers, and for the first time in a long time, the sledders didn't take a back seat to the sleds: while the previous four Games were largely determined by sled technology, the federation's new standards—dictating sled design, dimensions, and materials—left little room for aerodynamic shoo-ins.

With sleds conceived by a former auto designer, and with NFL ironman Herschel Walker entered as brakeman in both the two-man and four-man events, the US team hoped to medal for the first time since 1956. The start, powered by Walker's 29 1/2-inch fast twitch quadriceps, was to be the team's strong point.

NFL star Herschel Walker lent power but too little speed as brakeman for the two-man bobsled in Albertville; he and driver Brian Shimer hoped for the first US medal since 1956, but placed seventh.

Instead, the US two-man team's start sealed their seventh-place fate. Walker and driver Brian Shimer—who had been on the '88 four-man team—started the heats with about one tenth the number of training runs the best teams had. It showed. Walker, not especially fleet of foot behind a 440-pound sled, pushed no better than a sixth-fastest time, and gracefully entering the sled proved *très difficile* for the 220-pound running back. Pulled at the eleventh hour from the four-man sled amidst more than a little brou-ha, Walker claimed not to have been soured by the experience. *Sans* Walker, the US four-man sled finished in ninth place, one second—an eternity in bobsleighdom—behind the winners.

The Swiss team of Gustav Weder and Donat Acklin, who had finished fourth in Calgary, were in fifth place at the end of the first two heats, but managed to smoke the final two heats to sneak into first place. Just behind them, the world champion German team settled for silver with the smallest time difference since 1968.

The four-man competition was an exercise in splitting hairs. Two hundredths of a second faster than Germany, the Austria I crew savored victory by the smallest time difference ever recorded in an Olympic four-man bob competition. Switzerland, the Calgary titlists, slid into third place, even though their time was only 23 hundredths of a second slower than their winning 1988 time.

Herschel Walker

Herschel Walker mastered football, track, and taekwondo. Strength, speed, and athletic ability have earned him million-dollar salaries.

But he didn't conquer the bobsled runs of La Plagne, France, as a member of the 1992 US Olympic team.

Hailed as possibly the best bobsled pusher ever, the super athlete and professional football star became a bobsled sensation. His presence raised the profile and expectations of the American team, but not its position in the standings.

The two-man sled of Walker and driver Brian Shimer finished seventh in the 1992 Games, a respectable showing given Walker's inexperience and the world-class competition. In the end, it was clear that Walker needed more practice.

After the two-man results, Walker was dropped from the four-man team and replaced by Chris Coleman, whom Walker had beaten during team push-off qualification trials.

A talented and sometimes controversial athlete, Walker tried bobsledding at the suggestion of another football pro, Willie Gault, in 1989. Gault was a member of the 1988 US team, along with sprinter Edwin Moses. Walker tried bobsledding in Europe and loved the speed.

His own speed during Olympic tryouts earned him a berth on the US team.

He wasn't bobsledding for the money. Walker had been earning $2 million annually as a Minnesota Viking, though he was unhappy with the team. He won the 1982 Heisman Trophy at the University of Georgia as college football's top running back. Reviews of his professional career were mixed.

Walker is serious about fitness. His daily regimen includes 2,000 sit-ups and 1,500 push-ups in the morning, and 500 sit-ups every night. His Olympic training diet was mostly bread, water, fruit juice, and french fries.

A black belt in taekwondo, Walker has wondered aloud about competing as an Olympian in that sport. He is six feet tall and, as a bobsledder, weighed 220 pounds. His waist measures 31 inches but his massive thighs require size-40 trousers. Not limiting his athleticism to sports, Walker has danced with the Fort Worth ballet.

He was a celebrity among the amateur athletes in Albertville, saying he wanted to push the Americans bobsledders, winless for 36 years, past powerhouse teams like Germany and Switzerland.

A good start is vital in bobsledding, and speed and timing are integral to a fast start. For 50 meters the crew pushes the sled at full speed, then jumps in. The brakeman is the speediest crew member and the last one in the sled, which is moving 28 miles per hour by the time he jumps in. Shimer and Walker suffered from slow starts. In one heat, Walker jumped in too soon. They finished a third of a second behind gold medalists Gustav Weder and Donat Acklin of Switzerland.

Ironically, Walker's training focused on pushing but not jumping in the sled. Before the Olympics, he had raced only once, a year earlier. He had made only about 50 runs; his teammates make 200 a year.

The Shimer–Walker top-10 finish compares favorably to the Americans' 1988 performance. Also, the 1992 American four-man team, with Coleman aboard, was ninth. —B.L.

Medalists

Bobsled—Two-Man

1992
1. Switzerland, 4:03.26, Gustav Weder, Donat Acklin
2. Germany, 4:03.55, Rudolf Lochner, Markus Zimmermann
3. Germany, 4:03.63, Christoph Langen, Gunther Eger

1988
1. Soviet Union (I), 3:53.48, Ianis Kipours, Vladimir Kozlov
2. East Germany (I), 3:54.19, Wolfgang Hoppe, Bogdan Musiol
3. East Germany (II), 3:54.64, Bernhard Lehmann, Mario Hoyer

1984
1. East Germany (II), 3:25.56, Wolfgang Hoppe, Dietmar Schauerhammer
2. East Germany (I), 3:26.04, Bernhard Lehmann, Bogdan Musiol
3. Soviet Union (II), 3:26.16, Zintis Ekmanis, Vladimir Aleksandrov

1980
1. Switzerland (II), 4:09.36, Erich Schaerer, Josef Benz
2. East Germany (II), 4:10.93 Bernhard Germeshausen, Hans Jurgen Gerhardt
3. East Germany (I), 4:11.08, Meinhard Nehmer, Bogdan Musiol

1976
1. East Germany (I), 3:44.42, Meinhard Nehmer, Bernhard Germeshausen
2. West Germany (I), 3:44.99, Wolfgang Zimmerer, Manfred Schumann
3. Switzerland (I), 3:45.70, Erich Schaerer, Josef Benz

1972
1. West Germany (II), 4:57.07, Wolfgang Zimmerer, Peter Utzschneider
2. West Germany (I), 4:58.84, Horst Floth, Pepi Bader
3. Switzerland (I), 4:59.33, Jean Wicki, Edy Hubacher

1968
1. Italy (I), 4:41.54, Eugenio Monti, Luciano De Paolis
2. West Germany (I), 4:41.54, Horst Floth, Pepi Bader
3. Romania (I), 4:44.46, Ion Panturu, Nicolae Neagoe

1964
1. Great Britain (I), 4:21.90, Anthony Nash, Robin Dixon
2. Italy (II), 4:22.02, Sergio Zardini, Romano Bonagura
3. Italy (I), 4:22.63, Eugenio Monti, Sergio Siorpaes

1960 **Not held**

1956
1. Italy (I), 5:30.14, Lamberto Dalla Costa, Giacomo Conti
2. Italy (II), 5:31.45, Eugenio Monti, Renzo Alvera
3. Switzerland (I), 5:37.46, Max Angst, Harry Warburton

1952
1. Germany (I), 5:24.54, Andreas Ostler, Lorenz Nieberl
2. USA (I), 5:26.89, Stanley Benham, Patrick Martin
3. Switzerland (I), 5:27.71, Fritz Feierabend, Stephan Waser

1948
1. Switzerland (II), 5:29.2, Felix Endrich, Friedrich Waller
2. Switzerland (I), 5:30.4, Fritz Feierabend, Paul Eberhard
3. USA (II), 5:35.3, Fred Fortune, Schuyler Carron

1936
1. USA (I), 5:29.29, Ivan Brown, Alan Washbound
2. Switzerland (II), 5:30.64, Fritz Feierabend, Joseph Beerli
3. USA(II), 5:33.96, Gilbert Colgate, Richard Lawrence

1932
1. USA (I), 8:14.74, Hubert Stevens, Curtis Stevens
2. Switzerland (II), 8:16.28, Reto Capadrutt, Oscar Geier
3. USA (II), 8:29.15, John R. Heaton, Robert Minton

1924-
1928 **Not held**

Bobsled—Four-Man

1992
1. Austria, 3:53.90, Ingo Appelt, Winkler, Haidacher, Thomas Schroll
2. Germany, 3:53.92, Wolfgang Hoppe, Bogdan Musiol, Kuhn, Hannemann
3. Switzerland, 3:54.13, Gustav Weder, Donat Acklin, Schindelholz, Morell

1988
1. Switzerland (I), 3:47.51, Ekkehard Fasser, Kurt Meier, Marcel Faessler, Werner Stocker
2. East Germany (I), 3:47.58, Wolfgang Hoppe, Dietmar Schauerhammer, Bogdan Musiol, Ingo Voge
3. Soviet Union (II), 3:48.26, Ianis Kipours, Gountis Ossis, Iouri Tone, Vladimir Kozlov

1984
1. East Germany (I), 3:20.22, Wolfgang Hoppe, Roland Wetzig, Dietmar Schauerhammer, Andreas Kirchner
2. East Germany (II), 3:20.78, Bernhard Lehmann, Bogdan Musiol, Ingo Voge, Eberhard Weise
3. Switzerland (I), 3:21.39, Silvio Giobellina, Heinz Stettler, Urs Salzmann, Rico Freiermuth

1980
1. East Germany (I), 3:59.92, Meinhard Nehmer, Bogdan Musiol, Bernhard Germeshausen, Hans Jurgen Gerhardt

2. Switzerland (I), 4:00.87, Erich Schaerer, Ulrich Baechli, Rudolf Marti, Josef Benz
3. East Germany (II), 4:00.97, Horst Schoenau, Roland Wetzig, Detlef Richter, Andreas Kirchner

1976
1. East Germany (I), 3:40.43, Meinhard Nehmer, Jochen Babcok, Bernhard Germeshausen, Bernhard Lehmann
2. Switzerland (II), 3:40.89, Erich Schaerer, Ulrich Baechli, Rudolf Marti, Josef Benz
3. West Germany (I), 3:41.37, Wolfgang Zimmerer, Peter Utzschneider, Bodo Bittner, Manfred Schumann

1972
1. Switzerland (I), 4:43.07, Jean Wicki, Hans Leutenegger, Werner Camichel, Edy Hubacher
2. Italy (I), 4:43.83, Nevio De Zordo, Adriano Frassinelli, Corrado Dal Fabbro, Gianni Bonichon
3. West Germany (I), 4:43.92, Wolfgang Zimmerer, Stefan Gaisreiter, Walter Steinbauer, Peter Utzschneider

1968
1. Italy (I), 2:17.39, Eugenio Monti, Luciano De Paolis, Roberto Zandonella, Mario Armano
2. Austria (I), 2:17.48, Erwin Thaler, Reinhold Durnthaler, Herbert Gruber, Josef Eder
3. Switzerland (I), 2:18.04, Jean Wicki, Hans Candrian, Willi Hofmann, Walter Graf

1964
1. Canada (I), 4:14.46, Victor Emery, Peter Kirby, Douglas Anakin, John Emery
2. Austria (I), 4:15.48, Erwin Thaler, Adolf Koxeder, Josef Nairz, Reinhold Durnthaler
3. Italy (II), 4:15.60, Eugenio Monti, Sergio Siorpaes, Benito Rigoni, Gildo Siorpaes

1960 **Not held**

1956
1. Switzerland (I), 5:10.44, Franz Kapus, Gottfried Diener, Robert Alt, Heinrich Angst
2. Italy (II), 5:12.10, Eugenio Monti, Ulrico Girardi, Renzo Alvera, Renato Mocellini
3. USA (I), 5:12.39, Arthur Tyler, William Dodge, Charles Butler, James Lamy

1952
1. Germany (I), 5:07.84, Andreas Ostler, Friedrich Kuhn Lorenz Nieberl, Franz Kemser
2. USA (I), 5:10.48, Stanley Benham, Patrick Martin, Howard Crossett, James Atkinson
3. Switzerland (I), 5:11.70, Fritz Feierabend, Albert Madorin, Andre Filippini, Stephan Waser

1948
1. USA(II), 5:20.1, Francis Tyler, Patrick Martin, Edward Rimkus, William D'Amico
2. Belgium (I), 5:21.3, Max Houben, Freddy Mansveld, Louis-George Niels, Jacques Mouvet
3. USA (I), 5:21.5, James Bickford, Thomas Hicks, Donald Dupree, William Dupree

1936
1. Switzerland (II), 5:19.85, Pierre Musy, Arnold Gartmann, Charles Bouvier, Joseph Beerli

2. Switzerland (I), 5:22.73, Reto Capadrutt, Hans Aichele, Fritz Feierabend, Hans Butikofer
3. Great Britain (I), 5:23.41, Frederick McEvoy, James Cardno, Guy Dugdale, Charles Green

1932
1. USA (I), 7:53.68, William Fiske, Edward Eagan, Clifford Gray, Jay O'Brien
2. USA (II), 7:55.70, Henry Homburger, Percy Bryant, Paul Stevens, Edmund Horton
3. Germany (I), 8:00.04, Hanns Kilian, Max Ludwig, Dr. Hans Melhorn, Sebastian Huber

1928
1. USA (II), 3:20.5, William Fiske, Nion Tocker, Charles Mason, Clifford Gray, Richard Parke

2. USA (I), 3:21.0, Jennison Heaton, David Granger, Lyman Hine, Thomas Doe, Jay O'Brien
3. Germany (II), 3:21.9, Hanns Kilian, Valentin Krempl, Hans Hess, Sebastian Huber, Hans Nagle

1924
1. Switzerland (I), 5:45.54, Eduard Scherrer, Alfred Neveu, Alfred Schläppi, Heinrich Schläppi
2. Great Britain (II), 5:48.83, Ralph H. Broome, T. A. Arnold, H. A. W. Richardson, Rodney E. Soher
3. Belgium (I), 6:02.29, Charles Mulder, Rene Mortiaux, Paul van den Broeck, Victor Verschueren, Henri Willems

Trivia Quiz

1. The first official bobsled race:

A) was staged by the British in 1877 in Davos, Switzerland. B) was staged by the Norwegians in the 17th century near Lillehammer. C) was not held until 1912, when the Canadians sponsored a race at St. Moritz.

2. The first bobsled used for sport:

A) was at the time a high-tech device designed by an alpine ski racer. B) consisted of two low "American" sleds bolted together. C) was named "Rosebud" and has been lost in a fire.

3. Bobsleds derive their name:

A) from the name of the inventor of the first steel bobsled, Bob Roberts. B) from the name of American medalist Robert Minton. C) from the "bobbing" motion used by crew members to gain speed on straightaways.

4. Bobsledding is not traditionally a woman's sport:

A) Lillehammer will be the first Games where women are allowed to compete in bobsled events. B) women competed in bobsled events for the first time in 1992 at Albertville. C) women have never competed in bobsled events in the Olympics.

5. Bobsledding events first appeared in the Games:

A) at Antwerp, in 1920, where ice hockey made its Olympic debut. B) at Chamonix, in 1924, the first Winter Games. C) at Los Angeles, in 1984, where Carl Lewis led the American team to a gold medal.

6. Bad weather and poor conditions:

A) never affect the bobsled events since they are held on man-made tracks. B) caused the bobsled events to be held after the official closing of the Games in 1932. C) have caused the postponement of some event in six out of the past eight Games.

7. While the East Germans and Swiss currently dominate the sport, prior to the mid-1950s fourteen Olympic medals went to:

A) Belgium. B) Italy. C) USA.

8. The following did not compete in a bobsled event at a Games:

A) a Jamaican bobsled team. B) Herschel Walker. C) Bo Jackson.

9. In the four-man event, the last man to jump onto the sled:

A) is the best pusher, who must wedge himself in between his teammates. B) is the brakeman, who sits in the last position in the sled. C) is the pilot, who steers from the back of the sled.

10. Technical specifications concerning the bobsled:

A) are very vague, and concern only the material from which a sled can and cannot be constructed. B) are very specific, and dictate the maximum distance permitted between the front tip of the front runners and the rear tip of the rear runners. C) call for sleds of different weights to compensate for weight differences among teams and individual sledders.

Answers: 1-a, 2-b, 3-c, 4-c, 5-b, 6-b, 7-c, 8-c, 9-b, 10-b

FIGURE SKATING

WARM-UP

The first known skates were carved out of rib or shank bones of elk and reindeer. Early northern Europeans tied the skates to their feet and propelled themselves across the ice with poles. The word "skate" probably is derived from the very old Low German word "schake," meaning a shank or leg bone, as well as from the Dutch "schaats," Danish "skoite," English "scatch," and Scottish "sketcher."

fact: A 1992 survey indicated that figure skater Dorothy Hamill (1976 Winter Games gold medalist) and gymnast Mary Lou Retton (1984 Summer Games multi-medalist) are the USA's most beloved athletes.

Although skating was born in Europe, figure skating as we know it traces its origins directly back to an American—Jackson Haines—who was born in New York in 1840 and died in Finland in 1875, a victim of pneumonia, infected during a raging blizzard while traveling by sled from St. Petersburg to Stockholm.

Prior to that rather cold but romantic demise, Haines enjoyed his 15 minutes of fame and glory. Just before the Civil War, a skating craze, accompanied by a dancing craze, swept the country, inspiring ballet master Haines to combine virtuoso skating skills with expressive dance movements. At that time, figure skating was a stiff and rigid exhibition, a favorite with European aristocrats who dabbled in "artistic skating" for the amusement of friends and family. Haines won figure skating's Championships of America (now called the US Championships). But continued cool reception in the US prompted him to leave for Europe, where he was, of course, warmly received. He made his home in Vienna, creating the "International Style of Figure Skating." Haines translated ballet steps to skates, and the ensuing craze that swept Europe inspired composers to create special waltzes for dancers on skates.

quote: "The jumps were never supposed to mean so much. You need it all: the lightness and the airiness; the music, the personality.... You need the caressing of the ice."
—1960 gold medalist and present-day coach Carol Heiss, the first woman to land a double axel.

But it was not until the first decade of the 20th century that this style was fully accepted in America. Haines, however, became known as the "American Ice Master" in Europe, opening skating schools in several countries.

One of the men influenced by Haines was Canadian Louis Rubinstein, who formed the Amateur Skating Association of Canada in 1878. Nine years later the Skating Club of the United States was established in Philadelphia. Rubinstein, who won the Canadian figure skating championship every year from 1878 to 1889, was the US champion in 1888 and 1889, and in 1890 he won the world championship in Russia.

Figure skating was added to the 1908 Olympic Games, 16 years prior to the start of the Winter Olympic Games. However, the sport continued to function informally in the US through local skating clubs until 1921, when the United States Figure Skating Association (USFSA) was formed.

But figure skating did not become widely popular in America until a 13-year-old Norwegian girl by the name of Sonja Henie created a figure-skating stir in the 1920s. At the mere age of 10 in 1924, Henie won the Norwegian figure skating championship. Starting in 1927 (at the more mature age of 13), she took the world championship 10 straight years, fitting in three Olympic gold medals during the same period (the first in 1928 and the last in 1936). It was Henie who made figure skating the most popular of the Olympic events and professionalized the sport as a lucrative career.

fact: Experts project that the ladies' figure skating winner could have $10 million earning power by the end of this century. Tennis is the only other sport in which women can net earnings comparable to men.

In 1961, with the US reigning supreme as the world's premier figure skating team, tragedy struck. In February, a plane carrying the American team to the world championship in Prague crashed near Brussels, killing all 73 people aboard, including 18 team members, five coaches, the team manager, and friends and relatives. The team was shattered; though they'd won gold medals in the men's and ladies' singles during the 1956 and 1960 Games, the US did not take the gold again in either of these events until 1968, when Peggy Fleming won the ladies' singles. In the men's singles competition, the US did not win a gold medal until 1984, when Scott Hamilton triumphed.

Ice dancing was added to the Winter Olympic program in 1976, joining men's and ladies' singles and pairs skating. As its name implies, ice dancing is based on different aspects of dance, with the emphasis on rhythm and steps. The beauty of ice dancing lies in its precise footwork, coordination, and creative flair. Another change in figure skating competition came during the 1992 Winter Games, where for the first time the compulsory figures, those 42 enticing variations on the figure eight, did not figure into the men's and ladies' singles competitions.

SPECTATOR'S GUIDE

Figure skaters actually skate on water; as the steel blade cuts through the ice, the friction causes the ice to momentarily melt; it immediately refreezes after the blade passes.

Rather than a flat blade with a single edge, the figure skate blade is concave, creating two sharp edges that must be continually sharpened to maintain an even speed for cutting through the ice. The skates have an outside edge, on the outside of the foot, and an inside edge toward the body. Each edge has a front and a back, so that the skate has four pressure points. Different moves and jumps are done from specific edges of the skate blade. Figure skating blades also feature little spikes on the toes called "picks." These toe picks are used to perform certain maneuvers, jumps, and spins.

Two basic types of jumps are attempted: edge jumps and toe-assisted jumps. In toe-assisted jumps, the picks on one skate are pushed into the ice to help propel the skater into the air. On edge jumps, a skater presses into the ice with a certain edge of the skate and swings into the air with the force of the arms and other leg (the free leg). The majority of skaters spin to the left (counterclockwise).

quote: "I like jumps because they bring me the greatest pleasure.... All I can really do is jump. Figure skating is a matter of beauty, and Westerners are so stylish, so slender. I wish I could be beautiful like them." —Midori Ito, 1992 silver medalist and first woman to land a triple axel.

Olympic figure skating competition includes four separate disciplines: men's singles, ladies' singles, pairs, and ice dancing. Each draws on similar basic skills and techniques, but adheres to different rules and guidelines. Judges award marks to each skater ranging from 0.0 (did not skate) to 6.0 (perfect). Decimal points are used for exact placements, such as 4.8 or 5.3. In skating, the low and high marks *are not dropped,* and all of the points *are not added together.* Each judge's mark is converted into places—1st, 2nd, 3rd, etc. The skater winning the majority of first placements wins that event.

When you see the judges' marks posted in the arena, you are seeing them "horizontally" for one skater. You must look at all of the marks "vertically" to see the judges' marks for the skaters in relation to one another. Following each event, the placement that a skater earns is multiplied by a percentage, which is determined according to the value of the event.

Whew!

Scoring in figure skating is often the cause of controversy, and political influence is frequently suspected. Judging observes no binding guidelines on which to base marks and occasionally a wide disparity in marks for a skater will result. With nine judges, however, excessively high or low marks can usually be balanced.

quote: "One shouldn't be afraid to lose; this is sport," says fifteen-year-old Oksana Baiul of Ukraine. "One day you win; another day you lose. Of course, everyone wants to be the best. This is normal. This is what sport is about. This is why I love it."

The rules are similar for both **men's and ladies' singles.** Each competition is composed of two separate events: an original program and a long program. The combined placement from all the events makes up a competitor's total score. A third event, the **compulsory figures** (also known as "school figures"), was

Canadian skater Lloyd Eisler lifts partner Isabelle Brasseur during the figure skating exhibition at Albertville. The couple later captured a bronze medal in the pairs event.

eliminated from international competition in 1990 but may be skated as a separate medal in some competitions.

In the **original program,** also called the short program, the skater must execute, in two minutes and 40 seconds, eight required moves within a choreographed program using music. The required moves can be performed in any sequence of the skater's choice. The elements include a double axel; a double jump; a jump combination (two jumps following each other without a step in between); a flying jump spin; a spin with at least two changes of foot for men and a layback spin for women; a spin with at least one change of foot and at least two changes of position; two sequences of steps or footwork done in either a straight

Dressed in red and black and performing to Bizet's "Carmen," East Germany's Katarina Witt defended her figure skating title at Calgary. She'll likely be skating again at Lillehammer, after being reinstated as an amateur.

line, serpentine, or circular shape (one step sequence must be done in a spiral position for women).

Each skater receives two marks from each judge for the original program. The first mark is for technical merit—how well each of the required moves is done and how difficult they are. The second mark is for presentation and style (sometimes called artistic impression), which evaluates the overall presentation of the program.

The **long program** (also called the freestyle) is skated free of required elements. Four and a half minutes in length for men and four minutes for women, the long program is the most demanding part of the singles competition, requiring extreme stamina and concentration. Skaters select their own music and choreography blended with many different jumps, spins, and interpretive moves in a program designed to best display their technical and artistic skills.

As in the original program, two sets of marks are given. The first is for technical merit, the second for presentation and style of the overall program. While spectators may find that the grace, strength, and expression in a performance is pleasing, the judges are looking for technical and artistic excellence. An error, such as a fall, does not mean that the skater will lose the competition. Difficulty of moves and jumps, how they are executed, and the overall presentation are all considered.

If two skaters are tied at the end of the competition, the winner is determined first by the one who received the highest placement in the long program. If they are still tied, then the one with the highest presentation and style marks in the long program is declared the winner.

quote: "I always tell my girls: think like a man, but act and look like a woman." —1960 gold medalist and present-day coach Carol Heiss, the first woman to land a double axel.

Pairs skating is essentially skating performed in unison by partners, with the addition of daring and often dangerous lifts and throw jumps.

The key to pairs skating is exact timing and togetherness. Whether the partners skate in physical contact or apart, their movements should be synchronized with matching body lines, spins, gestures, and footwork.

In pairs skating, you will see "shadow skating," in which the couple skates in unison without touching, as well as "mirror skating," in which each skates identical moves in different directions, giving the illusion of a mirror. You will also see a variety of lifts and throws.

The pairs skating competition involves two parts—the original program and the long program. Each event is skated to the couple's own choice of music and choreography and includes scores for technical merit as well as style and presentation.

The **original program,** at two minutes, 40 seconds and worth 33.3% of the final score, includes eight required elements. These are: an overhead lift; a double twist lift; side-by-side solo double jumps; a solo spin in unison; a pair spin with at least one change of position and one change of foot; a death spiral; a spiral sequence; a step or footwork sequence of the skaters' choice. The required moves may be performed in any order.

The **long program** consists of technical and artistic moves choreographed to best display the skaters' individual strengths and abilities. Four and a half minutes long and 66.7% of the final score, the long program involves double and triple throw jumps, different overhead lifts and spins, variations on standard moves, and many original moves. Creativity, strength, endurance, and technical skills are all important.

fact: The International Skating Union no longer refers to "amateur" and "professional" skaters, preferring the terms "eligible" and "ineligible."

When watching **ice dancing,** watch for the flow of the program, the apparent ease with which difficult technical steps and moves are performed, and how well the music is interpreted. Ice dancers skate extremely close to each other and must remain in unison and contact during the program. They cannot separate for more than a few seconds. The strong, athletic moves seen in pair skating, such as overhead lifts and jumps, are prohibited in dance.

Ice dancing is comprised of three events: two compulsory dances, amounting to 20% of the final score; an original set pattern dance that is 30% of the final tally; and a four-minute free dance that counts for 50% of the total score.

Compulsory dances—such as the foxtrot, tango, blues, rhumba, Viennese waltz, and Yankee polka—are international dances frequently performed by ice dancers worldwide. From this list of dances, the couple selects two dances at random. To prescribed rhythms, the skaters execute specific steps in an exact manner. The skaters receive one score for each dance. The marks are added together to determine placements, and the couple scoring the highest mark finishes first.

The **original set pattern dance** is an original dance created by the couple to a previously announced rhythm, such as a waltz, tango, or polka. While the rhythm is preselected by skating officials, the music and choreography are chosen by the individual dancers. A definite dance pattern is created by the skaters, using the full surface of the ice. The skaters are judged on how well they interpret the rhythm and create an appropriate dance. Two marks are given: one for composition, which includes originality, difficulty of steps, variety, and the placement of steps in the pattern; the second mark is given for presentation, which reflects such components as timing, harmony of movements to the rhythm, and the interpretive style of the couple.

The **free dance** is performed to musical selections and choreography selected by the skaters. You may see different popular dances and rhythms used, such as graceful waltzes or fast jitterbugs, or you may see classical presentations. Although certain types of small lifts and original moves are used, free dance is differentiated from pairs skating by restrictions on the execution and number of these moves. Judges look for style and interpretation, expression of the music, difficulty of standard and original steps, and an overall harmonious blending of the couple's performances throughout the program. Two sets of marks are awarded, one for technical merit and the other for style and presentation.

Quick Skating Glossary

AXEL is the easiest jump to recognize because it is the only jump taken from a forward position. The skater glides forward on one foot, takes off from a forward outside edge, rotates (1.5 revolutions for a single, 2.5 for a double, and 3.5 for a triple axel), and lands on the opposite foot skating backward.

DEATH SPIRAL is a required move in pairs skating in which the man spins in a pivot position while holding one hand of the lady, who is spinning in a horizonal position on one edge of the skate with her body parallel to the ice.

FLIP is a toe-assisted jump, taken off from the left foot going backward and landed on the right foot.

LOOP is taken off and landed on the same foot and edge. At the point of takeoff, the skater's feet may look as if they are together. The free leg is then thrown sideways and upward in the direction of the jump.

LUTZ is one of the few jumps that takes off counter to the natural rotation of the edge. The skater usually approaches in a long curve, takes off from the left back outside edge with assistance from the right toe, and turns counter-clockwise, landing on the outside back edge of the right foot.

SALCHOW is a jump with a wide leg swing. At the moment before takeoff, the back inside edge of the skating foot curves sharply and the free leg is brought forward to initiate rotation. The skater lands on the back outside edge of the opposite foot of takeoff.

SPIN is the rotation of the body in one spot on one foot. Many different kinds of spins exist; if a skater leaps into the air before coming down into the spin, it is usually called a jump or flying spin.

SPLIT JUMP is a flashy move seen in single skating, in which the skater jumps into the air and performs a split in mid-air with the hands touching the ankles or toes. Also called a "Russian split," the move is referred to as a split flip when a half-revolution is added after touching the toes.

THREE TURN is a turn on one foot from forward to backward or backward to forward (from outside to inside edge or inside to outside edge).

THROW JUMPS are seen in pair skating, when the male partner assists the lady in the air into a jump.

TOE LOOP is rarely performed as a single jump but is very popular as a double and triple. The skater takes off from the back outside edge, strikes the toe of the free foot into the ice, turns in the air, and lands on the original back outside edge. The free leg stretches along the line of travel before takeoff.

HOPEFULS

Men's Singles: Several skating superstars are likely to vie for the medals at Lillehammer in 1994. Leading the pack of contenders is probably Ukranian Viktor Petrenko, who captured the gold at the 1992 games in Albertville. Another strong contender is Kurt Browning, the Canadian skater whose status as world champion of 1993 marks the fourth time that he has held top honors in a heatedly contested field. Foremost among the American skaters is Brian Boitano, whose reinstatement as an amateur enables him to vie again for the gold medal he secured at the 1988 Games. Mark Mitchell is also a strong American candidate, as is Todd Eldredge. Russians Alexei Urmanov and Oleg Tataurov and French skater Erik Millot may also prove worthy of top honors.

Ladies' Singles: Although America's star skater, 1992 gold medalist Kristi Yamaguchi, will most certainly not compete in the Lillehammer Games, the field of ladies' singles nonetheless remains a strong and exciting one. Ukranian Oksana Baiul, the fifteen year old who secured the world championship at the 1993 Prague competition, must be acknowledged as the likely front runner. Among the other prominent contenders is Germany's Katarina Witt, gold medalist in both 1984 and 1988, who turned pro after 1988 but has been reinstated as an amateur. American Nancy Kerrigan, bronze medalist at the

The Unified Team's Viktor Petrenko, who ranked second in the world going into the Albertville Games, captured the 1992 gold medal. He is pictured here in the original program.

Albertville Games in 1992, failed to win a medal in Prague and will doubtless be looking to match her earlier success when the 1994 Games take place. Other American possibilities include Lisa Ervin and Tonia Kwiatkowski, though neither seemed at their strongest in Prague. A more likely contender for the Olympic gold is French skater Surya Bonaly, who finished behind only Baiul at the Prague championships. And China's Lu Chen, who won a bronze medal in Prague, must be counted as well.

Pairs: This field appears wide open. The Canadian team of Isabelle Brasseur and Lloyd Eisler captured the gold at the 1993 Prague championships. They were followed by a German pair, Mandy Woetzel and Ingo Steuer, while

101

US figure skater Nancy Kerrigan performs during the women's free skating program at Albertville. Despite falling on a triple toe loop and missing another jump, Kerrigan turned in a bronze-medal performance.

Russians Evgenia Shishkova and Vadim Naumov captured the Prague bronze. Other Russian pairs also remain strong competitors here. Marina Eltsova and Andrei Bushkov fared impressively in Prague, and Russian professionals Natalia Mishkutenok and Artur Dmitriev, gold medalists at the 1992 Olympics, have regained amateur status, thus enriching an already imposing cast of contestants. Other leading couples include American tandems Jenni Meno–Todd Sand and Calla Urbanski–Rocky Marval, two pairs that finished in the top ten at the Prague championships. Look for Czech-Slovak couple Radka Kovarikova and Rene Novotny, fourth-place finalists at Prague, to also figure prominently in Lillehammer.

Ice Dancing: Russian couples remain among the strongest contenders in this competition. Both the Marina Kimova–Sergei Ponomarenko and Maia Usova–Alexander Zhulin teams are especially prominent candidates for the gold medal. Brother-sister skaters Isabelle and Paul Duchesnay, former world champions for France, must also be counted among the contenders. American hopefuls here include Susan Wynne and Russ Witherby and the Detroit-based duo Jerod Swallow and Liz Punsalan. Still another possibility for an Olympics medal is the US team of Renee Roca and Russian expatriate Gorsha Sur. Remember, though, that the Russians have secured four of the five gold medals contested since the ice dancing event was added to Olympic competition in 1976.

Brian Boitano

Brian Boitano is among America's most exciting skaters. Two-time world amateur champion, Olympic gold medalist, and four-time champion of the NutraSweet World Professional Figure Skating Championships, Boitano would appear to have already proven himself the best at all levels of his field. But in 1993 he decided that even all these championships and triumphs are not enough, so he applied for reinstatement as an amateur. His intentions are to compete for the United States in the 1994 Olympics in Lillehammer.

Only two years earlier, Olympic competition would have appeared beyond Boitano's grasp. After winning the gold medal in the Calgary Olympics, Boitano entered, and won, the NutraSweet World Professional Figure Skating Championships, a competition that is not sanctioned by the International Skating Union (ISU). Undaunted, Boitano entered the NutraSweet competition for the next three years, winning on each of those occasions as well. But when he considered entering the 1992 Olympic Games held in Albertville, Boitano was rejected. "The ISU turned me down because of the NutraSweet," Boitano told *Sports Illustrated.*

Banned from the 1992 competition, Boitano teamed instead with former Olympic gold medalist Katarina Witt, Germany's star skater, for a series of lucrative, acclaimed ice shows. But he also remained competitive, winning the aforementioned NutraSweet championships repeatedly and triumphing as well in the Hershey's Kisses Pro-Am Championships of 1993. Shortly before winning the Hershey's competition, Boitano expressed uncertainty about competing in the

US skater Brian Boitano revels in applause after his short program routine at Calgary. After having skated professionally, Boitano applied for reinstatement as an amateur to compete at the Lillehammer Olympics.

Lillehammer Games. When asked by *Sports Illustrated* whether he would consider the Olympics if he regained eligibility, he responded: "By '94, I'll probably think ... I've done everything that I really want to do in skating, it's time to move on."

But skating has always been a major aspect of Boitano's life. Born in 1963 in Sunnyvale, California, Boitano began ice skating at age eight after showing remarkable prowess on roller skates. His teacher, Linda Leaver, readily discerned Boitano's extraordinary talent and skill, and for sixteen years she remained his primary trainer. By age eighteen Boitano was excelling at the national level, though he often found himself trailing world champion Scott Hamilton in the various competitions. In 1984 Boitano skated in his first Olympic Games and finished fourth, just out of the medals. His rival, Hamilton, won the gold.

After Hamilton retired, Boitano quickly established himself as America's premier male skater, capturing the US championship for four consecutive years beginning in 1985. Despite these triumphs, Boitano was still dissatisfied with his performances, feeling that he was athletic but not convincingly expressive.

Working hard to improve himself in a competitive event that calls for both execution and expression, Boitano gained increasing success in the mid-1980s. He finished third in the 1985 world championships and first the following year.

During this period Boitano developed a rivalry with Canadian skater Brian Orser, who held his own nation's championship every year from 1981 to 1988. In addition, Orser finished third, just ahead of Boitano, in the 1984 Olympics and twice finished second in the world championships. Orser was actually expected by many observers to capture the world title in 1986, but on that occasion he succumbed to anxiety and twice failed to execute difficult triple doubles. The next year Orser did triumph as world champion, and thus he entered the 1988 Olympics as the favorite. But Boitano, who had decided that he could further improve the more aesthetic aspects of his skating routine, engaged a new choreographer, Sandra Bezic, who concocted a notably flamboyant piece, *Napoleon,* that included eight triple jumps and a demanding triple axel, at which Boitano was next to flawless. Orser was less successful in his more dramatic program, *The Bolt,* and thus the gold was awarded to Boitano.

By this time, though, Boitano was less keen on prizes than on fulfilling his own expectations. "It really didn't matter which color medal I won," he told the *Los Angeles Times* after completing *Napoleon.* "I just wanted to skate my best." Boitano summarized his 1988 Olympic performance as "the best that I've ever skated in my life."

As for the noted Boitano–Orser rivalry, otherwise known as the "Battle of the Brians," Boitano disclosed to the *Los Angeles Times* that the two skaters enjoyed a great friendship and were unaffected by the on-ice competition. "On the ice, we have our own jobs to do, and we both want to win," Boitano explained, "but we're very good friends off the ice."

It was after winning the Olympic gold that Boitano turned to the NutraSweet competitions, where he continued to prove his skating supremacy. The appeal of the Olympics, however, remained strong, so Boitano seized the opportunity to regain amateur status after the United States Figure Skating Association and the International Skating Union allowed reinstatement.

But competing and qualifying are two different things, and even fellow skaters cautioned that Boitano would not reach the Olympics merely by regaining the necessary status. "Brian Boitano is just another skater," proclaimed American rival Todd Eldredge to the *Detroit Free Press*'s Michelle Kaufman. "He's been out of competition since 1988, and we've been here every year. He'll have a lot more pressure on him than we will." Another American skater, Mark Mitchell, was more critical, claiming that Boitano was jeopardizing the opportunities of other skaters to compete in the Olympics. But Boitano seemed unmoved by such complaints. "I've gotten a lot of support from everyone but the skaters," he told Kaufman, "and they're entitled to their opinions."

Since applying for reinstatement as an amateur, Boitano has won the Hershey's Kisses Pro-Am competition, thus sending a message to his fellow skaters. And it may be that Boitano, as usual, ultimately finds it easier to impress others than to please himself. "I'm nowhere near ready for the Olympics," he was quoted in *USA Today* after winning the Hershey's Kisses Pro-Am. "But I'm on the right track." —*L.S.*

Schedule

The tentative figure skating schedule is as follows:

Sunday, February 13
Originals, pairs

Tuesday, February 15
Freestyle, pairs

Thursday, February 17
Originals, men

Friday, February 18
Compulsories, ice dancing

Saturday, February 19
Freestyle, men

Sunday, February 20
Originals, ice dancing

Monday, February 21
Freestyle, ice dancing

Wednesday, February 23
Originals, women

Friday, February 25
Freestyle, women

Saturday, February 26
Exhibitions

Colorado native Paul Wylie—an unexpected medalist—shows off his silver at the Olympic ice rink in Albertville.

MEN'S SINGLES

▼

HIGHLIGHTS

Ulrich Salchow of Sweden, a world champion ten times between 1901 and 1911, was the first Olympic gold medalist in the men's singles, leading two other Swedes into the medals. Russian Nikolai Panin, who withdrew from illness or in protest, is the record holder in perpetuity of the special figures title, a discontinued event that required elaborate patterns cut into the ice. His real name was Nikolai Kolomenkin, and in 1912 he competed in Stockholm as a member of the fourth-place Russian pistol team.

Beginning in 1920 Sweden's Gillis Grafström won three consecutive gold medals in the men's competitions; he was among the first to embrace the artistic advantage of interpreting music on the ice. The bronze medalist in 1920, Norway's Martin Stixrud, was 44 years old when he garnered his medal. Grafström's elegant reign ended when he took second place to Karl Schäfer of Austria in 1932—but Grafström remains the only skater to win medals in four Games.

Ernst Baier of Germany was silver medalist behind Schäfer in 1936 and also won the gold in the pairs with his future wife Maxi Herber; Baier thus became the only figure-skating competitor to have won a gold and silver in two different events.

fact: The axel—named for 19th century Norwegian skater Axel Paulsen—involves a leap and 1 1/2 revolutions forward, and is considered to be one of the most difficult moves in the sport.

US skater Dick Button, a superlative jumper, captured Olympic golds in 1948 and 1952. He had only mastered the double axel two days before he performed it in his 1948 freeskating program, and brought a newly developed triple loop to the 1952 Games.

Button was followed by countryman Hayes Alan Jenkins, gold medalist in 1956, whose brother, David Jenkins, won the bronze that year; silver medalist Ronald Robertson came between the brothers to effect an American sweep of the event. Hayes Jenkins later married 1960 ladies' gold medalist Carol Heiss. David Jenkins came back in 1960 to win the gold with some spectacular triple jumps.

West German Manfred Schnelldörfer, a former roller-skating champion, captured the gold in 1964, besting Alain Calmat of France and an exuberant Scott Allen of the US; Allen was two days short of his 15th birthday when he won the bronze, becoming the youngest person to medal in the Winter Games. Austrian Wolfgang Schwartz, gold medalist in 1968, narrowly took the field over Tim Wood of the US and third-place Patrick Pera of France. Pera was back as bronze medalist in 1972, behind Ondrej Nepela of Czechoslovakia (who won on his school figures and fell trying a triple-toe loop) and silver medalist Sergei Chetveroukhin of the USSR. Ken Shelley, the US national champion, took fourth place in the men's singles and also placed fourth along with partner JoJo Starbuck in the pairs.

fact: 1992 pairs gold medalist Artur Dmitriev was trained by the Kirov Ballet, whose other alumnae include Rudolf Nureyev and Mikhail Baryshnikov.

US skater Terry Kubicka is famous for being the first and last skater to perform a backflip in the Olympics, part of his program at Innsbruck in 1976. The move was later banned as too dangerous. That year John Curry of Britain, a magnificent stylist known as the "Nureyev of the Ice" for his ballet-like movements, won the gold, followed by Vladimir Kovalev of the USSR and Canadian Toller Cranston. US skater David Santee placed sixth.

In 1980 British skater Robin Cousins got off to a disappointing start at Lake Placid when he stood only fourth after the compulsories. But Cousins, then the finest freeskater in the world, moved into second place in the short program, then skated past his competitors in the final to bring Britain its second consecutive men's champion. Silver medalist Jan Hoffman of East Germany was competing in his fourth Olympics. US skater Charles Tickner claimed the bronze. Santee moved up to fourth in this Olympiad, while US skater Scott Hamilton took fifth place.

Hamilton's turn came in 1984, when he edged out Canada's Brian Orser for the gold, mostly based on their scores for the school figures. Czechoslovakia's Jozef Sabovtchik took the bronze.

In 1988 the "battle of the Brians" matched the 1984 silver medalist from Canada, Brian Orser, against Brian Boitano of the US. Boitano was best known for the quadruple toe loop, which he did not attempt for the Calgary competition. In 1982 he was the first skater to land a triple axel in the Nationals, and the following year he was the first skater to land all six triple jumps in the world championships: the salchow, lutz, axel, toe loop, loop, and flip. He also developed a trademark 'Tano triple, which adds to a triple lutz the gravitational challenge of one arm upstretched overhead while the other is cupped away from the body, cradled in front. The arm position slows down rotation, and so requires towering height on the jump.

Orser, who had to settle for the silver medal in 1984 because of a seventh place finish in the figures, boasted a trademark triple axel jump in his 1988 Olympic repertoire. Orser won the competition's only perfect 6.0 score, but bobbled in his long program and simplified a jump at the end. Boitano skated at

Canadian world champion figure skater Kurt Browning falls while attempting a triple axel during his original program at Albertville, eliminating his chance to medal.

his peak to claim the gold. Canadian Kurt Browning performed the only quadruple jump of the 1988 Games, but fell in the process.

Albertville Highlights

Albertville looked more like a tumbling match than a competition among the world's best skaters. In both the men's and ladies' singles, medals were sometimes default rewards for the handful of athletes who managed to stay vertical through most of their programs. Even skaters who fell were rewarded, and not just with the baser metals; those who fell least medaled best.

Trouble was, Albertville suffered from the jumps: the ever-more complicated air-grabbing maneuvers have changed (some say disfigured) the face of figure skating. And they seem to afflict some skaters as a compulsive disorder. Pressured by a competitor's arsenal of air-time, skaters attempt to tackle jumps in competition that their success-to-failure ratio in practice would clearly contraindicate.

The men displayed a number of surprises. Kurt Browning, with three world championship titles under foot, was supposed to be a shoo-in. When a triple axel landed him, Browning had to settle for fourth place in the short program. Christopher Bowman, meanwhile—then US National champion—hand-dabbed an attempted triple axel combination. And fellow American Todd Eldredge, another favorite, biffed on a double axel in the short program.

Artur Dmitriev and Natalia Mishkutienok of the Unified Team perform their gold-medal freestyle routine at the 1992 Olympic Games.

quote: *New York Times* reporter to Paul Wylie ('92 silver medalist) following a press conference introducing the US men who would skate for the stars-and-stripes in Albertville: "Paul, not to be impertinent, but why are you here?"

Gravity played the villain in the long program, as well. Browning retreated to sixth place after muffing a couple of triple axels, and the Unified Team's Viktor Petrenko, who led the short program, abridged both a triple jump and a double axel. He fell on a triple axel, but the judges were impressed enough by the rest of his program to reward him with gold-medal scores. The decision wasn't unanimous, though: two judges placed American Paul Wylie, who wasn't expected to be a top contender, in first place. Wylie—whose history of choking in competition earned him a reputation as a "practice skater"—glided through a flawless short program, and, concluding his long program with three Russian splits, earned the silver medal and the evening's sole standing ovation. Czech Petr Barna, who came out of the short program in second place, landed the Games' first quadruple axel and the bronze medal.

US skaters Calla Urbanski and Rocky Marval—dubbed "the waitress and the truck driver"—placed eleventh in the freestyle event, and tenth overall at Albertville.

Salchow and Button

Instruction for performing a salchow: 1. Jump up from the back inside edge of either skate. 2. Complete a full turn in the air. 3. Land on the back outside edge of the second skate. Repeat as necessary. Ulrich Salchow, the legendary Swede, was the first to do what is now a compulsory jump in any figure skating program. Then, a single Salchow was revolutionary. Contemporary programs now require two or three revolutions in the air.

By the 1908 London Olympics—the debut of figure skating as an Olympic event—Salchow was already a seven-time world champion. However, he had lost earlier that year to Russian Nikolai Panin. In London, though, Salchow won three first-place votes for his compulsory figures to Panin's two. The Russian, complaining of bias, dropped out, setting the stage for a Swedish sweep of all three medals, led by Salchow.

Until separate Winter Games began in 1924, figure skating events were held only if there happened to be a convenient skating rink. Salchow's next chance to defend his Olympic title came in Antwerp in 1920. Salchow, then 43, lost to countryman Gillis Grafström.

The American Richard Button first executed salchows, winning two gold medals in 1948 an 1952, and then talked about them as a network television commentator for the Olympics. At both Games, Button tossed new and exciting jumps into his freestyle program, including the first triple (a loop) in the 1952 Games. Over the two Games he earned 17 of 18 first place votes from judges. Button, born July 18, 1929 in Englewood, New Jersey, is author of the autobiography *Dick Button on Skates*. After the 1952 Games, Button turned professional, touring with the Ice Capades as well as earning a law degree. —*H.D.*

Medalists

Figure Skating—Men's Singles

1992	1. Viktor Petrenko, Unified Team, 1.5
	2. Paul Wylie, USA, 3.5
	3. Petr Barna, Czechoslovakia, 4.0
1988	1. Brian Boitano, USA, 3.0
	2. Brian Orser, Canada, 4.2
	3. Viktor Petrenko, Soviet Union, 7.8
1984	1. Scott Hamilton, USA, 3.4
	2. Brian Orser, Canada, 5.6
	3. Jozef Sabovtchik, Czechoslovakia, 7.4
1980	1. Robin Cousins, Great Britain, 189.48
	2. Jan Hoffman, East Germany, 189.72
	3. Charles Tickner, USA, 187.06
1976	1. John Curry, Great Britain, 192.74
	2. Vladimir Kovalev, Soviet Union, 187.64
	3. Toller Cranston, Canada, 187.34
1972	1. Ondrej Nepela, Czechoslovakia, 2,739.1
	2. Sergei Chetveroukhin, Soviet Union, 2,672.4
	3. Patrick Pera, France, 2,653.1
1968	1. Wolfgang Schwarz, Austria, 1,904.1
	2. Tim Wood, USA, 1,891.6
	3. Patrick Pera, France, 1,864.5
1964	1. Manfred Schnelldörfer, West Germany, 1,916.9
	2. Alain Calmat, France, 1,876.5
	3. Scott Allen, USA, 1,873.6
1960	1. David Jenkins, USA, 1,440.2
	2. Karol Divin, Czechoslovakia, 1,414.3
	3. Donald Jackson, Canada, 1,401.0
1956	1. Hayes Alan Jenkins, USA, 1,497.95
	2. Ronald Robertson, USA, 1,492.15
	3. David Jenkins, USA, 1,465.41
1952	1. Richard Button, USA, 1,730.3
	2. Helmut Seibt, Austria, 1,621.3
	3. James Grogan, USA, 1,627.4
1948	1. Richard Button, USA, 1,720.6

2. Hans Gerschwiler, Switzerland, 1,630.1
3. Edi Rada, Austria, 1,603.2
1936 1. Karl Schafer, Austria, 2,959.0
2. Ernst Baier, Germany, 2,805.3
3. Felix Kaspar, Austria, 2,801.0
1932 1. Karl Schafer, Austria, 2,602.0
2. Gillis Grafström, Sweden, 2,514.5
3. Montgomery Wilson, Canada, 2,448.3
1928 1. Gillis Grafström, Sweden, 2,698.25
2. Willy Bockl, Austria, 2,682.50
3. Robert van Zeebroeck, Belgium, 2,578.75

1924 1. Gillis Grafström, Sweden, 2,575.25
2. Willy Bockl, Austria, 2,518.75
3. Georges Gautschi, Switzerland, 2,233.50
1920 1. Gillis Grafström, Sweden, 2,838.50
2. Andreas Krogh, Norway, 2,634.00
3. Martin Stixrud, Norway, 2,561.50
1912 **Not held**
1908 1. Ulrich Salchow, Sweden, 1,886.5
2. Richard Johansson, Sweden, 1,826.0
3. Per Thoren, Sweden, 1,787.0

LADIES' SINGLES

▼

HIGHLIGHTS

British skater Madge Syers had finished second to Sweden's Ulrich Salchow in the 1902 world championships, which was then open to both genders. Syers came out of retirement to win the first ladies' Olympic gold in 1908; she also took a bronze in the pairs. In 1920 Sweden had a champion in Magda Julin; that year the bronze medalist from the US, Theresa Weld, was reprimanded by the judges for making the unfeminine mistake of including a salchow in her program. Weld also placed fourth in the pairs competition with Nathaniel Niles. Austria's Herma Planck-Szabó took the gold in 1924, with US skater Beatrix Loughran earning a silver. Loughran came back to win a bronze in 1928, and in 1932 came back for a silver in the pairs with Sherwin Badger.

Skating's first mega-star, Sonja Henie of Norway, competed in the 1924 Games at age 11, then took the gold in 1928, 1932, and 1936, leading skating to new areas of athleticism. Henie was influential in popularizing figure skating, first as an Olympic event and later as an entertainment vehicle, when she performed in ice shows and motion pictures. Her skating eventually earned her a fortune estimated at nearly 50 million dollars.

US skater Maribel Vinson won the bronze in 1932; as the mother of two promising skaters on the US team she perished along with them in the 1961 Brussels plane crash that killed 73 people, including 18 team members, five coaches, the team manager, and friends and relatives. Canadian Barbara Ann Scott earned the gold in 1948, followed by British skater Jeannette Altwegg in 1952. Shunning the ice capades route, Altwegg retired to work at the Pestalozzi Children's Village in Trogen, Switzerland.

fact: In 1993, fifteen-year-old Oksana Baiul became the youngest world champion since fourteen-year old Norwegian Sonja Henie stole the hearts of spectators around the world in 1927. Only one year earlier, Baiul had placed 12th in the Soviet Union's national championship.

American women have periodically captured the singles gold, including Tenley Albright in 1956 (silver medalist in 1952) and Carol Heiss in 1960 (silver medalist in 1956). Albright had been stricken with nonparalytic polio when she was 11 years old; after retiring from skating she followed her father's career path and became a surgeon. Heiss married men's 1956 champion Hayes Alan Jenkins. The silver medalist in 1960, Sjoukje Dijkstra of the Netherlands, earned the gold in 1964. US skater Peggy Fleming was champion in 1968, skating in costumes sewn by her mother. Fleming won the only US gold medal of the Grenoble Games.

Austrian Beatrix Schuba won the gold in 1972 on her compulsory figures, while the real dazzler in the free-skating program that year was US skater Janet Lynn, who took the bronze behind Canada's Karen Magnussen. The compulsory figures were subsequently reduced in overall importance, and US skater Dorothy Hamill turned in a sparkling free program for the gold in 1976. Dianne de Leeuw, an American citizen who competed for the Netherlands, was the silver medalist and Christine Errath of East Germany took the bronze.

US skater Linda Fratianne, hurt by her compulsory figures, earned a silver medal in 1980 behind East German Anett Pötzsch, in the closest competition in 60 years. Rosalynn Sumners won another silver for the US in 1984, behind East Germany's glamorous ice queen, Katarina Witt.

The American contender in 1988, Debi Thomas, was famous for a triple salchow double toe loop combination, a treacherous maneuver. She faced off in 1988 against Witt, the reigning Olympic queen. They both skated their long program to music from Bizet's *Carmen*. When it was all over, Thomas had to settle for the bronze—thereby becoming the first black athlete to win a medal in the Winter Games. Canada's Elizabeth Manley turned in an exciting and lively routine in front of a hometown crowd for the silver medal, and Witt, claiming the gold for the second time, became the first woman figure-skating champion to repeat at the Olympics since Sonja Henie. Especially charming was Japan's Midori Ito, who finished fifth with a triple lutz and a standing ovation from the crowd.

Albertville Highlights

1992 was billed as the year of the athlete versus the artist, and the press made the ladies' singles showdown between Kristi Yamaguchi and Midori Ito into a case study in athleticism and artistry. Ito—the first woman to land a triple axel—

USA's Kristi Yamaguchi skates her way to a gold medal in the freestyle program at Albertville. Although Yamaguchi won't be competing in Lillehammer, she may make an appearance as a commentator.

Japanese figure skater Midori Ito performs during the women's freestyle program at Albertville. In fourth place after the first round, Ito finished second to take the silver medal.

arrived at Albertville as the odds-on favorite; Yamaguchi, *sans* triple axel, was not favored as '92's golden girl, even though she had picked up world championship and US national titles en route to the Savoie showdown.

The short program set the stage for things to come. Ito, whose early practices had caused much hand-wringing among the competition, entered the short program fresh on the heels of a spate of crash-landed triple axels. Her confidence shaken, she scaled down to a triple lutz, a combination she'd never botched—until now. Yamaguchi, on the other hand, skated a picture-perfect short program.

Tonya Harding, the only other woman to arrive at Albertville with the triple-A to her name, seemed to have forgotten how to land the jump the day she landed in France. Arriving three days before her first event, Harding took a sixteen-hour post-flight snooze; not that she had jet lag—Harding claims never to suffer from jet lag—it's just that she performed with the panache of someone who was skating in her sleep.

In the long program, all six of the top competitors fell. And fell, and fell. Ito, whose first attempt to triple an axel in the long program caused her to spend some horizontal ice time, landed her second try. As clearly as her confidence had been shaken by her failed jumps, her success brought back the Midori the judges had come to know and love: the cloud that hung over Ito's early performance turned out to have a silver lining.

Yamaguchi, although not overextending herself in the long program, fell nonetheless. After failing a triple loop, the imperturbable artist scaled back her program *in medias* rink, and finished with a triple lutz and composure to spare. Judges gave her a 5.8 and 5.9s for artistic impression, 5.7s and 5.8s for technical merit, and a Lalique gold necklace to add to her growing collection.

Nancy Kerrigan, too, scaled back her long program, eliminating jumps before entering the rink; tainting her elegant style only a little with a couple of technical demerits, she charmed a bronze medal from the nine-judge panel.

Henie and Other Greats

Sonja Henie of Norway became the most famous figure skater of all time, and possibly the best. Henie skated in four Olympics, beginning with the 1924 Games in Chamonix when she was just 11 years old, then winning gold medals at the next three.

Henie, born in Oslo on April 8, 1912, won her first major title at the 1927 World Championships held, for Henie, on familiar ice in Oslo. Of the five judges, three were Norwegian, all of whom voted for her. The Austrian and German judges voted for Austrian Herma Planck-Szabó. After that competition, only one judge from any one country was included on the panel. Henie won her first gold at the St. Moritz Games in 1928 when she was still 15. Her style combined grace with a solid athleticism.

Henie dominated the first two Olympics in which she participated, although by 1932 in Lake Placid she was already facing Sonja Henie imitators. At St.

Moritz she won six of seven first place votes in the freestyle portion of the competition, and four years later she was the unanimous selection in Lake Placid.

But the 1936 Games at Garmish-Partenkirchen saw the first chink in her armor—and perhaps helped Henie decide on retirement from amateur competition: Following compulsory figures, the young Brit Cecilia Colledge, who skated in the Henie school, was just 3.6 points behind her role model. Henie barely edged her in the freestyle portion of the competition, but was able to take the gold.

fact: At the apex of her career, Sonja Henie's box office appeal was second only to that of Shirley Temple and Clark Gable.

By the time she retired, Henie had won 10 straight world championships (only Swede Ulrich Salchow won more) and more than 1,400 prizes in all. When Henie turned professional, 20th Century-Fox handed her a film contract, and she made 11 movies between 1938 and 1960. In 1941, Henie became a US citizen. She married, then divorced, two Americans (to attendant Liz Taylor-style publicity) before wedding her childhood boyfriend, a fellow Norwegian. Henie, who developed cancer, died on October 12, 1969, in a plane carrying her from Paris to Oslo for medical treatment.

America has also produced a long string of female figure skaters who set new standards for the sport. Tenley Albright of Newton Center, Massachusetts, who had suffered from a mild form of polio as a child, fell during training two weeks before the 1956 Cortina Olympics and badly cut her right ankle. Her surgeon father stitched her up and she won the gold. Peggy Fleming easily captured the gold at the 1968 Grenoble Games—wearing costumes sewn by her mother. In 1976, Dorothy Hamill claimed a unanimous victory and ushered in a new hairstyle, the wedge, to a waiting America. —*H.D.*

Medalists

Figure Skating—Ladies' Singles

1992
1. Kristi Yamaguchi, USA, 1.5
2. Midori Ito, Japan, 4.0
3. Nancy Kerrigan, USA, 4.0

1988
1. Katarina Witt, East Germany, 4.2
2. Elizabeth Manley, Canada, 4.6
3. Debi Thomas, USA, 6.0

1984
1. Katarina Witt, East Germany, 3.2
2. Rosalynn Sumners, USA, 4.6
3. Kira Ivanova, Soviet Union, 9.2

1980
1. Anett Potzsch, East Germany, 189.00
2. Linda Fratianne, USA, 188.30
3. Dagmar Lurz, West Germany, 188.04

1976
1. Dorothy Hamill, USA, 193.80
2. Dianne de Leeuw, Netherlands, 190.24
3. Christine Errath, East Germany, 188.16

1972
1. Beatrix Schuba, Austria, 2,751.5
2. Karen Magnussen, Canada, 2,673.2
3. Janet Lynn, USA, 2,663.1

1968
1. Peggy Fleming, USA, 1,970.5
2. Gabriele Seyfert, East Germany, 1,882.3
3. Hana Maskova, Czechoslovakia, 1,828.8

1964
1. Sjoukje Dijkstra, Netherlands, 2,018.5

2. Regine Heitzer, Austria, 1,945.5
3. Petra Burka, Canada, 1,940.0
1960 1. Carol Heiss, USA, 1,490.1
2. Sjoukje Dijkstra, Netherlands, 1,424.8
3. Barbara Roles, USA, 1,414.9
1956 1. Tenley Albright, USA, 1,866.39
2. Carol Heiss, USA, 1,848.24
3. Ingrid Wendl, Austria, 1,753.91
1952 1. Jeannette Altwegg, Great Britain, 1,455.8
2. Tenley Albright, USA, 1,432.2
3. Jacqueline du Bief, France, 1,422.0
1948 1. Barbara Ann Scott, Canada, 1,467.7
2. Eva Pawlik, Austria, 1,418.3
3. Jeannette Altwegg, Great Britain, 1,405.5
1936 1. Sonja Henie, Norway, 2,971.4
2. Cecilia Colledge, Great Britain, 2,926.8

3. Vivi-Anne Hulten, Sweden, 2,763.2
1932 1. Sonja Henie, Norway, 2,302.5
2. Fritzi Burger, Austria, 2,167.1
3. Maribel Y. Vinson, USA, 2,158.50
1928 1. Sonja Henie, Norway, 2,452.25
2. Fritzi Burger, Austria, 2,248.50
3. Beatrix Loughran, USA, 2,254.50
1924 1. Herma Planck-Szabó, Austria, 2,094.25
2. Beatrix Loughran, USA, 1,959.00
3. Ethel Muckelt, Great Britain, 1,750.50
1920 1. Magda Julin-Mauroy, Sweden, 913.50
2. Svea Noren, Sweden, 887.75
3. Theresa Weld, USA, 898.00
1912 **Not held**
1908 1. Madge Syers, Great Britain, 1,262.5
2. Elsa Rendschmidt, Germany, 1,055.0
3. Dorothy Greenhough-Smith, Great Britain, 960.5

PAIRS

▼

HIGHLIGHTS

Germans Heinrich Burger and Anna Hubler won the first pairs gold in 1908; that year the ladies' singles gold medalist, British skater Madge Syers, won a bronze in the pairs with her partner, Edgar Syers. In 1920 the ladies' singles bronze medalist, US skater Theresa Weld, took fourth place in the pairs with her partner Nathaniel Niles; that year Finland won its first skating gold with the husband-and-wife team of Walter and Ludovika Jakobsson; Walter was 38 when they won their gold and Ludovika 35. The Jakobssons were edged out of the gold in 1924 by Austrian pair Alfred Berger and Helene Engelmann.

Andrée Joly and Pierre Brunet of France, bronze medalists in 1924, came back to claim the gold in 1928 and 1932; they earned their second gold as Monsieur & Madame Brunet. The 1932 silver medalists were US skater Sherwin Badger paired with Beatrix Loughran, the ladies' singles silver medalist in 1924 and bronze medalist in 1928.

fact: Women run nine of the forty national governing bodies that work with the US Olympic Committee. Of these, only one is a Winter Games sport, and two represent sports that are women-only events on the Olympic level.

The men's singles silver medalist in 1932, German Ernst Baier, also won a gold in the pairs with Maxi Herber, who later became his wife; Baier is the only figure-skating competitor to have won gold and silver in two different events. Herber was only 15 when they won their gold. They were known for pioneering "shadow skating," in which both skaters perform the same moves without touching.

In 1952 West Germans Ria and Paul Falk took the gold; the US had silver medalists in Karol and Michael Kennedy. The 1956 competition was marred by dubious judging; the disgruntled crowd in Cortina pelted the officiators with oranges, requiring the ice to be cleared repeatedly. That year Austrian skaters Elisabeth Schwarz and Kurt Oppelt claimed the gold, closely contended by Canadian silver medalists Frances Dafoe and Norris Bowden.

The 1960 gold went to Canadians Barbara Wagner and Robert Paul, with US skaters Nancy and Ronald Ludington capturing the bronze. Paul became choreographer for future skating champions Peggy Fleming, Dorothy Hamill, and Linda Fratianne—as well as for entertainers Donny and Marie Osmond.

The Soviet Union has dominated pairs skating for the past three decades, claiming every Olympic pairs gold medal since 1964. The Soviet pair Lyudmilla Belousova and Oleg Protopopov skated to the gold in 1964 and, as a married couple, in 1968; the legendary couple was known for their balleticism and almost oblivious passion on ice. The Protopopovs invented the haunting death spiral, now a mainstay of pairs programs. They were followed to the gold in the next three Games by Irina Rodnina and her two partners, Alexei Ulilov (in 1972) and Aleksandr Zaitsev (in 1976 and 1980), who skated a more powerful and technical style. The silver medalists in 1972 were also a Soviet pair, Lyudmila Smirnova and Andrei Suraikin. Rodnina's partner Ulilov developed a romance with Smirnnova that broke up the top Soviet pair. Smirnova and Ulilov married, and Rodnina trained for the gold with a new partner, Zaitsev; the latter couple was married in 1975.

quote: "You have to kiss a few toads before you find the right prince."
—US pairs champion Calla Urbanski, six times separated from her
pairs partners

US pair Randy Gardner and Tai Babilonia had upset the Soviets in the 1979 world championships and had been expected to break the Soviet gold streak at Lake Placid in 1980. They stunned American fans when their bid for the medal was shattered by a serious groin injury that Gardner sustained just before heading to Lake Placid. Warming up on the ice before the Olympic short program Gardner, shot with painkillers, fell four times; the pair was forced to withdraw. Rodnina and Zaitsev took their second gold, less than a year after the birth of their son. Marina Cherkasova, half of the Soviet pair that placed second in 1980, turned 15 just three days before medaling.

In 1984 US pair Kitty and Peter Carruthers won a tight competition for the silver, the first silver for the US in pairs skating since the 1952 Olympics in Oslo. The 1984 gold medalists, Elena Valova and Oleg Vassiliev, skated to the silver in Calgary. The new Soviet pair appearing in 1988, Ekaterina Gordeeva and Sergei Grinkov, brought a trademark quadruple twist lift to the Games. This appealing couple skated with a lively and youthful simplicity and came away with a gold and spectators' hearts worldwide. US pair Peter Oppegard and Jill Watson won a bronze in Calgary, demonstrating their trademark swoop, in which Oppegard swung Watson's face just inches from the ice.

Albertville Highlights

The pairs competition held fewer surprises than other skating events, but plenty of spills: six consecutive pairs bought ice. While Viktor Petrenko was the first Soviet to capture the gold in a singles competition, Soviet-trained pairs have traditionally owned the pairs event. Albertville was no exception: Natalia Michkouteniok and Artur Dmitriev skated away with the eighth consecutive "Soviet" gold, while fellow Unified teammates Elena Betchke and Denis Petrov added a silver to the Big Red coffer. Despite two falls, Canadians Isabelle Brasseur and Lloyd Eisler swung the bronze medal, while the rocky story of "The Waitress and the Truck Driver" lost its fairy tale fizzle when Rocky Marval and Calla Urbanski lumbered to a tenth-place finish.

Medalists

Figure Skating—Pairs

1992
1. Natalia Michkouteniok, Artur Dmitriev, Unified Team, 1.5
2. Elena Betchke, Denis Petrov, Unified Team, 3.0
3. Isabelle Brasseur, Lloyd Eisler, Canada, 4.5

1988
1. Ekaterina Gordeeva, Sergei Grinkov, Soviet Union, 1.4
2. Elena Valova, Oleg Vassiliev, Soviet Union, 2.8
3. Jill Watson, Peter Oppegard, USA, 4.2

1984
1. Elena Valova, Oleg Vassiliev, Soviet Union, 1.4
2. Kitty Carruthers, Peter Carruthers, USA, 2.8
3. Larissa Selezneva, Oleg Makorov, Soviet Union, 3.8

1980
1. Irina Rodnina, Aleksandr Zaitsev, Soviet Union, 147.26
2. Marina Cherkosova, Sergei Shakrai, Soviet Union, 143.80
3. Manuela Mager, Uwe Bewersdorff, East Germany, 140.52

1976
1. Irina Rodnina, Aleksandr Zaitsev, Soviet Union, 140.54

2. Romy Kermer, Rolf Oesterreich, East Germany, 136.35
3. Manuela Gross, Uwe Kagelmann, East Germany, 134.57

1972
1. Irina Rodnina, Aleksei Ulanov, Soviet Union, 420.4
2. Lyudmila Smirnova, Andrei Suraikin, Soviet Union, 419.4
3. Manuela Gross, Uwe Kagelmann, East Germany, 411.8

1968
1. Lyudmila Belousova, Oleg Protopopov, Soviet Union, 315.2
2. Tatiana Zhuk, Aleksandr Gorelik, Soviet Union, 312.3
3. Margot Glockshuber, Wolfgang Danne, West Germany, 304.4

1964
1. Lyudmila Belousova, Oleg Protopopov, Soviet Union, 104.4
2. Marika Kilius, Hans-Jurgen Baumler, West Germany, 103.6
3. Debbi Wilkes, Guy Revell, Canada, 98.5

1960
1. Barbara Wagner, Robert Paul, Canada, 80.4
2. Marika Kilius, Hans-Jurgen Baumler, West Germany, 76.8
3. Nancy Ludington, Ronald Ludington, USA, 76.2

1956 1. Elisabeth Schwarz, Kurt Oppelt, Austria, 101.8
2. Frances Dafoe, Norris Bowden, Canada, 101.9
3. Marianna Nagy, Laszlo Nagy, Hungary, 99.3

1952 1. Ria Falk, Paul Falk, West Germany, 102.6
2. Karol Kennedy, Michael Kennedy, USA, 100.6
3. Marianna Nagy, Laszlo Nagy, Hungary, 97.4

1948 1. Micheline Lannoy, Pierre Baugniet, Belgium, 123.5
2. Andrea Kekessy, Ede Kiraly, Hungary, 122.2
3. Suzanne Morrow, Wallace Diestelmeyer, Canada, 121.0

1936 1. Maxi Herber, Ernst Baier, Germany, 103.3
2. Ilse Pausin, Erik Pausin, Austria, 102.7
3. Emilie Rotter, Laszlo Szollas, Hungary, 97.6

1932 1. Andrée Brunet-Joly, Pierre Brunet, France, 76.7
2. Beatrix Loughran, Sherwin C. Badger, USA, 77.5

3. Emilie Rotter, Laszlo Szollas, Hungary, 76.4

1928 1. Andree Joly, Pierre Brunet, France, 100.50
2. Lilly Scholz, Otto Kaiser, Austria, 99.25
3. Melitta Brunner, Ludwig Wrede, Austria, 93.25

1924 1. Helene Engelmann, Alfred Berger, Austria, 74.50
2. Ludovika Jakobsson-Eilers, Walter Jakobsson, Finland, 71.75
3. Andree Joly, Pierre Brunet, France, 69.25

1920 1. Ludovika Jakobsson-Eilers, Walter Jakobsson, Finland, 80.75
2. Alexia Bryn, Yngvar Bryn, Norway, 72.75
3. Phyllis Johnson, Basil Williams, Great Britain, 66,25

1912 Not held
1908 1. Anna Hubler, Heinrich Burger, Germany, 56.0
2. Phyllis Johnson, James Johnson, Great Britain, 51.5
3. Madge Syers, Edgar Syers, Great Britain, 48.0

ICE DANCING

▼

HIGHLIGHTS

Ice dancing became an Olympic sport in 1976, and the Soviet Union captured the first two places. Ludmilla Pakhomova and Alexandr Gorshkov edged out Irina Moiseeva and Andrei Minenkov; the surprise bronze medalists were US skaters Colleen O'Connor and Jim Millns. The 1980 gold went to Soviets Natalia Linichuk and Gennadi Karponosov; Hungary got the silver and another Soviet couple won the bronze. Gold medalists Jayne Torvill and Christopher Dean of Britain were awarded a maximum nine 6.0 scores for artistic impression in their 1984 program, and three 6.0 scores for technical merit.

In 1988 Soviet ice dancers Natalia Bestemianova and Andrei Bukin claimed the gold with three perfect 6.0 scores. Another Soviet pair, Sergei Ponomarenko and Marina Klimova, won the silver, while Canadians Tracy Wilson and Robert McCall took the bronze. But it was a non-medaling performance that stirred the crowd: Isabelle and Paul Duchesnay, siblings raised in Québec but skating for France, who finished eighth but pushed the sport in a new direction with their innovative style and technique.

Albertville Highlights

Ice dancing—thanks to rules that prohibit jumps in favor of good old-fashioned skating—was the only figure-skating event that didn't feature tumbling moves. Isabelle Duchesnay-Dean and Paul Duchesnay, who skated for France and hoped to win big with their *West Side Story* routine, settled for silver behind Marina Klimova and Sergei Ponomarenko, who elegantly flouted a couple of rules en route to the roster of Unified gold medalists.

Medalists

Figure Skating—Ice Dancing

1992
1. Marina Klimova, Sergei Ponomarenko, Unified Team, 2.0
2. Isabelle Duchesnay-Dean, Paul Duchesnay, France, 4.4
3. Maia Usova, Alexander Zhulin, Unified Team, 5.6

1988
1. Natalia Bestemianova, Andrei Boukin, Soviet Union, 2.0
2. Marina Klimova, Sergei Ponomarenko, Soviet Union, 4.0
3. Tracy Wilson, Robert McCall, Canada, 6.0

1984
1. Jayne Torvill, Christopher Dean, Great Britain, 2.0

2. Natalia Bestemianova, Andrei Boukin, Soviet Union, 4.0
3. Marina Klimova, Sergei Ponomarenko, Soviet Union, 7.0

1980
1. Natalia Linichuk, Gennadi Karponosov, Soviet Union, 205.48
2. Krisztina Regoeczy, Andras Sallay, Hungary, 204.52
3. Irina Moiseeva, Andrei Minenkov, Soviet Union, 201.86

1976
1. Ljudmila Pakhomova, Alexandr Gorshkov, Soviet Union, 209.92
2. Irina Moiseeva, Andrei Minenkov, Soviet Union, 204.88
3. Colleen O'Connor, Jimmy Millins, USA, 202.64

Trivia Quiz

1. Figure skating first appeared at the Games:

A) in 1908, sixteen years prior to the first Winter Games. **B)** in 1896, the year of the first modern Games. **C)** in 1928, the second time the Winter Games were held.

2. Figure skating was not popular in the United States:

A) until 1968, when USA's Peggy Fleming garnered the gold medal in Ladies' Singles. **B)** until 1956, when Tenley Albright was the first American woman to capture a gold medal in Ladies' Singles. **C)** until Norwegian Sonja Henie created a stir at the age of 13.

3. The only time 1988 gold medalist Katarina Witt lost the World Championship between 1983 and 1986, she took second place to:

A) Kristi Yamaguchi (US). **B)** Elizabeth Manley (Canada). **C)** Debi Thomas (US).

4. The only US gold medal at the Grenoble Games went to:

A) Tim Wood. **B)** Dick Button. **C)** Peggy Fleming.

124

5. *The first woman ever to perform the triple axel in international competition was:*

A) Dorothy Hamill (US). **B)** Debi Thomas (US). **C)** Midori Ito (Japan).

6. *The only skater to surpass Sonja Henie's 10-straight World Championship winning streak was:*

A) the United States's Brian Boitano. **B)** Sweden's Ulrich Salchow. **C)** the Soviet Union's Viktor Petrenko.

7. *One of the few jumps to take off counter to the natural rotation of the skater's edge is:*

A) the death spiral. **B)** the lutz. **C)** the zamboni.

8. *The only jump taken from a forward position is:*

A) the lutz. **B)** the axel. **C)** the szabo.

9. *Nine judges mark skaters on a scale of 0.0 to 6.0, and:*

A) the skater's lowest mark is dropped. **B)** each judge's mark is converted into places (for example, first and second). **C)** scores that vary by more than 2.5 points are subject to a re-vote.

10. *The axel, a leap with one and one-half forward revolutions, was named:*

A) to note the skater's position with respect to the axis of the turn. **B)** after Axel Rose, a famous Norwegian figure skater. **C)** after Axel Paulsen, a famous Norwegian figure skater.

Answers: 1-a, 2-c, 3-c, 4-c, 5-c, 6-b, 7-b, 8-b, 9-b, 10-c

ICE HOCKEY

WARM-UP

An electric Olympic moment: 1980, Lake Placid, the US hockey team erupts on the ice, having defeated Finland for their first gold medal since 1960 and only the second since the Olympics began. Against the odds. The miracle on ice. In the stands, they begin to chant. "USA! USA! USA!" Goose bump time. Sports columns overflow with emotion, the public joyously celebrates, the country beams with pride, the young men on the American hockey team are canonized as national heros.

And hockey was temporarily embraced as the national American sport. Never mind that it has been the national sport of Canada for most of this century.

But hockey actually began hundreds of centuries before that shining American moment at Lake Placid. Hockey is the oldest known game played on ice. The ancient Greeks and Romans played a form of field hockey and the principle of knocking an object with a stick into a designated area was adopted by the French, who called the game "hocquet," or curved shepherd's crook. A monk in the 12th century described a scene near the walls of London:

> When it is frozen, many young men run over the ice. Some of them have bones tied to their feet and use a stick with a sharp end. They slide as quickly as a bird flying in the air or the arrow from a bow. Sometimes from two opposite points, at a large distance, two young men race towards each other and one of them, or perhaps both, falls to the ground after beating each other with their sticks. Many of them incur head wounds, and most of them break an arm or a leg; but in our day and age young is forever seeking glory and these mock fights make them more courageous when it comes to real fighting.

Sounds somewhat like a typical National Hockey League game.

In the 19th century, the game made its way across the Channel from France to Britain, then was brought over by Scottish settlers to Canada, where it was known as "shinty." The long Canadian winter provided plenty of ice, so it was that children adapted the sport to their environment, playing with broomsticks and stones on the frozen ponds. Groups of up to fifty a side would gather in the harbor at Halifax and go at each other all afternoon.

Even today, many of the players in the National Hockey League have their first taste of hockey on an outdoor sheet of ice, often playing in subzero temperatures.

The cities of Montreal, Quebec, and Halifax all lay claim to having staged the earliest ice hockey game (or near ice hockey game), but the first documented game was played in 1855 at Kingston, Ontario, involving soldiers of the Royal Canadian Rifles. The first organized league was formed in Kingston soon thereafter, while the first set of rules are credited to John George Alwyn Creighton, an engineer from Halifax who was working in Montreal. A rugby and lacrosse player, Creighton embraced hockey apparently because he and his friends were searching for a new game that would allow them to stay in shape during the long Canadian winters. On March 3, 1875, Creighton and 17 others appeared at the Victoria Skating Rink in Montreal, armed with bandy sticks, skates, and a lacrosse ball.

In 1893, ice hockey was introduced to two US universities, Yale and Johns Hopkins. The Amateur Hockey Association of the United States was formed in 1894. Two years later a four-team league was started in New York, and soon after that, the Baltimore Hockey League was founded.

fact: North Americans skate with short, chopping strides, pushing off the inside edge of skates placed widely apart, with the power generated by thigh and groin muscles; Swedish and Czechoslovakian skaters use the more powerful quadriceps and buttock muscles to thrust skates that start closer together, pushing straight back and gliding on the outside edge of the front skate—results are faster and smoother skating.

The sport continued to grow in the northern climes of the US and Canada. In 1893 (hockey's watershed year?), Lord Stanley, the Governor of Canada, donated a $50 trophy cup that still bears his name (and has presumedly appreciated), to be awarded to the world's best amateur ice hockey team. The first recipients of the trophy were the Montreal Wheelers of the Amateur Hockey Association of Canada. In 1908, the Ontario Professional Hockey League was organized, with the Cup as the championship prize. Since 1910, the Stanley Cup has been emblematic of professional hockey supremacy, and is now awarded to the National Hockey League's champion.

The first US team to win the Stanley Cup was the Seattle Metropolitans in 1917, the same year that the NHL was formed. Strictly a Canadian circuit until Boston joined the league in 1924, the NHL added Chicago, Detroit, and New York in 1926. Montreal and Toronto completed the "original six." In 1967, the league doubled to 12 teams and in the next few years expanded to 21.

Worldwide, hockey has continued to grow. In 1908, the International Ice Hockey Federation (IIHF) was formed in London, with Great Britain, France, Belgium, Switzerland, and Bohemia as founding members.

fact: The first gold-medal team was not a Canadian national team; it was the Winnipeg Falcons.

Today the sport is very popular in several European countries, particularly Sweden, Finland, Czechoslovakia, Switzerland, Poland, Germany, and, of course, Russia. Their chief incentive for playing, apart from sheer recreation, is the Olympics. The international style of play, popularized by the superb Soviet teams, has changed hockey throughout the world in the last decade. Typified by speed and razor-sharp passing, the new style of hockey relies less on muscle and reaction and more on play planning.

SPECTATOR'S GUIDE

Hockey is a high-speed game where much of the action occurs away from the puck, that hard rubber disc the players swat with such abandon and is so hard to see on a television screen. During three 20-minute periods, the teams furiously battle up and down the ice with one basic goal in mind: scoring more goals than their opponents. Preventing the other team from knocking the puck past your goalie (the one wearing the mask) is also admirable and highly desired.

fact: International hockey is played on a rink that is as much as 30 feet wider than an NHL rink. On the wider rink, players who pass well have the advantage.

The route to a goal is often a rough-and-tumble path. Hockey combines the grace of figure skating with the brawn of boxing, offering intricate teamwork as well; nothing is quite as exciting as two teams playing full-out, dashing from "end-to-end," creating continuous action. Everything is fast about hockey; forward line changes are made every 60 seconds or so, the puck is just a blur as it is passed about the ice, changing hands moment by moment, and even the referees must move quickly as they try to keep up with the flow of the play.

The cardinal rule for an attacking team is that the puck must precede the first player across the offensive blueline. Otherwise, and this is a frequent

Ice Hockey

violation, an offside is called, resulting in a faceoff. The puck cannot be sent from one end of the ice to the other without being touched or carried by members of the offensive team, unless that team is playing shorthanded. Such an infraction is called icing, and the puck is brought back for a faceoff deep in the offending team's zone. A shorthanded team is permitted to clear the puck from one end to the other; this is considered very good defense in these situations.

A team at full strength consists of a goaltender and five skaters: the forward line, consisting of a center and two wings, plus two defensemen. Numerous infractions of the rules may prevent a team from playing at full strength much of the time; players are sent to the penalty box, where they serve two minutes, for such rule violations as tripping, slashing (using the stick as a weapon), high sticking (ditto), and cross-checking. If the opposing team scores during the penalty period, the player in the box is released. Up to two players may serve these "minor" penalties at a time, so a team may play two men short. A five-minute major penalty for fighting or other more serious offenses may be called as well; a player receiving a major will serve his full penalty, regardless of how many goals the opponent scores during this time period.

fact: Hockey has become a great melting pot sport: North American players have signed up with European leagues, while European pucksters have signed with the NHL. The 1992 Swedish team, for example, had four current and former NHL All-Stars.

When a team gains an advantage in the number of men on the ice because of a penalty situation, it is said to be on its "power play," and usually puts forth its best shooters on the ice. The team on the power play will try to maintain the puck in the opponent's zone and pepper the goalie (the guy wearing the mask) with as many shots as possible.

Olympic hockey rules differ in several respects from those of the National Hockey League. An offside pass crossing the center, or red line, would be called immediately in the NHL, and play would stop. In the Olympics, extenuating circumstances may permit play to continue at the referee's discretion. Similarly, play is stopped in the NHL for any offside or when a player enters the faceoff circle at the time of a faceoff. But in the Olympics, no whistle is blown if the non-offending team gains possession of the puck.

fact: Olympic ice hockey consists of patient weaving and passing, vastly different from the NHL brawls that North American fans are used to.

In Olympic hockey, a second major penalty carries an automatic game misconduct and a trip to the locker room. Any Olympian starting a fight is assessed a match penalty.

For the Winter Olympics, twelve countries are eligible, based on their finish in the previous year's world championships. The defending Olympic champion (in this case, the Unified Team) is given an automatic berth, as is the host nation.

The countries will be split into two groups, with each group engaging in a five-game round-robin series. The two teams with the best records from each division will advance to the semifinals, where the winner of each group meets the second place team of the other. The two survivors then will play for the championship.

HOPEFULS

Usually you can tell the hopefuls in Olympic ice hockey by looking back at the last World Championships. The past will not be the usual prologue this year, mostly because the NHL players who performed at the World Championships last April and May will not be at Lillehammer. With nearly one in six NHL players coming from Europe, the league's decision to continue play during the Olympics affects almost every national team. This is good news for the US team and bad news for almost everybody else. Still, it is worth remembering how the national teams did at the World Championships. Russia defeated Sweden 3 to 1 in the finals while the Czech Republic defeated Canada for the bronze medal. Look for the same four teams to be in the Olympic medal round.

Since the last Olympic hockey tournament was only two years ago, the fortunes of teams there may be more telling than usual. At Meribel, the site of the last Olympic hockey games, the Unified Team defeated Canada 3–1 to win the gold medal, giving the Canadians the silver and their first medals in 24 years. Czechoslovakia beat the US team 6–1 for the bronze medal. Some of the names and circumstances have changed, but similar national teams will be back. This year the Czech Republic figures to be in the medal hunt along with the Russian team.

Although the Soviet's Big Red Machine is no more, its various parts parceled out to bigger money in the NHL and European leagues than the Russians can afford, watch out for an inspired and motivated Russian team to win the gold. Forwards Andrei Khomoutov and Vyacheslav Bykov have been playing in Switzerland and will not be under the same ban as NHL players; they were dominant in 1992 and could be an even more powerful combination this time. Andrei Trefilov, who made 35 saves in the World Championship game against Sweden last spring and was Russia's MVP in that game, belongs, at this writing,

US goalie Ray LeBlanc raises his stick in victory after a 2–0 shutout over Germany at the 1992 Albertville Games—the first for the US since 1964. LeBlanc manned a second shutout later in the tournament, and led Team USA to a fourth-place finish.

to the Calgary Flames. But if the Flames have as little use for him this year as they did last, Trefilov could be back in goal for the Russian team.

Tim Taylor, hockey coach at Yale University for seventeen years and for the US National Team the last five, will serve as head coach for the US Olympic ice hockey team. Taylor is considered to be an excellent strategist, so look for the recently assembled US team to be well coached but less experienced than the team that played at the World Championships in Germany. They won't have played together for as long as some other teams, such as France, and will be relatively young. They will miss Mike Richter who tended goal at the World

Championships but has returned to the New York Rangers. Mike Dunham, a 21 year old from the University of Maine who played in the 1992 Olympics and on the US National Team at the World Championships, might be in the nets this time and could play a pivotal role there. The team with the hottest goalie is often the one to watch in a short tournament like the Olympics. Harvard senior Ted Drury could make a big difference at forward; he also has some international experience, including seven appearances in the 1992 Games.

During the last Games most Canadian fans watched 19-year-old Eric Lindros. This year their attention will focus on his younger brother Brett who, at the age of 17, joined Team Canada last summer. The expectations placed on sports siblings are usually unfair, but hockey fans will be interested to see whether Brett Lindros will do for Team Canada what the then-underconditioned but high-flying Eric did in 1992. Don't get your hopes up, but have fun watching him.

France made the medal round in 1992 and will be a dark horse this time. They played poorly at the World Championships, losing their first five games by a combined score of 24 to 10. In fact, if you love underdogs and want to pick a long shot looking for a miracle, take France. The lack of NHL players may hurt them less than anyone else, except perhaps Italy and Germany, both of which have strong professional leagues of their own. If you want a reasonably likely winner, look to Finland.

The changing international style of play will also make a difference in who gets to the medal round this time and their chances once they get there. These Games will be more like the NHL and less like the international style of play usually associated with the Olympics. As in 1992, a lot of players are hoping for North American professional contracts. To be sure, skating and passing are rewarded in Olympic hockey; but look for more aggressive play too. The gentleness and grace associated in the past with the Swedes, Finns, and Czechs will still be there, but less so. If the officials allow a rougher style of play, the Canadians might nab another medal. Still, the officiating will be tougher than in the NHL; players won't get away with nearly as much here. The bigger rink also will make a difference in the style of play and that favors the Swedes.

NHL scouts will be the other hopefuls at the Games; they'll be looking for new stars to bring to North America. By the end of the last Olympics twelve players from the Unified Team had been drafted by NHL teams, although not all became starters for North American professional teams. The Russians reportedly are looking to the NHL to help finance the professional hockey leagues in Russia. Their effort to reclaim Russian hockey players from Western Europe and the United States led to the plan to support 64 of their teams. A year's support will cost the NHL roughly the equivalent of Eric Lindros's salary from the Philadelphia Flyers. A deal like that, plus the return of NHL stars in 1998, makes the prospects for future Olympic hockey tournaments even better.

133

The tentative ice hockey schedule is as follows:

Saturday, February 12
Three games

Sunday, February 13
Three games

Monday, February 14
Three games

Tuesday, February 15
Three games

Wednesday, February 16
Three games

Thursday, February 17
Three games

Friday, February 18
Three games

Saturday, February 19
Three games

Sunday, February 20
Three games

Monday, February 21
Three games

Tuesday, February 22
Two medal round games

Wednesday, February 23
Four medal round games

Thursday, February 24
Four medal round games

Friday, February 25
Two medal round games

Saturday, February 26
Three medal round games

Sunday, February 27
Final

HIGHLIGHTS

Ice hockey first appeared at the Summer Games at Amsterdam in 1920. Canada took the first four gold medals, ceding to Great Britain (whose team included some renegade Canadians) in 1936, then captured the last two golds before the USSR entered the arena.

Between 1920 and 1952, Canadian teams played 41 Olympic Games in which they scored 403 goals and allowed only 34. The Soviets were late in coming to the sport; it is thought that they might never have taken up hockey at all if it had not been an Olympic sport. Since the Soviets appeared in the Winter Olympics in 1956, they have won the gold in hockey seven times, losing only to the US, in 1960 at Squaw Valley and in 1980 at Lake Placid. The US has won six silver medals and one bronze to add to their two golds, including a surprise silver at the 1972 Games in Sapporo. Canada has earned two silver and two bronze medals to add to their pile of gold, while Sweden has won two silver medals and four bronze.

The diverse definitions of the amateur versus professional status accorded their teams by different nations has caused such controversy that even Canada chose to boycott its national sport in the 1972 and 1976 Games.

fact: In 1948 two teams showed up to represent the United States.

The 1980 competition was overlain with political tensions between the USSR and the US. When the heavily favored Soviet team was upset by an inexperienced US team, the crowd at Lake Placid was jubilant, as were television audiences across the nation. But the US squad still had to beat Finland in the final to capture the gold. In typical fashion, fighting from behind for the sixth time in seven Games, the gallant Americans behind coach Herb Brooks produced a 4–2 victory with three goals in the final period.

fact: Swiss hockey player Richard "Bibi" Torriani won a bronze medal in 1928 and another in 1948.

The 1980 Games were the third Olympics for the great Soviet goaltender Vladislav Tretiak. His countrymen recaptured the gold in 1984, ahead of Czechoslovakia. The medal round of the hockey competition was expanded from four teams to six in 1988. That year Canada's team made it to the medal round, but the gold was captured once again by the Soviet team, the silver going to Finland. In 1980, 1984, and 1988 Sweden maintained a lock on the hockey bronze.

Albertville: Still No Miracle

Although Albertville didn't set the stage for another Miracle on Ice, Team USA had a one-man miracle in goal keeper Ray LeBlanc, on loan from the Chicago Blackhawks' farm team. A softspoken man of 5'10", Ray—who was apparently on a first-name basis with the European crowds who chanted his name—allowed only 17 goals out of the 298 shots that barreled his way. That's a 94.29 save percentage. In spite of LeBlanc's show-stopping saves, however, dreams of a miraculous Team USA were grounded by the fact that none of the top fifteen scorers was wearing the American jersey; nor were the US boys heavy on the big "D." What's more, the in-your-face American-style hockey doesn't score well on the larger international rinks, which favor teams whose skaters display a certain measure of finesse. The American team didn't distinguish itself by its finesse: Czech goalie Petr Briza—whose team precision shot the Americans out of the bronze medal by a score of 6–1—complained, "They don't play hockey. They just hurry around."

LeBlanc wasn't in a big hurry to give away any goals, though: in an early match against Germany—who had soundly throttled the US team in Calgary—he

1960's Team USA celebrates its upset victory over Canada in Squaw Valley, California.

manned the first Olympic shutout by an American goalie since 1964. Then he manned a second shutout, earning an American record at the Games. By tournament's end, Team USA was in fourth place, not a dream come true, but a lot better than the seventh- or eighth-place finish experts had predicted, and a lot closer than they've come to precious metals in over a decade.

Canada, led by center Eric Lindros and goalie Sean Burke, had its best shot at the gold since 1952. In the final match between Canada and the Unified Team on the day of the closing ceremony—with both teams holding seven Olympic titles—the gold fell to what was probably the last of the Big Red hockey machine, with a 3–1 score. The Unified victory brought coach Victor Tikhonov his third gold medal, equalling the medal record of Anatoli Tarasov, the granddaddy of

Soviet hockey. By the end of the '92 Games, the Unified Team—the youngest and least penalized team at Albertville—had already lost 12 of its 23 players to the NHL draft.

A Lifetime Ago

For many fans—and certainly for the players—it was, and will remain, the most memorable sporting event of their lifetime. There has been little—could there ever be *anything?*—to match the excitement, emotion and pride generated by the 1980 US hockey team's Cinderella story at the Lake Placid Winter Games. The US team, 20 hockey players in their early to mid-20s, defeated the superb Soviets, 4–3, in one heart-stopping game, then rallied to beat spunky Finland, 4–2, in the gold-medal game.

During one incredible weekend in February, "USA! ... USA! ... USA!," and "Do you believe in miracles?" gave a discouraged America, a country besieged by high prime-lending and inflation rates, unnerved by the Soviet invasion of Afghanistan, and frustrated by the plight of 52 hostages held by Iran, something to really cheer about.

"For a lot of people, it was more than just a hockey game," team captain Mike Eruzione told the *St. Paul Pioneer Press.*

"It was a case," said Eruzione, who scored the game-winning goal against the Soviets with 10 minutes to play, "of a country not feeling as powerful as we once did, going up against a power at their own game and beating them with a bunch of kids."

fact: The 1980 Team USA broke the Soviet's sixteen-year winning streak.

The US hadn't defeated the Soviets since winning the gold medal at the 1960 Games and had been outscored 28–7 by the men in red in subsequent Olympic matchups. Less than a week before the 1980 Games, the Soviets had clobbered the US team, 10–3, in an exhibition at Madison Square Garden.

And after winning the gold medal?

"Here we (were)," Rob McClanahan told the *Pioneer Press,* "a team that was together 10 months and had just done something incredible, and the next day it was over. We're still a team in a sense, but we would never play together again. We didn't get a chance to celebrate as a team. It's kind of sad."

Indeed, life went on, even for these immortalized Boys of Winter.

Ten years later, in 1990, on the anniversary of their triumph, while many recapped their Olympian feats for reporters, the players had far different stories to tell each other.

In the intervening years, Coach Herb Brooks went on to coach the New York Rangers and Minnesota North Stars in the NHL, then provide color commentary on SportsChannel NHL cable telecasts. He was later inducted into

Coach Herb Brooks follows the 1980 US–USSR competition at Lake Placid. Team USA beat the Soviets for the first time since 1960, then defeated Finland for the gold.

the US Hockey Hall of Fame and then signed to coach the New Jersey Devils farm team in Utica, New York.

Twelve players had NHL tales to tell, some better than others. The most notable pro careers belonged to Neal Broten, Mark Johnson, Dave Christian, Mike Ramsey, and Ken Morrow. Broten became the first American-born player to score 100 points in an NHL season (105 in 1985–86); Morrow was the only player from the 1980 team to win a Stanley Cup ring, winning four with the New York Islanders. Retiring in 1990, he went on to become a professional coach.

Off the ice, Mike Eruzione seemed to capitalize the most on the team's success, parlaying his involvement into a TV-commentating and motivational-speaker career, as well as providing hockey color commentary at the 1992 Games in Albertville. Goalie Jim Craig had a brief and disappointing stint in the NHL and was involved in a traffic accident that resulted in the death of a 29-year-old woman. He became a salesman for a newspaper advertising-insert company.

McClanahan became a trader at a Chicago brokerage house; Phil Verchota played on the 1984 Olympic team, then turned to commercial banking; Eric Strobel was selling AT&T equipment; Buzz Schnieder was a supervisor with a moving company; Steve Christoff became a Northwest Airlines pilot; Bill Baker, graduating second in his dentistry class, was well on his way to becoming an oral surgeon and serving as the dentist for the University of Minnesota hockey team.

John Harrington played on the 1984 Olympic hockey team and became an assistant coach at the University of Denver, later moving on to St. Cloud (Minnesota) State; Steve Janaszak, the back-up goalie to Craig, was a Long Island real estate developer; Jack O'Callahan was a stock broker in Chicago; Mark Pavelich was a businessman in Eveleth, Minnesota; Dave Silk was playing in West Germany, where he was the MVP of his league; Bob Suter was running a sporting goods store in Madison, Wisconsin, and Mark Wells was managing a family restaurant in suburban Detroit.

Times had, indeed, changed.

"I work 70 to 75 hours a week," Wells told the *Detroit Free Press.* "I only have time to go home and do the laundry."

He tried to explain the 1980 miracle from the inside. "In '80 we were all placed at a village ... (and) all we did in '80 was go from the ice arena to the village and back. Everything was kind of blurry to me; a lot of guys felt the same way. Everything was too fast. That's because all we did was focus on our event."

Said Verchota, in the *Pioneer Press:* "It's almost like someone else's life, to be honest with you."

"Sometimes," Craig said, "it seems like a another lifetime ago."

Said Wells: "What we're doing today doesn't really matter. What it comes down to is lasting friendship."

And a lasting memory. —*E.K.*

Ice Hockey

1992 1. Unified Team, Alexandre Andrievski, Pavel Boure, Viatcheslav Boutsayev, Viktor Grodiouk, Yevgueni Davydov, Aleksei Jamnov, Aleksei Jitnik, Valeri Kamenski, Andrei Kovalenko, Viatcheslav Kozlov, Igor Kravtchouk, Vladimir Malakhov, Serguei Martyniouk, Aleksei Mariine, Dmitri Mironov, Andrei Potaitchouk, Vitali Prokhorov, Alexandre Semak, Alexandre Smirnov, Guerman Titov, Andrei Trefilov, Vladimir Tiourikov, Viatcheslav Ouvayev, Dmitri Filimonov, Mikhail Chtalenkov, Dmitri Youchkevitch

2. Canada, Dave Archibald, Todd Brost, Sean Burke, Devin Dahl, Karl Dykhuis, Curt Giles, Dave Hannan, Gordon Hynes, Fabian Joseph, Joe Juneau, Trevor Kidd, Chris Lindberg, Eric Lindros, Kent Manderville, Adrien Plavsic, Dan Ratushny, Stephane Roy, Sam Saint-Laurent, Brad Schlegel, Wally Schreiber, Randy Smith, David Tippett, Brian Tutt, Jason Wooley

3. Czechoslovakia, Patrick Augusta, Petr Briza, Jaromir Dragan, Leo Gudas, Miloslav Horava, Petr Hrbek, Otakar Janecky, Tomas Jelinek, Drahomir Kaadlec, Kamil Kastak, Robert Lang, Igor Liba, Ladislav Lubina, Frantisek Prochazka, Petr Rosol, Richard Shenlik, Robert Svehla, Betrich Scerban, Jiri Slegr, Oldrich Svoboda, Radek Toupal, Petr Veselovsky, Richard Zemlicka

1988 1. Soviet Union, Ilia Biakin, Igor Stelnov, Vyacheslav Fetisov, Alexei Gusarov, Alexei Kasatonov, Sergei Starikov, Vyacheslav Bykov, Sergei Yachin, Valeri Kamensky, Sergei Svetlov, Alexander Tchernykh, Andrei Khomutov, Vladimir Krutov, Igor Larionov, Andrei Lomakin, Sergei Makarov, Alexandre Nogilny, Anatoli Semyonov, Alexander Kozhevnikov, Igor Kravchuk

2. Finland, Timo Blomqvist, Kari Eloranta, Raimo Helminen, Iiro Jaervi, Esa Keskinen, Erkki Laine, Kari Laitinen, Erkki Lehtonen, Sakari Lindfors, Jyrki Lumme, Reijo Mikkolainen, Jarmo Myllys, Teppo Numminen, Janne Ojanen, Arto Ruotanen, Reijo Ruotsalainen, Simo Saarinen, Kai Suikkanen, Timo Susi, Jukka Tammi, Jari Torkki, Pekka Toumisto, Jukka Virtanen

3. Sweden, Anders Bergman, Peter Lindmark, Peter Aslin, Peter Andersson, Anders Eldebrink, Tomas Eriksson, Lars Ivarsson, Lars Karlsson, Mats Kihlstroem, Tommy Samuelson, Mikael Andersson, Bo Berglund, Jonas Bergovist, Thom Eklund, Peter Eriksson, Michael Hjaelm, Mikael Johansson, Lars Molin, Lars-Gunnar Pettersson, Thomas Lundqvist, Ulf Sandstroem, Hakan Soedergren, Jens Oehling

1984 1. Soviet Union, Viatcheslav Fetissov, Aleksei Kassatonov, Sergei Makarov, Igor Larionov, Vladimir Kroutov, Vassili Pervoukhin, Zenetoula Biliatletdinov, Sergei Chepelev, Alexandre Guerassimov, Andrei Khomoutov, Igor Stelnov, Sergei Starikov, Nikolay Drozdetskiy, Victor Tumenev, Alexandre Kozhevnikov, Alexandre Skvortsov, Vladimir Kovin, Mikhail Vasilev, Vladimir Zoubkov

2. Czechoslovakia, Milan Chalupa, Jaroslav Benak, Jiri Lala, Vladimir Kyhos, Frantischek Tchernik, Arnold Kadlec, Miloslav Horava, Igor Liba, Darius Rusnak, Vincent Lukatch, Radoslav Svoboda, Eduard Uvira, Pavel Richter, Vladimir Ruzsitchka, Vladimir Cladr, Jiri Hrdina, Duschan Paschek, Jaroslav Korbela

3. Sweden, Arne Michael Thelven, Bo Ericsson, Jens Erik Ohling, Per-Erik Eklung, Peter Olog Gradin, Thomas Valter Ahlen, Mats Gunnar Thelin, Karl Hakan Soedergren, Mats Stefan Waltin, Tommy Jan Motrh, Goeran Folke Lindblom, Leif Hakan Nordin, Thomas Sandstroem, Lars Hakan Eriksson, Thom Lennart Eklund, Peter Michael Hjalm, Thomas Per Rundquist, Mats Gunnar Hessel

1980 1. USA, James Craig, Kenneth Morrow, Michael Ramsey, William Baker, John O'Callahan, Bob Suter, David Silk, Neal Broten, Mark Johnson, Steven Christoff, Mark Wells, Mark Pavelich, Eric Strobel, Michael Eruzione, David Christian, Robert McClanahan, William ''Buzz'' Schneider, Philip Verchota, John Harrington

2. Soviet Union, Vladimir Myshkin, Vladislav Tretiak, Vyacheslav Fetisov, Vasily Pervukhin, Varery Vasiliev, Aleksei Kasatonov, Sergei Starikov, Zinetulla Bilyaletdinov, Vladimir Krutov, Aleksandr Maltsev, Yuri Lebedev, Boris Mikhailov, Vladimir Petrov, Valery Kharlamov, Helmut Balderis, Viktor Zlukov, Aleksandr Golikov, Sergei Makarov, Vladimir Golikov, Aleksandr Skvortsov

3. Sweden, Per-Eric "Pelle" Lindbergh, William Lofqvist, Tomas Jonsson, Sture Andersson, Ulf Weinstock, Jan Eriksson, Tommy Samuelsson, Mats Waltin, Thomas Eriksson, Per Lundqvist, Mats Ahlberg, Hakan Eriksson, Mats Naslund, Lennart Norberg, Bengt Lundholm, Leif Holmgren, Dan Soderstrom, Harald Luckner, Lars Mohlin, Bo Berglund

1976 1. Soviet Union, Vladislav Tretiak, Aleksandr Sidelnikov, Boris Aleksandrov, Sergei Babinov, Aleksandr Gusiev, Valeri Kharlamov, Aleksandr Yakushev, Viktor Zlukov, Sergei Kapustin, Vladimir Lutchenko, Yuri Lyapkin, Aleksandr Maltsev, Boris Mikhailov, Vladimir Petrov, Vladimir Chadrin, Viktor Szalimov, Gennady Tsygankov, Valeri Vasiliev

2. Czechoslovakia, Jiri Holecek, Jiri Crha, Oldrich Machac, Milan Chalupa, Frantisek Pospisil, Miroslav Dvorak, Milan Kajkl, Jiri Bubla, Milan Novy, Vladimir Martinec, Jiri Novak, Bohuslav Stastny, Jiri Holik, Ivan Hlinka, Eduard Novak, Jaroslav Pouzar, Bohuslav Ebermann, Josef Augusta

3. West Germany, Erich Weishaupt, Anton Kehle, Rudolf Thanner, Josef Volk, Udo Keissling, Stefan Metz, Klaus Auhuber, Ignaz Berndaner, Rainer Phillip, Lorenz Funk, Wolfgang Boos, Ernst Kopf, Ferenc Vozar, Walter Koberle, Erich Kuhnhacki, Alois Schloder, Martin Hinterstocker, Franz Reindl

1972 1. Soviet Union, Vladislav Tretiak, Aleksandr Pachkov, Vitali Davydov, Vladimir Lutshenko, Alexsandr Ragulin, Viktor Kuzkin, Gennady Tsygankov, Valeri Vasiliev, Valeri Kharlamov, Yuri Blinov, Vladimir Petrov, Anatoli Firsov, Aleksandr Maltsev, Vladimir Chadrin, Boris Mikhailov, Vladimir Vikulov, Aleksandr Yakushev

2. USA, Michael Curran, Peter Sears, Walter Olds, Thomas Mellor, Frank Sanders, James McElmury, Charles Brown, Richard McGlynn, Ronald Naslund, Robbie Ftorek, Stuart Irving, Kevin Ahearn, Henry Boucha, Craig Sarner, Timothy Sheehy, Keith Christiansen, Mark Howe

3. Czechoslovakia, Vladimir Dzurilla, Jiri Holecek, Vladimir Bednar, Rudolf Tajcnar, Oldrich Machac, Frantisek Pospisil, Josef Horesovksy, Karel Vohralik, Vaclav Nedomansky, Jiri Holik, Jaroslav Holik, Jiri Kochta, Eduard Novak, Richard Farda, Josef Cerny, Vladimir Martinec, Ivan Hlinka, Bohuslav Stastny

1968 1. Soviet Union, Viktor Konovalenko, Viktor Zinger, Viktor Blinov, Aleksandr Ragulin, Viktor Kuzkin, Oleg Zaitsev, Igor Romichevsky, Vitali Davydov, Yevgeny Zymin, Vyacheslav Starshinov, Boris Mayorov, Viktor Polupanov, Anatoly Firsov, Yuri Moiseyev, Anatoli Ionov, Yevgeny Michakov, Veniamin Aleksandrov, Vladimir Vikulov

2. Czechoslovakia, Vladimir Nadrchal, Vladimir Dzurilla, Oldrich Machac, Josef Horesovsky, Jan Suchy, Frantisek Pospisil, Karel Masopust, Frantisek Sevcik, Josef Golonka, Jaroslav Jirik, Jan Havel, Petr Hejma, Jiri Holik, Jan Hrbaty, Jiri Kochta, Josef Cerny, Vaclav Nedomansky, Jan Klapac

3. Canada, Kenneth Broderick, Wayne Stephenson, Marshall Johnston, Barry MacKenzie, Brian Glennie, Paul Conlin, Terrence O'Malley, Ted Hargreaves, Raymond Cadieux, Francis Huck, Morris Mott, Stephen Monteith, Gary Dineen, Herbert Pinder, William MacMillan, Danny O'Shea, Roger Bourbonnais, Gerry Pinder

1964 1. Soviet Union, Veninaim Aleksandrov, Aleksandr Alyimetov, Vitaly Davidov, Anatoli Firsov, Eduard Ivanou, Viktor Konovalenko, Viktor Kuzkin, Konstantin Loktev, Boris Mayorov, Yevgeny Mairov, Stanislaus Petuchov, Aleksandr Ragulin, Vyacheslav Starshinov, Leonid Volkov, Viktor Yakushev, Boris Zaitsev

2. Sweden, Kjell Svensson, Lennart Haggroth, Gert Blome, Nils Johansson, Roland Stoltz, Bert-Ola Nordlander, Nils Nilsson, Ronald Pettersson, Lars-Erik Lundvall, Eilert Maatta, Anders Andersson, Ulf Sterner, Carl-Goran Oberg, Sven Johansson, Uno Ohrlund, Hans Mild, Lennart Johansson

3. Czechoslovakia, Vladimir Dzurilla, Vladimir Nadrchal, Rudolf Potsch, Frantisek Tikal, Frantisek Gregor, Stanislav Sventek, Ladislav Smid, Vlastimil Bubik, Jaroslav Walter, Miroslav Vlach, Jiri Dolana, Jiri Holik, Josef Cerny, Stanislav Pryl, Josef Golonka, Jaroslav Jirik, Jan Klapac

1960 1. USA, John McCartan, Laurence Palmer, Robert Owen, John Kirrane, John Mayasich, Rodney Paavola, Richard Rodenheiser, Paul Johnson, Weldon Olson, Roger Christian, William Christian, Thomas Williams, Eugene Grazia, Richard Meredith, William Cleary, Robert Cleary, Robert McVey

2. Canada, Harold Hurley, Donald Head, Harry Sinden, John Douglas, Darryl Sly, Maurice Benoit, George Samolenko, Robert Attersely, Fred Etcher, Clifford Pennington, Robert Forhan, Robert McKnight, Floyd Martin, Kenneth Laufman, Donald Rope, James Connelly, Robert Rousseau

3. Soviet Union, Veniamin Aleksandrov, Aleksandr Alyimetov, Yuri Baulin, Mikhail Bychkov, Vladimr Grebennikov, Yevgeny Groshev, Viktor Yakushev, Yevgeny Yerkin, Nikolai Karpov, Alfred Kuchevsky, Konstantin Loktev, Stanislav Petuchov, Viktor Prjazhnikov, Nikolai Puchkov, Genrich Sidorenkov, Nikolai Sologubov, Yuri Tsitsinov

1956 1. Soviet Union, Yevgeny Babich, Usevolod Bobrov, Nikolai Chlystov, Aleksey Guryshev, Yuri Krylov, Alfred Kuchevsky, Valentin Kusin, Grigory Mkrtchan, Viktor Nikiforov, Yuri Pantyuchov, Nikolai Puchkov, Viktor Shuvalov, Genrich Sidorenkov, Nikolai Sologubov, Ivan Tregubov, Dmitri Ukolov, Aleksandr Uvarov
2. USA, Willard Ikola, Donald Rigazio, Richard Rodenheiser, Daniel McKinnon, Edward Sampson, John Matchefts, Richard Meredith, Richard Dougherty, Kenneth Purpur, John Mayasich, William Cleary, Wellington Burnett, Wendell Anderson, Eugene Campbell, Gordon Christian, Weldon Olson, John Petroske
3. Canada, Denis Brodeur, Keith Woodall, Floyd Martin, Howard Lee, Arthur Hurst, John McKenzie, James Logan, Paul Knox, Donald Rope, Byrle Klinck, William Colvin, Gerald Theberge, Alfred Horne, Charles Brooker, George Scholes, Robert White, Kenneth Laufman

1952 1. Canada, Eric Paterson, Ralph Hansch, John Davies, Robert Meyers, Allen Purvis, William Dawe, Donald Gauf, Robert Watt, George Abel, Bruce Dickson, David Miller, Francis Sullivan, Louis Secco, William Gibson, Gordon Robertson, Thomas Pollock
2. USA, Richard Desmond, Donald Whiston, Allen Van, Joseph Czarnota, Robert Rompre, Gerald Kilmartin, Kenneth Yackel, Leonard Ceglarski, Ruben Bjorkman, John Noah, Andre Gambucci, James Sedin, Clifford Harrison, Arnold Oss, John Mulhern
3. Sweden, Thord Flodqvist, Lars Svensson, Ake Andersson, Rune Johansson, Sven Thunman, Gote Almqvist, Lars Bjorn, Ake Lassas, Gote Blomqvist, Gosta Johansson, Erik Johansson, Stig Tvilling, Hans Tvilling, Lars Pettersson, Hans Oberg, Sven Johansson, Holger Nurmela

1948 1. Canada, Murray Dowey, Bernard Dunster, John Lecompte, Henri-Andre Laperriere, Walter Halder, George Mara, Reginald Schroeter, Thomas Hibberd, Albert Renaud, Jean Orval Gravelle, Patrick Guzzo, Irving Taylor
2. Czechoslovakia, Bohumil Modry, Zdenek Jarkovsky, Dr. Miroslav Slama, Josef Trousilek, Premysl Hajny, Vilibald Stovik, Oldrich Zabrodsky, Miloslav Pokorny, Ladislav Trojak, Vladimir Zabrodsky, Stanislav Konopasek, Vaclav Rozinak, Jaroslav Drobny, Karel Stibor, Gustav Bubnik, Vladimir Bouzek, Vladimir Kobranov
3. Switzerland, Hand Banninger, Reto Perl, Emil Handschin, Ferdinand Cattini, Hans Cattini, Heinrich Boller, Hans Durst, Walter Durst, Richard Torriani, Gebhard Poltera, Ulrich Poltera, Hans Trepp, Beat Ruedi, Alfred Bieler, Heini Lohrer, Werner Lohrer, Otto Schubiger

1936 1. Great Britain, James Foster, Carl Erhardt, Gordon Dailley, Archibald Stinchcombe, Edgar Brenchley, John Coward, James Chappell, Alexander Archer, Gerry Davey, James Borland, Robert Wyman, John Kilpatrick
2. Canada, Francis Moore, Arthur Nash, Herman Murray, Walter Kitchen, Raymond Milton, David Neville, Kenneth Farmer-Horn, Hugh Farquharson, Maxwell Deacon, Alexander Sinclair, William Thomson, James Haggarty, Ralph Saint Germain
3. USA, Thomas Moone, Francis Shaugnessy, Philip LaBatte, Frank Stubbs, John Garrison, Paul Rowe, John Lax, Gordon Smith, Elbridge Ross, Francis Spain, August Kammer

1932 1. Canada, William Cockburn, Hugh Sutherland, Roy Hinkel, Walter Monson, Victor Lindquist, Romeo Rivers, Harold Simpson, Norman Malloy, Aliston Wise, Clifford Crowley, Albert Duncanson, George Garbutt, Kenneth Moore, Stanley Wagner
2. USA, Franklin Farrell, John Garrison, Osborn Anderson, John Chase, Douglas Everett, Winthrop Palmer, John Bent, John Cookman, Joseph Fitzgerald, Edward Frazier, Gerard Hallock, Robert Livingston, Francis Nelson, Gordon Smith
3. Germany, Walter Leinweber, Alfred Heinrich, Erich Romer, Rudi Ball, Martin Schrottle, Gustav Jaenecke, Erich Herker, Werner Korff, Marquardt Slevogt, Georg Strobl

1928 1. Canada, Dr. Joseph Sullivan, Ross Taylor, John Porter, Dr. Louis Hudson, David Trottier, Norbert Mueller, Hugh Plaxton, Frank Sullivan, Frank Fisher, Herbert Plaxton, Roger Plaxton, Charles Delahay
2. Sweden, Nils Johansson, Kurt Sucksdorff, Carl Abrahamsson, Henry Johansson, Emil Bergman, Wilhelm Petersen, Gustaf Johansson, Birger Holmqvist, Sigurd Oberg, Ernst Karlberg, Bertil Linde, Erik Larsson
3. Switzerland, Arnold Martignoni, Charles Fasel, Mezzi Andreossi, Giannin Andreossi, Robert Breiter, Richard Torriani, Dr. Luzius Ruedi, Albert Geromini, Fritz Kraatz, Heini Meng, Anton Morosani, Louis Dufour

1924 1. Canada, Duncan Munro, W. Beattie Ramsay, Harry Watson, Reginald Smith, Albert McCaffery, Cyril Sig. Slater, Harold McMunn, Jack Cameron, Ernest Collett
2. USA, Alphonse Lacroix, Irving Small, Clarence Abel, Herbert Drury, Justin McCarthy, Willard Rice, John Lyons, Frank Synott, John A. Langley
3. Great Britain, Colin Carruthers, Eric Carruthers, Ross Cuthbert, Edward Pitblado, Hamilton Jukes, W. H. Anderson, Lorne Carr-Harris, Blane Sexton, George Holmes, Guy Clarkson

1920 1. Canada, Walter "Wally" Byron, Konrad Johannessen, Robert Benson, Allan "Huck" Woodman, Haldor "Slim" Halderson, Frank Fredrickson, Mike Goodman, Chris Fridfinnson

2. USA, Raymond Bonney, Cyril Weidenborner, George Geran, J. Edward Fitzgerald, Frank Goheen, Leon Tuck, Anthony Conroy, Herbert Drury, Joseph McCormick, Lawrence McCormick, Frank Synott

3. Czechoslovakia, Jan Peka, Karel Walzer, Jan Palous, Otakar Vindys, Dr. Karel Hartman, Vilem Loos, Josef Sroubek, Dr. Karel Pesek

Trivia Quiz

1. The current Team USA coach is:

A) Tim Taylor. B) Al Wilson. C) Gordie Howe. D) Buzz Schneider.

2. Ice hockey made its first Olympic appearance:

A) in 1924, at the first Winter Games. B) in 1920, at Amsterdam. C) in 1936, at Garmisch-Partenkirchen. D) in 1940, at Sapporo, Japan.

3. What American scored the game-winning goal against the Soviets in 1980?

A) Richard Dougherty. B) Buzz Schneider. C) Mike Eruzione. D) Ray LeBlanc.

4. Who coached the 1980 American team to the "Miracle on Ice"?

A) Tim Taylor. B) Buzz Schneider. C) Herb Brooks. D) Don Cherry.

5. What team earned the first Olympic gold medal?

A) the US team. B) the Canadian team. C) the Finnish team. D) the Winnepeg Falcons.

6. The "international" style of hockey favors:

A) skaters who skate with finesse and pass well. B) skaters with boxing backgrounds. C) skaters who maneuver with short, choppy strides. D) skaters who have NHL backgrounds.

7. Hockey first appeared at American universities:

A) in 1893, at Yale and Johns Hopkins. B) in 1926, at the University of Minnesota. C) in 1932, at Vassar. D) in 1928, at Princeton.

8. In Olympic hockey, an offside pass crossing the red line:

A) is always allowed. B) is never allowed. C) is sometimes allowed.

9. How many countries are eligible to play hockey at the Winter Games?

A) twelve, based exclusively on their finish in the previous year's world championships. B) twelve, automatically including the host nation. C) twelve, automatically including the Russian team. D) as many as want to, provided they entered the previous year's world championships.

143

10. "Icing" is a penalty that refers to:

A) knocking down an opponent. **B)** sending the puck from one end of the rink to the other without appropriate handling. **C)** rubbing snow in an opponent's face. **D)** using the hockey stick as a weapon.

LUGE

WARM-UP

Luge probably has the distinction of being considered by American viewers as the strangest Winter Olympic sport. Although it has roots in prehistoric sledding and bears a close resemblance to the familiar childhood sport of "belly-whomping" on a winter hill, luge has yet to catch on in a big way in the USA. This may be because the US has not yet come close to winning a medal, and Americans are a success-oriented people. And though Americans love daredevils, riding down a bending track at 70 miles per hour while on your back with no particular way to steer may be a stretch for the average sledder.

fact: Sliders use what they call "black magic"—sharpening and preparing their blades—to get an extra edge on the course. Coating the blades with silicone is illegal magic. Adding to the sport's gravity, lugers refer to the building at the top of the run as the "morgue."

Historians have found evidence that sleds resembling the modern-day luge were used in Norway more than 1,000 years ago. Luge, the French word for sleigh, had practical origins several centuries ago as a means of travel in the alpine mountainous regions of Austria, Poland, Germany, northern Italy, and Russia.

The first international luge race took place in Switzerland in 1883, sponsored by a group of Swiss hotel owners. Seven countries took part, including the US. In 1914, the first European championship was held in Austria. But it was not until 1953 that luge formally separated itself from bobsledding with the formation of the International Luge Federation. And in 1964, luge was added to the Winter Olympic program.

fact: Luge is the only Olympic sport that is timed to the thousandth of a second.

145

At that time, critics protested that the sport was too dangerous for the Olympics. Their fears were well founded; two weeks before the first Olympic event in Innsbruck, Austria, a member of the British team died after a crash during a trial run. Stricter safety regulations have eliminated fatalities in recent years, but for the luger, fear is still the co-pilot. 1984 men's singles gold medal winner Paul Hildgartner of Italy, who broke his back on a bumpy natural ice run in 1981, says, "Certainly I know fear. After a heavy injury, I am scared to go down the chute again."

Until the Olympic run was completed on Mt. Van Hoevenberg for the 1980 Games, not a single "bahn" (course or road) suitable for international competition was located in the Western Hemisphere. Before Lake Placid, the only available bahn in the Western Hemisphere was a 750-foot practice track in Toronto. This meant that American lugers had to use the bob run at Mt. Van Hoevenberg when it was available, or train in Europe. Consequently, the US has yet to win a medal in an Olympic contest, while East Germany (now Germany) has dominated the medal awards, particularly in the women's singles.

SPECTATOR'S GUIDE

Luge has been described as the most dangerous of Olympic sports, with the sleds careening downhill at speeds of more than 120 kilometers per hour, the riders flat on their back, feet extending beyond the runners. For roughly 40 seconds the pressure that flattens them against the sled could be up to seven times the force of gravity, or twice that exerted on an astronaut during a shuttle launch. From a spectator's point of view, it looks like a mighty uncomfortable ride. One hand grips the reins and the other the sled. A luge is so flexible that even a slight repositioning of the head can cause the sled to veer into a wall or off the track altogether.

fact: Metabolically speaking, a slider—who's subjected to up to 5G of compression—is just about on the verge of seizure.

"If you start to veer out of control, you can't let yourself panic," former US champion Frank Masley once noted. "If you let up your concentration for a split second, you'll crash into the wall." That wall always in mind, the luger lies on his or her back with shoulders resting on the seat in the rear, head up and feet forward. Except for a steering strap, no panels or straps hold the competitor on the sled. A luge cannot contain any mechanical steering or braking devices. The driver steers the luge by exerting foot and leg pressure, downward and sideways, on the forward extensions of the runners and by shifting his or her body.

fact: Each time a luger raises her head to check her path she loses precious time; she may only look up two or three times during a run that takes about 50 seconds.

So luge has its exciting moments. Olympic luge consists of men's and women's singles and men's doubles. Singles competition consists of four heats, while doubles has only two. In doubles competition, one luger lies flat on top of his teammate. The rider on top is the driver, while his partner assists with body positioning and acts as ballast.

The bahn must be between 1,000 and 1,200 meters long and between 1.35 and 1.5 meters wide, with an incline measuring between 9 and 12%. Included among the curves must be one hairpin, one left and one right, one "S" and one labyrinth. The start platforms must be between three and 10 meters high. The length of the run is 20% shorter for men's doubles and the women's singles.

fact: If a luger loses a tenth of a second in the pretimed part of the race, when he's pushing the sled down a steep incline toward the starting line, he's probably blown his chances entirely.

The highly customized luge can weigh a maximum of 22 kilograms (48.4 pounds) for a one-person sled, and 24 kilograms (52.8 pounds) for a two-person sled. The maximum width between runners is about 18 inches. Most sleds are about four feet long, although length is not restricted.

For the one-person sleds, the maximum weight total for men is 242 pounds and for women, 220. The heavier driver has an advantage on the straightaway while the lighter driver is quicker on the curves. If a luger is under the weight limit, he or she may carry half the weight that is missing. Thus, if a man weighs 200 pounds, he may carry an additional 21 pounds.

HOPEFULS

Leading an impressive pack of strong competitors in the men's singles is Germany's Georg Hackl, gold medalist at the 1992 Olympic Games in Albertville. Hackl, who has twice held the world title, will be strongly challenged in Lillehammer by the current World Cup holder, Austria's Markus Prock, who was silver medalist at the Albertville Olympics. Prock's fellow Austrians Markus Schmidt, bronze medalist at Albertville, and Robert Manzenreiter, who finished fifth in the 1992–94 World Cup standings, are also imposing candidates for the Olympic gold. American luger Wendel Suchow, holder of the 1992–93 world championship, is still another formidable contender, as is fellow American Duncan Kennedy, who finished second in the 1991–92 World Cup games and third in the 1992–93 cup competition. Among doubles contenders, the German men's tandems of Stefan Krausse–Jan Behrendt and Yves Mankel–Thomas Rudolph loom large, as does the American team of Mark Grimmette–Jon Edwards.

fact: Since weight gives lugers an advantage, lighter sliders wear weights. But it isn't that simple. Since smaller weighted bodies are faster than larger bodies of the same weight, there's a formula for weight-wearing in luge events.

Americans also stand prominent among the women lugers. Foremost among the American contestants is Cammy Myler, who finished second in the 1991–92 World Cup season and fifth in Albertville. Myler's principal rivals would appear to be Italian Gerda Weissensteiner, World Cup champion for the 1992–93 season, and Austrian sisters Doris and Angelika Neuner. Other contenders include German lugers Susi Erdmann, the 1991–92 World Cup champion, and Gabriele Kohlisch.

Duncan Kennedy

Duncan Kennedy ranks with 1992–93 world champion Wendel Suchow as one of America's most promising candidates for the Olympic gold medal in the luge competition. Kennedy is a colorful figure who first began sliding at age twelve after attending the luge slides at the 1980 Olympics held in Lake Placid. In only a year's time he realized the US Junior National Singles title, and the next year he repeated that championship and shared in the doubles title as well. In 1982 Kennedy also became the first American luger to capture an international medal

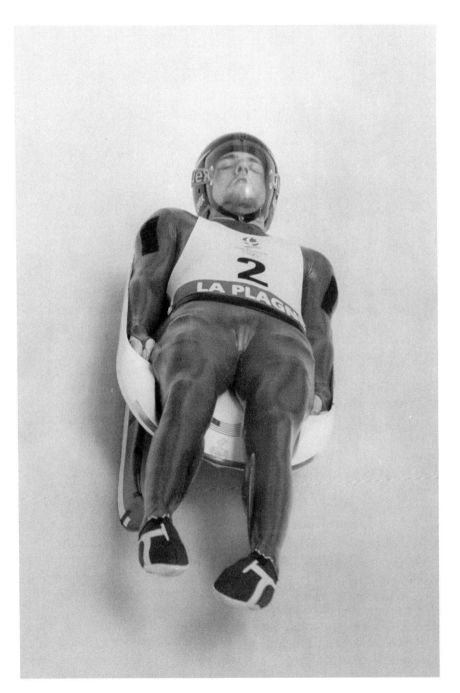

USA's Duncan Kennedy hurtles down the final run of the men's singles competition at the Albertville Olympics. Kennedy finished tenth—a record for American lugers in the men's events.

Wendel Suchow and Bill Tavares race to ninth place in the Olympic men's doubles competition in 1992—the best ever for an American team.

when he placed second at a junior race conducted in Igls, Austria. And he closed the decade by capturing the first of his three US National Singles Championships.

In the 1990s Kennedy achieved increasing success on the international luge circuit. During the 1990–91 season he raced to first at the NYNEX international tournament and closed with a fourth-place finish at the Grand Prix in Albertville. In his next season of international competition, Kennedy won a slew of medals, including two golds and two silvers, and finished only one point behind Austrian winner Markus Prock in total World Cup points.

On the domestic front, Kennedy maintained his stronghold, winning further championships in 1991 and 1992. He thus figured prominently in America's plans to compete for the gold medal at the 1992 Olympic Games in Albertville. Expectations were no doubt fueled by Kennedy's relatively high public profile. A *Newsweek* profile, for example, characterized Kennedy as a candid, speed-loving luger determined to promote his sport domestically by triumphing in Albertville. But the Olympics ultimately proved somewhat of a disappointment for the ambitious, hard-training Kennedy, who finished a distant tenth. But though he finished well out of the medals, Kennedy realized at least a small measure of success, for his tenth-place standing was the highest finish ever secured by an American luger in the men's Olympic competition—a finish, incidentally, that constitutes but one of twenty-seven American records held by Kennedy, which puts him twenty-four ahead of his nearest rival.

Gold medalist Doris Neuner, right, and her sister, silver medalist Angelika, are carried by fellow Austrian team members following their finish in the 1992 Olympics.

In the ensuing World Cup competitions Kennedy recovered impressively from his disappointing Olympics showing. He was accorded a silver medal in Lillehammer and a bronze medal in Winterberg, and he eventually closed the season in third-place overall, trailing only Austria's Markus Prock, Olympic silver medalist at Albertville, and Germany's Georg Hackl, who captured the gold at the same Games. It thus appears likely that Kennedy, along with world champion Suchow and prominent women's-singles luger Cammy Myler, will play a key role in America's performance in the Lillehammer Olympic Games. —L.S.

Cammy Myler

Cammy Myler is probably the United States's leading contender for an Olympic medal in the luge competition. She became active in the sport when she was only eleven years old and readily won the National Junior Olympics. In the early 1980s she continued her success by winning three consecutive titles in the US Junior Women's Championships, and in 1985, at age sixteen, she became the premier athlete at the American senior competition when she triumphed as Senior Women's Champion.

Myler entered international competition in 1989 and realized sixth place in the 1989–90 World Championships. The following year she secured a bronze medal at the World Cup races held in Altenberg, Germany. The next year she improved on that success by winning a silver medal in Altenberg and finishing second in the World Cup games to Germany's Susi Erdman.

At the 1992 Olympic Games held in Albertville, Myler finished fifth—a standing, although out of the medals, that proved the highest ever realized by an American luger. During the ensuing 1992–93 season Myler, who had undergone surgery to repair an injured shoulder, managed to fare ninth in the World Cup competition. This standing, though well back of Italian winner Gerda Weissensteiner and Austrians Doris Neuner and Andrea Tagwerker, still managed to lead all Americans in the competition. Myler served further notice of her leadership among America's women lugers when she captured her fifth national championship—and third consecutive title—in 1993. —*L.S.*

Schedule

The tentative luge schedule is as follows:

Sunday, February 13
Single, men

Monday, February 14
Single, men

Tuesday, February 15
Single, women

Wednesday, February 16
Single, women

Friday, February 18
Double, men

HIGHLIGHTS

Luge competition was not part of the Winter Games until the Innsbruck Games in 1964. Since then, East Germany has won 38 of the 72 Olympic medals awarded in luge. Bad weather shortened the competition in 1968, but not before three East German women were disqualified for heating the metal runners on their sleds—a practice that had been legal in 1964. Manfred Schmid, taking the Olympic gold in singles in 1968, is the only Austrian to have done so. A problem with the starting gate canceled the results of the first run in the two-man event in 1972; a disputed tie was finally resolved by the awarding of a double gold, to East Germany and Italy.

fact: Many lugers draw their knees up at the start of the race to delay by a fraction of a second triggering the electric beam of the timer, which is placed three inches above the ice and begins recording the time elapsed during the run; at the end of the race the lugers extend their toes as far in front of the sled as possible, to trigger the timer beam at the bottom of the run a fraction of a second sooner.

While East German Ute Rührold was capturing her second straight silver medal at age 21 at the 1976 Olympics, the US team took pride in the fact that the whole team finished all their runs in the three events. East Germans Hans Rinn and Norbert Hahn became the first repeat gold medalists in luge when they won the 1980 two-man event. That year the USSR picked up a rare gold, and Italy clinched two silvers. One of Italy's 1980 silver medalists, Paul Hildgartner, was 31 when he took the 1984 gold in men's singles; another 1984 gold medal winner, Hans Stangassinger of the West German two-man team, weighed 244 pounds.

In 1988 the East German women swept the medals in luge singles. That year East German men and women won six of the nine luge medals, and all the gold. US luger Bonny Warner came in sixth, the best US finish until that time.

Albertville: The US Slides Closer to Victory

1992 produced the best US finishes ever in both the men's and women's singles events, but Duncan Kennedy's 10th-place slide was still a disappointment. Having rocketed to the top in world cup competition, Kennedy had a shot at winning the overall world cup title, which would be a first-time honor for an American. Finishing twelfth in the race—held one month before the Games, in Calgary—he was only one point behind champion Markus Prock in the standings, but way behind in morale. After his disappointing finish, Kennedy confessed, "After Calgary I was extremely defeated mentally." Not good when you're screaming downhill at 70 mph under five Gs of pressure. In the first run at Albertville, Kennedy finished sixth; by the second run, he slid out of medal contention, having skidded through two turns en route to a 12th-place finish. His next two runs held him in 10th place overall, a full 1.489 behind the winning time.

Georg Hackl, who captured the silver at Calgary and had won the world championships twice since then, was 1992's prohibitive favorite. At Albertville, he was unbeatable: despite sled-slowing fresh snow on the second day, Hackl turned in the three fastest runs in the singles competition. The margin of victory: .306 seconds.

Germany's Georg Hackl celebrates his gold-medal run in the men's singles competition at the Albertville Games—a first for Germany.

In second place, 1991 world cup winner Markus Prock slid by teammate Markus Schmidt, leaving Jens Muller, the 1988 Games champion, out in the cold. In the doubles competition, Germany hogged the podium, leaving only third place for the world-cup-champion Italians.

In the women's event, Austria's Neuner sisters both medaled, relegating Germany's reigning world champion, Susi Erdmann, to third place. Meanwhile, in fifth place, Cammy Myler earned the best US finish ever.

The 1992 Games banned toe pointers—straps that contort a slider's feet in the name of aerodynamics—and required lugers to leave the finish line of their own power. It made for less dramatic exits than those of previous Games, where vertically challenged lugers required escorts to help them from the track.

Austrian gold medalist Doris Neuner is greeted by members of her team after winning the women's event in at the 1992 Games. Her sister Angelika garnered the silver.

Luge—Men's Singles

1992 1. Georg Hackl, Germany, 3:02.363
2. Markus Prock, Austria, 3:02.669
3. Markus Schmidt, Austria, 3:02.942
1988 1. Jens Mueller, East Germany, 3:05.548
2. Georg Hackl, West Germany, 3:05.916
3. Iouri Kharchenko, Soviet Union, 3:06.274
1984 1. Paul Hildgartner, Italy, 3:4.258
2. Serguev Danilin, Soviet Union, 3:4.962
3. Valeri Doudin, Soviet Union, 3:5.012
1980 1. Bernhard Glass, East Germany, 2:54.796
2. Paul Hildgartner, Italy, 2:55.372
3. Anton Winkler, West Germany, 2:56.545
1976 1. Detlef Guenther, East Germany, 3:27.688
2. Josef Fendt, West Germany, 3:28.196
3. Hans Rinn, East Germany, 3:28.574
1972 1. Wolfgang Scheidl, East Germany, 3:27.58
2. Harald Ehrig, East Germany, 3:28.39
3. Wolfram Fiedler, East Germany, 3:28.73
1968 1. Manfred Schmid, Austria, 2:42.48
2. Thomas Kohler, East Germany, 2:52.66
3. Klaus-Michael Bonsack, East Germany, 2:53.33
1964 1. Thomas Kohler, East Germany, 3:26.77
2. Klaus-Michael Bonsack, East Germany, 3:27.04
3. Hans Plenk, West Germany, 3:30.15
1924-1960 Not held

Luge—Men's Doubles

1992 1. Germany, 1:32.053, Stefan Krausse, Jan Behrendt
2. Germany, 1:32.239, Yves Mankel, Thomas Rudolph
3. Italy, 1:32.298, Hansjorg Raffl, Norbert Huber
1988 1. East Germany, 1:31.940, Joerg Hoffmann, Jochen Pietzsch
2. East Germany, 1:32.039, Stefan Krausse, Jan Behrendt
3. West Germany, 1:32.274, Thomas Schwab, Wolfgang Staudinger
1984 1. West Germany, 1:23.620, Hans Stangassinger, Franz Wembacher
2. Soviet Union, 1:23.660, Yevgeny Beloussov, Alexandar Belyakov
3. East Germany, 1:23.887, Joerg Hoffmann, Jochen Pietzsch
1980 1. East Germany, 1:19.331, Hans Rinn, Norbert Hahn
2. Italy, 1:19.606, Peter Schnitzer, Karl Brunner
3. Austria, 1:19.795, George Fluckinger, Karl Schrott
1976 1. East Germany 1:25.604, Hans Rinn, Norbert Hahn

2. West Germany, 1:25.899, Hans Brner, Balthasar Schwarm
3. Austria, 1:25.919, Manfred Schmid, Franz Schachner
1972 1. Italy, 1:28.35, Paul Hildgartner, Walter Plaikner
1. East Germany, 1:28.35, Horst Hornlein, Reinhard Bredow
3. East Germany, 1:29.16, Klaus-M. Bonsack, Wolfram Fiedler
1968 1. East Germany, 1:35.85, Klaus-M. Bonsack, Thomas Kohler
2. Austria, 1:36.34, Manfred Schmid, Ewald Walch
3. West Germany, 1:37.29, Wolfgang Winkler, Fritz Nachmann
1964 1. Austria, 1:41.62, Josef Feistmantl, Manfred Stengl
2. Austria, 1:41.91, Reinhold Senn, Helmut Thaler
3. Italy, 1:42.87, Walter Aussendorfer, Sigisfredo Mair
1924-1960 Not held

Luge—Women's Singles

1992 1. Doris Neuner, Austria, 3:06.696
2. Angelika Neuner, Austria, 3:06.769
3. Susi Erdmann, Germany, 3:07.115
1988 1. Steffi Walter-Martin, East Germany, 3:03.973
2. Ute Oberhofner, East Germany, 3:04.105
3. Cerstin Schmidt, East Germany, 3:04.181
1984 1. Steffi Martin, East Germany, 2:46.570
2. Bettina Schmidt, East Germany, 2:46.873
3. Ute Weiss, East Germany, 2:47.248
1980 1. Vera Zozulia, Soviet Union, 2:36.537
2. Melitta Sollmann, East Germany, 2:37.657
3. Ingrida Amantova, Soviet Union, 2:37.817
1976 1. Margit Schumann, East Germany, 2:50.621
2. Ute Ruehrold, East Germany, 2:50.846
3. Elisabeth Demleitner, West Germany, 2:51.056
1972 1. Anna-Maria Muller, East Germany, 2:59.18
2. Ute Ruehrold, East Germany, 2:59.49
3. Margit Schumann, East Germany, 2:59.54
1968 1. Erica Lechner, Italy, 2:28.66
2. Christa Schmuck, West Germany, 2:29.37
3. Angelika Dunhaupt, West Germany, 2:29.56
1964 1. Ortrun Enderlein, East Germany, 3:24.67
2. Ilse Geisler, East Germany, 3:27.42
3. Helene Thurner, Austria, 3:29.06
1924-1960 Not held

1. **Toe pointers, which are used to streamline the sliders' feet:**

   A) have always been illegal in the Olympics. B) were first allowed at Albertville. C) were last allowed at Calgary.

2. **Luge was added to the Olympic program:**

   A) in 1956, three years after the sport formally separated from bobsledding. B) in 1964, at Innsbruck. C) in 1944, at Cortina d'Ampezzo.

3. **Who is the highest-placing US man in Olympic singles competition?**

   A) Duncan Kennedy. B) Nigel Kennedy. C) Theodore Kennedy.

4. **The luge run is refered to as:**

   A) the chute. B) the bahn. C) the morgue.

5. **The word "luge" comes from:**

   A) a German word meaning rosebud. B) a French word meaning sled. C) a Scandinavian word meaning gonzo.

6. **How many luge runs are there in the US?**

   A) three, in Colorado Springs, Colorado; Marquette, Michigan; and in Lake Placid, New York. B) one, in Lake Placid, New York. C) none: the only luge run in the Western Hemisphere is in Toronto.

7. **Sliders steer by shifting body weight and:**

   A) by exerting foot and leg pressure. B) by manipulating mechanical steering devices. C) by praying.

8. **Which of the following is not illegal in Olympic luge competition?**

   A) carrying balast. B) heating sled runners to more than five degrees above air temperature. C) using silicone on the sled runners. D) employing braking devices.

9. **Women's luge events were first included:**

   A) in 1964, at Innsbruck. B) in 1992, at Albertville. C) women have never competed in Olympic luge.

10. **The US team:**

    A) dominated Olympic luge competition through the 1950s. B) has won only one luge medal. C) has never medaled in Olympic competition.

Answers: 1-c, 2-b, 3-a, 4-b, 5-b, 6-b, 7-a, 8-a, 9-a, 10-c

SKIING—ALPINE

WARM-UP

Skiing, once the province (or at least the hill) of the rich in the US, became a sport popular with the masses after World War II, with former members of the famed 10th Mountain Division (the "hallowed ski troops") invigorating the ski industry. Other returning servicemen, who had been given a chance to ski in Europe after or even during the war, also contributed to the growing popularity of the sport. Everyone wanted to forget the hard times of the war; silently traversing the winter landscape on skis proved a tonic for some.

Although the American interest in skiing is relatively new, skiing has been practiced in northern Europe for centuries. The oldest known ski, found in a peat bog at Umea, Sweden, goes back nearly 45 centuries to 2500 BC. However, a Stone Age petroglyph in Rodoy, Norway showing a skier has been dated at 5000 BC, a sure sign that someone, now very old, was on skis more than 7,000 years ago. A sled runner about 10 feet long was pulled out of a Finnish bog and carbon-dated to 7000 BC, or 9,000 years ago. As Ted Bates notes in his book *Nine Thousand Years of Skis*, "Where there were sled runners, there were probably skis." But thousands of years of relying on skis for transportation did not naturally give way to sport; only in the last century has it become a recreational and competitive sport.

In the early days, skiing invariably meant nordic: ski jumping and cross-country. When the British began to popularize skiing in central Europe during the late 19th century, the Alps gave their name to alpine skiing.

fact: Downhillers are considered by other skiers to be insane.

Henry Lunn of Great Britain, a travel agent, founded the Public Schools Alpine Sports Club and promoted alpine skiing to lure elite Britons to Switzerland and the Alps. In 1911, Lunn organized the first downhill race, the Roberts of Kandahar Challenge (so named because the trophy was put up by Lord Kandahar), held in what is now Crans-Montana, Switzerland. His son, Arnold Lunn, staged the first modern slalom in 1922 in Murren, Switzerland.

For the first three Olympics, only nordic events were staged, and were only held for men. In 1948, alpine events were fully integrated into the Olympic

Alberto "La Bomba" Tomba charges through the first of two runs in the
men's giant slalom race on Mt. Allan in Nakiska at the Calgary Games. 1.14
seconds ahead of the second-place finisher after the first run, Tomba held the
lead to capture the 1988 giant slalom gold.

program. The inaugural alpine event, the combined, which was introduced in 1936 and included women, was dropped as an Olympic event after 1948, not to reappear until 1988. The 1948 Olympics saw the introduction of men's and women's downhill and slalom events. Men's and women's giant slalom was added to the Olympic lineup in 1952, and super giant (super-G) slalom and combined events placed on the program in 1988.

SPECTATOR'S GUIDE

Downhill and super giant slalom are generally grouped together as speed events, while slalom and giant slalom are considered technical events. Generally, skiers compete in either the speed or the technical events, since each involves unique skills and equipment and requires different strategies to be successful.

The top 15 skiers are seeded and unless course conditions are poor, this group has the advantage of going down first on a fresh course. When conditions are poor, lower-ranked skiers are sent off first to create a firmer trail. If two heats are involved, the top 15 reverses its order for the second run. Virtually all of the medalists will come from the top-seeded group, although an unseeded skier will occasionally surprise and grab a medal.

fact: Swiss skier Paul Accola (1988 bronze men's combined) didn't always see eye-to-eye with his coaches, and refused to wear the official Swiss uniform in Albertville because it was "too tight." With a reputation as a downhill badboy, Accola was once on the guest register of a Swiss army brig (for petty larceny).

Alpine skis are more durable and wider than those used for cross country. The slalom ski has a more defined side cut and is a little narrower at the center. The giant slalom side cut isn't as defined while the downhill model is almost straight. Built for speed, the downhill ski is the longest of the racing models, measuring approximately seven feet. Slalom racers tend to favor shorter skis for greater maneuverability, while the length of the giant slalom ski falls between the downhill and slalom.

Slalom is an event requiring the execution of many short, quick turns through two heats on two different courses. The times for the two heats are added together to determine the final finish order.

A slalom course is required to have 55–75 gates for men and 40–60 gates for women. The competitors are required to pass between all the gates (alternate red/blue pairs of flag poles) in sequence down the course. The course is composed of various gate combinations designed to test a skier's skill and strategy. As long as a racer's feet pass between the markers, no penalty is charged for knocking down the flags with arms or shoulders. But if a gate is missed, the racer will be disqualified unless he or she returns to the gate and passes through it. The vertical drop on slalom courses is between 140–220 meters for men and 120–180 meters for women.

Giant Slalom is characterized as the discipline that requires the most technical skill; skiers race down the mountain through a faster, longer, and more open course than in slalom. The number of gates on the course is determined by the vertical drop of the course. The FIS requires that all giant slalom races be run on courses with vertical drops of 250–400 meters for men and 250–350 meters for women. The minimum distance between gates is 13 feet. Competitors stay low between gates and straighten up for turns.

> **fact:** Albertville drew skiers from forty-seven countries, including Bolivia, Brazil, Costa Rica, India, Lebanon, Morocco, Swaziland, and Taiwan. Also-rans outnumbered the medalists 132 to 3.

Speed and drama go hand and hand during the **downhill,** run in one cutthroat heat with the fastest time winning. And it's all over in less than two minutes. Skiers tear down the course at speeds of 60 to 80 miles per hour between a series of red poles set at about the same distance as in the giant slalom. To make conditions safer and inhibit the reckless nature of the skiers, a minimum number of control and direction flags are set up along the course. The men's course has at least an 800-meter vertical drop, while the women's course is between 500 and 700 meters.

Super giant slalom, or super-G, is a hybrid of downhill and giant slalom. Like downhill, the winner is decided in one run. Long, sweeping, high-speed turns make this event popular with spectators.

HOPEFULS

A little bit about the mountain: Probably the biggest Olympic hurdle that the Norwegians had to overcome was the fact that they didn't have a "true" downhill course for the alpine skiers. Three years and 20 million dollars later they built one. A single run accessed by three chair lifts, the new Kvitfjell downhill is not even a ski area. Its sole use will be a once-a-year World Cup stop and the venue for the most exciting of the Olympic skiing events. Drawn up with the help of famed downhiller Bernhard Russi (who designed the Albertville course), the technical Kvitfjell course drops 837 meters (2,746 feet) to its finish next to the scenic Glomma river. Racers should average about 65 mph through out the course that will favor the technical experts over the gliders because of its blind rolls and jumps. And the trademark jump on the course—known as the Russi Sprung—will launch skiers almost the length of a football field (80 meters) through the air before they land. The course, already likened to the famed Kitzbuehel, Austria downhill, opened to great reviews in the World Cup's stop there last March. The technical events (giant slalom and slalom) will be held at nearby Hafjell mountain.

The Speed Events—Men

Downhill: The Norwegians will have to hold off the invading Austrians and a Heinzer-led Swiss team that placed three skiers in the top five in last year's World Cup. When the $20 million Kvitfjell downhill course opened for competition in the 1993 World Cup, Skaardal was the top overall Norwegian placer in the two-day event (third and ninth). And despite the home-mountain advantage that Atle Skaardal and teammate Kjetil Andre Aamodt will enjoy, watch out for Italy's Werner Perathoner (second on both days), Austria's Armin Assinger and Switzerland's William Besse.

US Outlook: New York's A.J. Kitt, who won the 1991–92 season opener in Val d'Isere—the first American to win a World Cup downhill since Bill Johnson's 1984 win in Sarajevo—is our best hope at a medal. Kitt also won a bronze medal in last year's World Championships at Morioka, Japan. Keep an eye as well on Alaskan Tommy Moe who finished ahead of Kitt in the overall World Cup standings and three-time US downhill champion Jeff Olson of Montana.

Super-G: If there is to be any race that the host country should dominate, the super-G is it. Kjetil Andre Aamodt's 113-point World Cup title victory over Guenther Mader last year was the largest margin of victory of all the events. He also won last year's World Cup super-G at Kvitfjell, Norway (where the 1994 Olympic giant slalom will be run). Back him with Jan Einar Thorsen (fourth World Cup super-G) and you've got a pretty impressive one–two national punch. Also, keep in mind that the best event at Albertville for five-time World Cup overall points champion Marc Girardelli (along with giant slalom) was the super-G, and he has yet to add a gold medal to his record five championship globes.

US Outlook: Jeff Olson's 12th at the 1992 Marioka, Japan super-G was the best American finish in that event all year. Both Tommy Moe and A.J. Kitt finished ahead of Olson in last year's World Cup standings and—like the one run downhill event—anything can happen in the super-G.

Skiing—Alpine

163

The Technical Events—Men

Slalom: In the Albertville slalom, traditionally the last of the five events, Alberto Tomba (having already won the giant slalom) was poised for his second gold. And though Finn Christian Jagge took a seemingly insurmountable one-and-a-half-second lead into the second and final run, Tomba's second slalom run was the best single run of the whole Olympics; Tomba lost the gold to Jagge by only two tenths of a second. Watch for Tomba, Thomas Stangassinger and Austrian teammate Bernhard Gstrein, Kjetil Andre Aamodt, and Tomas Fogdoe at the top.

US Outlook: Colorado's Matt Grosjean is perhaps our best shot at a medal, and more realistically, a top-ten Lillehammer slalom finish. The 23 year old was the only American to score any World Cup slalom points (42) last season.

Giant Slalom: The names atop the giant slalom shoot-out could very well be the same as in Albertville. Again, you have to look to Aamodt as the favorite. In last season's home-mountain World Cup race at Oppdal, Norway, Aamodt clocked a combined 2:12.87. Second through 12th place were in the 2:14s. Still, you can't count out Alberto Tomba—and his zany Italian followers—in his best event in front of the whole world. Norwegian Lasse Kjus (who placed fourth for the World Cup giant slalom) and Marc Girardelli (third-place World Cup finisher) could also figure in the medal hunt.

US Outlook: Coming back from a knee injury suffered in the 1991–92 World Cup season, Wisconsin's Jeremy Nobis put up the best American giant slalom numbers (31st overall). And though Nobis was the only American to score points in last year's World Cup, teammate Matt Grosjean (a slalom specialist) hopes this season to carry his fine slalom ability into the other technical event.

Downhill/Slalom Combined: This event is the toughest to call. The combined event in Albertville turned into a comedy of errors that saw Josef Polig as one of the few skiers to stand up in both courses. Figure that if the Lillehammer officials took note of the reported sloppy preparation at Albertville, you have an event made for Luxembourg's Marc Girardelli. Also figure in Steve Locher, Guenther Mader and Kjetil Andre Aamodt somewhere near the medals.

US Outlook: A.J. Kitt, who finished 10th in the downhill portion of the event—then failed to finish the slalom—was ranked 15th overall in the World Cup downhill/slalom combined standings following the 1992–93 World Cup season. Also right up there are Kyle Rasmussen (tied for 21st) and Tommy Moe (28th).

Marc Girardelli

Some athletes deal with pain much better than others. And in a sport like skiing, where athletes are frequently on the brink of disaster at 60-plus miles per hour, a slight miscalculation can lead to an abrupt and painful stop. In December of 1989, skier Marc Girardelli was at highway-type speed on a super-G course in Sestriere, Italy, when he lost control. Flying completely off the course, Girardelli crashed not into fresh snow (due to the dry season) but into dirt—frozen like rock.

The results were hideous. A concussion, a lacerated kidney, and enough internal bleeding to rob him of two and a half quarts of blood within two hours of the crash. And it wasn't until a month later that doctors found a hole (ripped by his pelvic bone) in his hip muscle that had also been bleeding since the crash.

When the 1990 World Cup season came around, Girardelli, and his father/coach Helmut, convinced Girardelli's doctors that he could race in the upcoming World Cup. After a 71st place finish in the opening race, Girardelli went on to an amazing 13 top-four finishes and his fourth overall World Cup title.

"I've had constant pain since 1989," said Girardelli, who damaged his knee so badly in a crash in 1983 that it led his orthopedic surgeon Dr. Richard Steadman to say that "in no sport that I'm aware of has anyone come back from an injury like that to become the best in the world."

Girardelli began skiing on the World Cup circuit at the age of 16. At 18, he finished sixth in the overall title hunt. Within three years he won his first World Cup. But in taking over the reins from Switzerland's Pirmin Zurbriggen as the most successful overall World Cup skier, Girardelli has yet to win an Olympic medal; he was 9th in the downhill, 20th in the giant slalom at the Calgary Games, during an injury-plagued season in which he finished 5th overall in the World Cup.

And at the 1984 Winter Olympics, the Austrian-born Girardelli (who refused to join the Austrian Ski Federation because he wanted to be coached by his father) declared himself a citizen of Luxembourg (the Rhode Island-sized country next to Belgium), but was disallowed entrance into the Sarajevo Games.

Though a gold medal at Lillehammer (following silvers in slalom and giant slalom at Albertville) would look nice next to his unprecedented fifth crystal World Cup overall championship globe, the skier referred to as a "robot" reached his ultimate goal last season with his overall World Cup win. Girardelli now stands alone ahead of Zurbriggen and Italian Gustavo Thoeni, each of whom had won four titles.

"A fifth would make me number one in history—the best ever," said Girardelli. —P.S.

A.J. Kitt

Not since Bill Johnson's stunning downhill win in the 1984 Sarajevo Olympics (and at Whistler and Aspen) has an American met with such success in skiing's best-known event as A.J. Kitt.

Kitt, who hails from New York, won the 1992 World Cup season-opening downhill at Val d'Isere, France—America's first World Cup downhill win since Johnson's. And to top that off he finished second at Austria's legendary Kitzbuehle Hahnenkamm, third at British Columbia and Val Gardena, and eighth at Garmisch and Aspen.

And when the 1991–92 World Cup season's final points were tallied, Kitt, a *Sports Illustrated* cover boy for the Albertville Olympic Games, had placed third

US skier A.J. Kitt charges through the downhill run at Val d'Isere. Kitt finished ninth, 1.61 seconds behind the gold-medal time.

in the overall downhill standings and an equally impressive 10th in the combined events overall standings.

But last year Kitt, along with the rest of the men's team, suffered through a trying season. Kitt finished 21st in the overall downhill race, just behind fellow American Tommy Moe (who tied for 19th with Norwegian Jan Einar Thorsen). Part of the reason for Kitt's slide in the 1993 World Cup standings can be linked to an early season basketball injury that kept him from competing at 100 percent—something that a speed specialist cannot afford to do at 70-plus miles per hour.

Kitt endured his injury and, at times, showed flashes of his previous season's brilliance—amidst controversy—during the 1993 season. Following a bronze medal at the Morioka, Japan, World Cup Championships, Kitt was involved in a heartbreaking decision at the Americas Downhill at Aspen when an FIS official's decision stripped him of an apparent title.

Kitt was leading the Americas Downhill by .96 of a second over Norwegian Atle Skaardal before the race was cancelled due to the development of what officials deemed to be an unsafe hole. "As far as I was concerned, conditions were fine," said Kitt, who lost $30,000 and the Roch Cup when they cancelled the race. "Courses like Garmisch were much worse."

After the decision, when spectators of the race had cooled down a bit, Kitt sprung for the first 900 beers at Schlomos at the base of Aspen Mountain and

Austria's Guenther Mader flies through a practice run for the men's downhill in Val d'Isere. Mader later captured the 1992 men's downhill bronze.

also announced that he would help sponsor 10 youths in the Aspen Supports Kids program.

At 26, Kitt still has some promising results ahead of him, according to US super-G/downhill coach Bill Eagan.

"I think A.J. could be one of the two or three brightest stars on the World Cup," he said. "He has such a great ability to focus." —*P.S.*

Tommy Moe

Named as the US Ski Team's male alpine Skier of the Year, Alaskan Tommy Moe was the shiny spot on a rather lackluster 1993 World Cup season for the American men.

At 23, Moe, a World Junior Super-G champion at age 18, scored the highest American finish in the super-G last year with a seventh at Whistler, British Columbia. He also scored a couple of fine downhill finishes to go with his team-leading tie for 19th ranking (along with Norwegian Jan Elnar Thorsen) in the overall World Cup downhill standings.

First, at the World Championships at Morioka-Shizukuishi, Japan, Moe backed A.J. Kitt's bronze medal with a fifth-place finish. He then followed it with a second-place finish (along with his seventh in the super-G) at Whistler the following weekend.

And this came off a slow start that saw Moe remove himself from the team in order to spend some time focusing on whether he wanted to compete anymore.

Obviously, he did.

Moe, a speed events specialist who's quickly becoming one of America's most versatile skiers, finished 30th in the overall World Cup standings. And from the looks of it, he hit his slide in the season prior to the rest of the team's fall in the rankings. In fact, men's downhill coach Bill Egan said before the season that he was looking for a comeback from Moe.

What Moe will need to do at Lillehammer is tap on the success he had at the Whistler speed events last year. In the icy and bumpy downhill, Moe blazed out of the 21st starting position to finish ahead of World Cup downhill champion Franz Heinzer of Switzerland—and the conditions of the Whistler course were much like those at Lillehammer last year. The following day Moe knocked down a respectable 12th (tied with Italy's Werner Perathoner) in the super-G.

So what will Lillehammer and the 1994 World Cup season hold for Tommy Moe?

One thing's for sure. Moe knows skiing. —P.S.

Alberto Tomba

At the post-race press conference following the final alpine skiing event in the 1988 Calgary Winter Olympics, a handsome, muscular 21-year-old Italian skier met with the press. There he propositioned the 1988 Olympics' other darling, East Germany's figure skater Katarina Witt, for a date. "If she doesn't win one she can have one of mine," Alberto Tomba boldly told the media, referring to his two gold medals (slalom and giant slalom). Witt won her gold medal that night and Tomba never got his date.

One of the top-ranked technical skiers (slalom and giant slalom) on the World Cup circuit over the last several years, Tomba did receive a compliment from another skiing great that may not have been as nice as dating Witt, but when he decides to finally garage his skis, it should make him awfully proud. "Tomba may be the greatest slalom skier ever," said the legendary Ingemar Stenmark, dual gold medal winner at the 1980 Lake Placid Games and 85-time World Cup giant slalom and slalom winner.

Tomba thoroughly dominated the 1990–91 World Cup giant slalom, topping the second place finisher Austria's Rudolf Nierlich (who died in an auto accident at season's end) by 51 points and placing him second behind Marc Girardelli for the overall title. Then, in the 1992–93 World Cup season, despite missing the Mt. Kotakakura, Japan, World Championships with the flu, Tomba continued to dominate the technical disciplines—scoring second-place finishes in both the slalom and giant slalom overall titles at the end of the season.

An interesting footnote to Tomba's skiing is that he really only concentrates on the technical events (slalom and giant slalom) and doesn't get involved too much in the speed events (downhill and super giant slalom). The reason for this is not just due to the danger factor, but mostly out of respect for his parents, with whom he still lives in a mansion on the outskirts of Bologna.

Alberto Tomba kisses his gold medal after winning the men's giant slalom at Val d'Isere. Having proclaimed himself the messiah of skiing, Tomba became the first skier to defend an Olympic alpine title.

Forgoing the speed events may have cost Tomba the 1991 overall World Cup title. Girardelli beat Tomba by 23 points that year, scoring 23 in the speed events. And again, in the 1992–93 World Cup season, Tomba failed to score a point in speed events but still wound up an impressive fifth in the overall standings, just 11 points out of third.

Heading into Lillehammer, Tomba will again (as he was in Calgary and Albertville) be the favorite to strike gold in the technical events. And another gold medal—he has three already—would put him in an Olympic skiing class by himself. —*P.S.*

The Speed Events—Women

Downhill: Remember this name in the speed events: Katja Seizinger. The German speed demon captured the last year's World Cup downhill crown with an amazing 604 points—281 ahead of second-place German teammate Regina Haeusl's 323. She would likely have won the overall World Cup title (instead of Austrian Anita Wachter) had it not been for the cancellation of the season's last downhill in Sweden. Only 19 years old at the last Olympics, Seizinger will have had two full seasons of World Cup competition experience heading into Lillehammer. Also look out for Canada's Kerrin Lee-Gartner and Austrian Anja Haas.

US Outlook: Alaskan Hilary Lindh's silver medal in Albertville was the first American downhill medal since Cindy Nelson's bronze at Innsbruck in 1976—and she may enter the Lillehammer downhill as the second-ranked American. The one to watch could be Picabo (pronounced *peek-a-boo*) Street who finished the 1992–93 season with a bang by capturing second place at the Hafjell, Norway downhill.

Super-G: Katja Seizinger won the overall World Cup super-G crown in the last race of the season at Are, Sweden, by capturing first place and vaulting herself from third to first in the overall standings. But of all the events, the super-G has the potential to be the most closely contested. Carole Merle, Ulrike Maier and 1992–93 World Cup champion Anita Wachter should be right up there with Seizinger and defending Olympic champion Deborah Compagnoni.

US Outlook: Alaskan native Megan Gerety may have found her niche on the team with the super-G. And with a year's experience on the World Cup circuit, the 23 year old looks to have the best shot out of the six Americans who scored in a World Cup super-G race.

The Technical Events—Women

Slalom: With Petra Kronberger out of the picture (she retired at 23), the question remains: Does Vreni Schneider have another gold-medal slalom run (1988 Calgary) left in her 30-year-old knees? If so, it will only strengthen her already legendary Olympic and World Cup feats. Chasing—or maybe leading— Schneider should be New Zealand's Annelise Coberger, who lost last year's World Cup title to Schneider by only six points. Also figure in Anita Wachter, France's Patricia Chauvet and Julie Parisien.

US Outlook: Perhaps our best shot at an alpine medal rides with Maine's Julie Parisien in the slalom. Ranked number one in the world two years ago, Parisien battled injuries to finish seventh last year, just 29 points out of fourth. As the highest-ranked American skier—man or woman—Parisien hopes to improve on her Albertville finish where she missed the bronze medal by 5/100 of a second.

Giant Slalom: Twenty-nine-year-old Carole Merle has dominated the World Cup giant slalom scene over the last several seasons. She had also won four consecutive super-G titles before Katja Seizinger broke up her streak last season.

Look for her to be the favorite heading into Lillehammer, but not by much. Anita Wachter, Martina Ertl and a host of other Europeans (including Switzerland's Vreni Schneider) should make the giant slalom nearly as close as the super-G.

US Outlook: Though Diann Roffe-Steinrotter dropped from third in the 1991–92 overall World Cup giant slalom standings to 19th last year, she is the only American with Olympic giant slalom medal experience. And maybe that will rub off on teammates Julie Parisien and Eva Twardokens—both of whom finished in the top 10 at Albertville.

Downhill/Slalom Combined: Austria's Anita Wachter should be the clear favorite in this race—especially if the downhill course resembles a super-G. At the end of last year's World Cup standings, Wachter ranked fourth in both slalom and super-G. Germany's Miriam Vogt and Italian Morena Gallizio should also fare well. And don't rule out a medal from Katja Seizinger.

US Outlook: Picabo Street has to be the favored American following her surprising second-place combined finish at the World Championships at Mt. Kotakakura, Japan. Krista Schmidinger was the highest-ranking American on the combined World Cup last season. And as the third-ranked American downhiller (behind Street and Hilary Lindh), if she can reel off an incredible downhill run and survive the following days' slalom—who knows? Look what happened at Albertville in the men's combined.

Julie Parisien

Looking back a year ago, Julie Parisien's freshman year on the World Cup was one to remember.

Ranked number one in the world in slalom, the Québec-born Maine native scored top-six finishes in seven events—including a slalom win at Sundsvall, Sweden—as well as two top-five finishes (fourth in slalom, fifth in giant slalom) at the Albertville Olympics.

This past season was a bit of a letdown for the high standards Parisien and her coaches set for her, though she did finish as the top overall American skier at 27th in the World Cup and had the best individual overall event place with a seventh in slalom.

What might have led to Parisien's drop from first to seventh in the slalom standings was the heartbreaking way she lost the gold medal at the Albertville games. After leading the slalom event after the first run, Parisien, playing it conservative, came up short in her quest for even the bronze medal by 5/100 of a second.

"The only thing I don't want to be is first after the first run," Parisien was quoted as saying before the race. "The pressure might be too much for a first Olympics."

And prior to the slalom, Parisien had been disqualified in the super-G (for leaving the starting gate too early) and missed the bronze medal in the giant slalom by 41/100 of a second.

171

Julie Parisien, of Auburn, Maine, dejectedly sits on her skis after finishing fourth in the women's slalom at Meribel. Having clocked the best time in the first run of the slalom, Parisien finished only .05 away from the podium.

Still, Parisien's accomplishments shouldn't be weighed by her first Olympic Games' results. Consider this: She entered the games with four false teeth in her mouth, the result of a collision with a recreational skier in Hinterstoder, Austria, and was recovering from a broken wrist she suffered a week later at Piancavallo, Italy.

Heading into Lillehammer, Parisien, whose older brother Robbie and younger sister Anna both ski for the US Ski Team, will likely be America's best choice at a medal (slalom). And should she get over her sophomore jinx on the World Cup circuit, there's surely a place at the top for her in the slalom and overall title race.

"No question, Julie can do it," says US Women's Coach Paul Major. "She's totally focused on winning. There are no distractions; skiing is first for her." —P.S.

Vreni Schneider

Switzerland's Vreni Schneider rode into the 1988 Calgary Games in the wake of two of the more popular Swiss skiers of the times: Michela Figini, the youngest skier ever to win a gold medal (17 when she won the downhill at Sarajevo) and 1988 World Cup downhill points leader, and Maria Walliser, who after her two Calgary bronzes (combined and super-G), told a tabloid newspaper that "I'm going to Hollywood." Funny how things can change.

Italy's Deborah Compagnoni—also known as "Tombagnoni"—leaves the competition in the dust en route to the 1992 women's super giant slalom gold.

The low-key Schneider, a technical specialist who just may be the greatest female giant slalom skier of all time, torched the rest of the field in slalom and giant slalom and led the 1988 Games (along with Italy's Alberto Tomba) with two gold medals. In the opening technical event, the giant slalom, Schneider was sitting in fifth place after the first run. On her second run she showed the greatest skiers in the world why she owns the giant slalom event—winning by a whole second.

In slalom, although she wasn't favored to medal, Schneider again put down a second run that was nothing short of breathtaking. Leading by only a couple hundredths of a second over the second- and third-place racers after the first run, Schneider's chance to sweep the Calgary technical events looked to be in place.

Sweden's Camilla Nilsson (who was in second place after the first run) fell on what turned out to be a very demanding new course. Yugoslavia's Mateja Svet then let go with a very fast second run to take the lead. Out of the starting gate, Schneider, in what's been called "the most brilliant single effort of the alpine in women's Olympic history," floored those in attendance by clocking a run that gave her the gold by an amazing 1.68 seconds.

Along with Walliser's two bronze medals, the heavily favored Figini managed only a silver in the super-G.

Near the end of the Olympic festivities, Yugoslavia's Svet asked Schneider if she "might be the second Tomba?" Schneider replied "Oh, no, I am not like Tomba ... I want to remain Vreni like I have always been."

The following ski season, the Olympic great from the small Swiss village known simply as "Elm," had her best year ever, winning the World Cup overall title and in the process setting a record with 14 wins. With four slalom titles and an overall title taken from New Zealand's Annelise Coberger at the last race of the 1992–93 season at Are, Sweden, the 29-year-old Swiss active legend will definitely be looking to Lillehammer to improve on her seventh-place finish in slalom at Albertville. —*P.S.*

Katja Seizinger

Since the retirement of Austria's Petra Kronberger, if there is one cut-and-dried favorite—among both men and women—to win multiple medals at the Lillehammer Olympics, it has to be Germany's Katja Seizinger.

The 21-year-old speed-events specialist so thoroughly dominated the World Cup downhill and super-G scene last year that she came within 20 points of winning the overall World Cup title over Austrian Anita Wachter—and probably would have won it had it not been for a downhill event cancellation at season's end.

But even more remarkable than her rule over her speed event competitors is that she could have won the World Cup overall title without scoring a single point in slalom. During the 1992–93 season Seizinger collected six World Cup wins and won both the downhill and super-G discipline titles.

Hailing from Eberbach, Germany, Seizinger is destined to become one of the greats. She has climbed through the ranks as an amateur, finishing 12th overall in the 1989 Europa Cup and 44th overall in her first year on the World Cup circuit (1990). Then, following a 15th overall place finish in the 1991 season, Seizinger blazed to the overall downhill championship—capturing wins at Schruns, Morzine, and Vail.

That season, when she was only 19 years old, Seizinger captured the bronze medal in the Albertville super-G, and she finished fourth in the downhill and eighth in the giant slalom. In only her third full World Cup season, Seizinger ranks third among the active woman skiers in career wins.

And to prove she isn't some kind of fly-by-night speed freak who's riding on luck and guts over skiing ability, Seizinger came on strong at the end of the season in the giant slalom, finishing third at the Hafjell, Norway giants, first at the Klovsjo-Vemdalen, Sweden giants, and fourth at the season finale giants in Are, Sweden.

Come Lillehammer, unless the German team changes its uniform colors, the person you'll really want to keep an eye out for will be a 21-year-old German whiz kid wearing a zebra-striped racing suit. —*P.S.*

174

Picabo Street

One could start by saying remember this name. But how could you forget it? Picabo (pronounced *peek-a-boo*) Street—voted as the outstanding US female alpine skier last year—has arrived.

As a 21-year-old B-team member entering the 1992–93 World Cup season, Street scored a huge silver medal in the downhill combined at the World Championships at Mt. Kotakakura, Japan. It was to be the United States's top combined finish all year.

And as a possible prelude to the 1994 Lillehammer Olympics, Street backed her amazing downhill run at Mt. Kotakakura with an equally impressive second-place finish at the season finale World Cup downhill in Lillehammer.

Street got her unusual name from her father, a stone mason, after the game by the same name and from a nearby town where she grew up in Idaho. And skiing aside for a moment, one aspect of Street that even non-skiers will find amusing is her personality.

One of her more noteworthy quotes from last year was her announcement that she was planning to buy a Harley with the money she earned from her silver-medal finish in Japan. And favorite pastimes include watching "The American Gladiators" and mud wrestling.

But it was Street's carefree attitude that nearly lost her a spot of the US team. After being booted from the 1990 team for a lack of commitment last summer, according to women's downhill coach Ernst Hager, "Picabo had to re-qualify for the team."

A two-time North American series champion, Street is in her seventh year on the US Ski Team. And though the downhiller has put up her best numbers in the speed events, women's head coach Paul Major is optimistic that she will broaden her event capabilities. "We still want Picabo to eventually be a four-event skier," Major said.

Street's combined silver at the World Championships proved that it was worth Major's time and effort to keep her in a US Ski Team jacket.

And keep an eye, or at least an ear, open for Street come Lillehammer. Because even if she's not in the medals, Americans will surely hear from Picabo. —*P.S.*

Schedule

The tentative alpine skiing schedule is as follows:

Sunday, February 13
Downhill, men

Monday, February 14
Combined downhill, men

Tuesday, February 15
Super-G, women

Thursday, February 17
Super-G, men

Saturday, February 19
Downhill, women

Sunday, February 20
Combined downhill, women

Monday, February 21
Combined, slalom, women

Wednesday, February 23
Giant slalom, men

Thursday, February 24
Giant slalom, women

Friday, February 25
Combined, slalom, men

Saturday, February 26
Slalom, women

Sunday, February 27
Slalom, men

MEN'S ALPINE EVENTS

▼

HIGHLIGHTS

Norwegian Birger Ruud won both the downhill and the jumping events when alpine skiing was in its infancy in 1936. At the 1948 Games Henri Oreiller of France was a double gold-medal winner, taking the downhill and combined (an event subsequently discontinued until 1988), and earned a bronze in the slalom. James Couttet of France and Karl Molitor of Switzerland also landed two medals apiece.

In the 1952 Games at Olso, Norwegian Stein Eriksen captured the giant slalom gold and won the silver in the slalom; he later became a legendary ski instructor who seemed to be straight from Central Casting. At age 33 Zeno Colò of Italy took a gold in the downhill despite his unorthodox style, finishing fourth in the other two events. Othmar Schneider of Austria, silver medalist in the downhill, took a gold in the slalom.

fact: The ideal downhiller is pearshaped, heavily muscled in the thighs and buttocks—for better absorption of the shocks encountered skiing at high speeds on bumpy slopes—and slight in the shoulders and upper arms, for the least wind resistance.

Austria's legendary Toni Sailer swept all three alpine events held in 1956; he took the downhill using a ski strap supplied at the last minute by the trainer for the Italian team. French skiers introduced waxless metal skis for the 1960 Games, and came away from Squaw Valley with three medals; in the downhill Jean Vuarnet captured the gold and Guy Perillat the bronze. Perillat took the downhill silver eight years later. In the slalom at Squaw Valley it was Ernst Hinterseer of Austria for the gold, and Swiss skier Roger Staub won an upset gold in the giant slalom.

Prince Karim, the Aga Kahn, skied the downhill and slalom for Iran at the 1964 Games, which were conducted under the shadow of tragedy; 19-year-old Australian Ross Milne was killed practicing on the downhill course just days before the final competition. That year the US men finally earned alpine medals when Billy Kidd and Jimmy Heuga placed second and third behind 26-year-old Austrian ski veteran Josef "Pepi" Stiegler in the slalom; Stiegler also won the bronze in the giant slalom. Austrian Egon Zimmerman took the downhill gold, and French skier François Bonlieu defied his coaches all the way to the gold in the giant slalom, with Austrian Karl Schranz taking the silver.

fact: Downhill racers crouch with their chests to their knees to cut wind resistance.

Twelve years after Toni Sailer swept the alpine events, French skier Jean-Claude Killy duplicated his feat at the Grenoble Games. Controversy over Killy's amateur status threatened to disqualify the handsome customs inspector, but Killy was eventually allowed to compete. Suspense mounted when Austrian legend Karl Schranz was allowed to restart his second run in the slalom due to spectator interference, and turned in a better time than Killy's; it was later determined, but not unanimously, that Schranz had missed a gate before the spectator interfered with him on his aborted run, and he was disqualified, giving the sweep to Killy.

Schranz was a great all-around skier, but never won an Olympic gold; he was barred from the 1972 Games for allowing "use of his name and pictures in commercial advertisements." The Austrian team felt Schranz had been scapegoated and threatened to pull out of the Games in sympathy, but Schranz insisted they continue. Spain claimed its first ever alpine medal in 1972 when Francisco "Paquito" Fernandez-Ochoa took the gold in slalom. Gustav Thoni of Italy won the very steep giant slalom and added a silver medal in the slalom. Bernhard Russi and Roland Collombin gave Switzerland a 1–2 finish in the downhill. Russi came back to take the downhill silver four years later and recently he helped design some of the ski runs for the Albertville Games.

fact: When Bill Johnson ran the downhill in 1984 his average speed was clocked at over 64 mph.

But at Innsbruck in 1976, hometown favorite Franz Klammer of Austria took the downhill gold from the defending Russi by one-third of a second. Italy's Thoni was back for a silver in the slalom, edged out for the gold by his teammate and protegé, Piero Gros. By 0.20 seconds over teammate Ernst Good, Swiss skier

Heini Hemmi won the giant slalom, where defending champion Thoni placed fourth behind Swedish come-from-behind legend Ingemar Stenmark. US skiers Phil and Steve Mahre competed in their first Games at Innsbruck.

Phil Mahre was medalist caliber in 1980, winning a silver in the slalom. Despite a serious injury in September 1979, Sweden's Ingemar Stenmark won both the slalom and the giant slalom at Lake Placid, with Andreas Wenzel, half of Liechtenstein's brother-sister ski team, claiming the giant slalom silver. The men's downhill delighted Austrian hearts, with Leonhard Stock and Peter Wirnsberger placing 1–2. Canada's Steve Podborski won a bronze at Lake Placid, the first medal ever won by a non-European in the downhill. He was the youngest of the so-called Crazy Canucks, a group of Canadian daredevils that in the late 1970s began to break the European stranglehold on the downhill.

Franz Klammer, skiing star of the 1970s and 1976 gold winner in the downhill, failed to make Austria's 1980 team but was back for a sentimental showing in the 1984 Games. But 1984 saw European skiing dominance shaken. That year the men's downhill gold was won by US skier Bill Johnson, and brothers Phil and Steve Mahre took a gold and silver, respectively, in the slalom, confirming North American emergence in the skiing arena. At the 1984 Games, champion skier Ingemar Stenmark was ruled out of Olympic competition for technicalities relating to his amateur status, and thus could not defend his 1980 Olympic golds.

quote: "Congratulations, Alberto. Thank you, me."

Stenmark was back in competition for the 1988 Games, a sentimental favorite at nearly 32 years of age without much hope to medal. Marc Girardelli of Luxembourg was barred from the 1980 and 1984 Games over a citizenship snafu; in 1988 he competed but did not medal. In a curious sidenote, Prince Hubertus von Hohenlohe skied the Alpine events for Mexico in 1988. Pirmin Zurbriggen of Switzerland was favored to win as many as five gold medals going into the 1988 Games in Calgary, but he managed only one gold, in the downhill, and a bronze in the giant slalom. Behind Zurbriggen, Swiss teammate Peter Müller won his second Olympic downhill silver. But 1988 was the year for Italy's Alberto Tomba, who took a gold in the giant slalom and another in the slalom. And France's Franck Piccard, after taking a bronze in the downhill, won the first Olympic gold awarded for the super-G, a race in which 33 of the 94 starters failed to finish. Piccard is a native of Albertville, France, a detail that was not lost on those looking to the 1992 Winter Games.

Albertville Highlights

"I am the messiah of skiing," declared the ever-modest Alberto in Madonna di Campiglio prior to the 1992 Games. The competition didn't argue with him: winning the giant slalom by a margin of .32 seconds, Alberto Tomba became the

On his way to a gold medal at Albertville, Norway's Kjetil Andre Aamodt grabs big air in the men's super-G.

first skier in Olympic history to retain an alpine title. Apparently, though, he's one of the lesser gods: despite a heroic effort to save his slalom title at Albertoville, Tomba lost to Norwegian Finn Christian Jagge by .28 seconds. A slim margin of victory, to be sure, but more decisive than Alberto's Calgary victory had been: a mere .06 seconds bequeathed Tomba the 1988 slalom championship by the slightest margin in Olympic history.

1972 downhill gold medalist Bernhard Russi had a hand in writing Olympic history, designing a downhill course that favored skiers with technical acumen and not a little chutzpah. Intended to put a little excitement back in the downhill, Russi's Roc de Fer—rife with some twenty jumps—did just that, and then some. First out of the gate was Austrian Patrick Ortlieb, who at Games' start had never captured an international title. Fifty-five runs later, he had an Olympic title, having bested the favorites with a time of 1:50.37. But not even the gold medalist was enamored with Russi's gut-wrenching run: he declared afterwards, "I hope I never have to race on it again." France's Franck Piccard, Calgary's bronze medalist, slipped into second place just five hundredths of a second behind Ortlieb.

The combined event held plenty of surprises for the reigning favorites. Marc Girardelli took himself out of the running when he fell in the downhill, and Calgary gold medalist Hubert Strolz missed a gate in the slalom. Even Paul Accola was guilty of poor judgement, preparing the way for Italians Josef Polig and Gianfranco Martin to make off with the gold and silver medals. Behind them, Steve Locher captured the bronze medal for the barely medaled Swiss team.

Anton "Toni" Sailer

Perhaps he's not as well known as Jean-Claude Killy to today's Olympic spectator, but his performance at the 1956 Olympics in Cortina, Italy, may have even been more dominating than Killy's three-gold performance in the Olympics.

Austrian Anton "Toni" Sailer, affectionately known at the "Blitz from Kitz" (after his hometown of Kitzbuhel, Austria), so thoroughly dominated the Winter Games that year that his performance may never be equalled.

In the giant slalom, Sailer won by over six seconds. Amazingly, he did this with only one run—not with combined times.

The giant slalom course set at Cortina was to be a very demanding one at that. It began on an extreme steep near the summit of Tondi di Faloria and wound down the mountainside, sometimes cutting through ridges and valleys that made for quite a rollercoaster ride on skis of that era, which amounted to not much more than planks of wood with boots nailed into them.

When the first Austrian, Anderl Molterer (starting sixth) raced down through the course, he was mobbed by Austrian fans at the finish line. Molterer waved them away.

"Toni hasn't come yet," said Molterer, who knew he was destined for the silver medal with a time of 3:06.3.

Starting from the 18th position, Sailer, who claimed that the Cortina giant slalom course was "the toughest I'd ever seen," kept the flats of his skis on the snow as much as possible and absorbed the worst of the depressions and bumps en route to a 3:00.1 finish—6.2 seconds ahead of teammate Molterer. And fellow Austrian Walter Schuster rounded out the Austrian sweep of the event with a 3:07.2.

Sailer went on to capture the downhill and slalom in similar fashion. In the seventh Winter Olympic Games, he pulled off what the Europeans back then called "The Olympic Hat Trick."

But it was probably Japan's Chiharu "Chick" Igaya (silver medal in the slalom) who put it best after he crashed in the downhill while chasing Sailer: "I made the mistake of trying to beat Sailer in the downhill," he said. —P.S.

The First US Men to Win Alpine Medals

By 1964 the US men had yet to win a medal in alpine skiing in four Winter Olympics. This changed on a snowy Saturday in February on the out-run of the mighty Birgitskopfl peak in Innsbruck, Austria. There, Americans Billy Kidd, from Stowe, Vermont, and Jimmy Heuga, of Lake Tahoe, California, upset the heavily favored Europeans for the silver and bronze medals.

The demanding course quieted a number of the favorites right from the start. France's Jean-Claude Killy torqued his binding right out of his ski after 20 gates and his teammate Guy Perillat hooked the last gate, spun around, and put himself into 27th position going into the second run. This set the stage for Kidd and Heuga.

Kidd had already logged a time putting him right up there with the leaders, when Heuga, racing out of the 24th slot, put forth a masterful run and found himself in third place. On their second runs (Heuga again raced from the back of the pack due to his first run placement), the Americans skied the 71-gate course to near-perfection and captured the silver and bronze medals behind Austria's Josef Stiegler. And to this day, no Olympic racer has started from a position similar to Heuga's and gone on to win a medal.

Billy Kidd went on to finish seventh in the giant slalom, which gave him a third place finish in the alpine combined category, although no medal was awarded for the combined finish that year. —P.S.

Jean-Claude Killy

A skier who had just arrived at the pearly gates noticed a skier who greatly resembled the legendary Jean-Claude Killy on the slopes, and who was in the process of signing autographs at the base of Heaven's ski area.

"Is that Jean-Claude Killy?" said the skier to St. Peter, pointing him out.

"Oh him," St. Peter laughed. "No that's not Killy. That's God. He only thinks He's Jean-Claude Killy."

In 1968, it had been 12 years since Austrian Toni Sailer completed the almost unthinkable—sweeping three gold medals in the three disciplines of alpine skiing. To this day, with one exception, no one has ever come close to duplicating Sailer's achievement.

That exception took place in the 1968 Olympics in Grenoble, France. There, coming off of the 1967 World Cup season in which he won all three categories (slalom, giant slalom, and downhill) and scored a maximum 225 points (a record that has yet to be equalled), Killy was thought to have a chance of matching Sailer's "Olympic Hat Trick."

"It wouldn't surprise anyone if Jean-Claude Killy were to repeat Toni Sailer's Olympic feat of 1956—sweeping all three gold medals," read an article in the February, 1968, Olympic preview issue of *Skiing* magazine.

"At the start of the Olympic season I wasn't skiing too well," recalls Killy, contesting that forecast.

And it was actually a second-place finish in the Hahnenkamm (Kitzbuhlen, Austria) downhill, which is the Indy 500 of the European downhill races, that gave Killy the confidence he needed heading into the Olympics. "I had made a serious error on a section of the course that forced me to lose a great deal of speed," explained Killy. "I knew that if I hadn't made that error I would have won, which told me I was back in shape, my skis were fast and I was skiing very well."

At the Olympics, Killy readied himself for a bout with history. A half-hour before his run in the downhill, he inadvertently skied over a patch of ice and stripped a good portion of the wax off of the base of his skis. This almost cost him his first gold medal. When he found his coach and explained to him what had happened, his coach had the right words. He replied simply, "Don't worry. Get a good start and you'll win anyway."

His confidence intact, Killy negotiated a rolling portion of the course better than anyone in the field, and although he almost lost the race near the finish in the warmer snow (where the wax he lost would have enabled him to glide better), Killy held on to win by 8/100 of a second.

"Winning the downhill gave me confidence and took some of the pressure off," said Killy. "So, in the giant slalom, I hardly had the feeling that I was racing in the Olympics at all."

Killy went on to capture the giant slalom by over two seconds and edged Austrian Herbert Huber by 9/100 of a second in the slalom.

An interesting note concerning the giant slalom was what happened to Killy the night before the race. It seems that the heater in the room he shared with Alain Penz (a former French alpine team member) was not working properly. The room became so cold that the two skiers were shaken out of their sleep by what they thought was a gun shot—but what actually turned out to be a bottle of champagne (that Killy intended to drink after his victory the next day) exploding.

After Penz left for another, warmer room, Killy swiped his blankets and went back to bed. Still freezing, he began to put on more clothes ... his long johns, warmup pants, ski coat, socks, gloves, and a hat. "When it was time to get up I was all dressed to go skiing," he said.

Killy hung up his skis for some five years after his three-gold performance at Grenoble. Then, at 30 years of age, he joined the International Ski Racers Association circuit.

Since 1986, Killy had represented France as the co-president of the Albertville organizing committee, sharing the post with national assembly representative Michel Barnier. In the early going, the position gave Killy more headaches than he could handle, to the point that he actually left the post in early 1987 for a year. International Olympic Committee president Juan Antonio Samaranch, understanding the impact of a Killy-less French Olympics, finally convinced Killy to get back aboard. Killy returned and applied the level of determination that once made him the world's most successful skier. The stamp of Killy was very evident on the Albertville Games. —P.S.

Franz Klammer

It's tough to agree on the greatest moment of a given sport. Was it Hank Aaron's 715th home run, or Don Larsen's perfect game in the World Series? Was it Wilt Chamberlain's 100-point performance? Or five-foot, seven-inch Spud Webb winning the NBA's Slam Dunk contest?

Skiing has its share of great moments as well. But one performance seems to stand out among all of the others.

Many within the inner ski racing circle believe that the greatest single run of all time was Austrian Franz Klammer's come-from-behind performance on the Patscherkofel downhill course at the 1976 Innsbruck Games.

World Cup champion and Olympic favorite Bernhard Russi, 27, of Switzerland, seemed to have a lock on the gold medal when the young Klammer—as his country's last hope for the gold—entered the starting gate.

The bright yellow suit, that would later become synonymous with his famous run, was shredded in spots after a high-speed tumble he'd taken at Val d'Isere, France prior to the Games; it was the same portion of the course that took the life of top French downhiller Michel Dujon during the same race.

"I've won wearing it and I've lost wearing it, too," Klammer would later comment.

As he exploded out of the start, the crowd—tens of thousands—that lined the course and the finish line erupted as well. As Klammer gained speed down the 10,379 foot course, he was followed by ABC cameras that had put together the most comprehensive top-to-bottom downhill coverage in Olympic history.

Gaining speed through the course, comprising a virtual minefield of gullies and unpredictable changes in terrain and bumps, Klammer, not known for his stellar technique, was all over the course. At midpoint he had only clocked the third fastest time.

The crowd got thicker toward the bottom of the course. The customary cowbells rang out. "Hup, up, up, up, up," the Austrians yodeled as he streaked by, still gaining speed.

As Klammer reached speeds of up to 80 mph, the bright yellow suit, tipped with a blazing red helmet, now looked liked a meteorite raging down the mountainside. At times he was airborne, looking as if he'd never pull out of it. Then, as if he could slow things down at 80 mph, evaluate the situation, and correct it, he'd regain control—in a split second.

Winning by four-tenths of a second, and already a European hero, the 1976 Olympics gave Franz Klammer to the world. —*P.S.*

Ingemar Stenmark

If you were to ask skiers who have competed at the last several Winter Olympics to name the greatest skier of all time, they would probably come up with several different answers.

Toni Sailer or Jean-Claude Killy, perhaps, because of their three gold-medal Olympic performances.

Or Franz Klammer, for his strength and bravery in the downhill.

Or Marc Girardelli, for his ability to succeed after injury.

But ask the same skiers who is the closest to technical perfection on a pair of skis and you'll inevitably receive just one answer: Ingemar Stenmark.

Growing up in the Arctic, some 1,000 miles north of Stockholm, Sweden, Stenmark began skiing on mountains. Much of his skiing plummeted through the dusk, for during certain days of the year in that area the sun only shines for some 30 minutes.

If he'd have grown up on Mt. Olympus with Zeus, he might have been dubbed "Stenmarkus, the God of Skiing."

The longest reigning and most consistent slalom and giant slalom specialist on the World Cup circuit, Stenmark achieved his Olympic highlight in the 1980 Lake Placid Games. There, he swept gold in those two events.

Stenmark fell behind after his first runs at the giant slalom and slalom courses, almost falling moments from the finish line in his giant slalom run. He found himself starting his second run from the third position.

On his second run, Stenmark carved through the course with surgeon-like precision and took the gold by almost a second—which in recent Olympics would be like the USA basketball team beating the Soviets by 60 points. It's just not supposed to happen.

In the slalom, Stenmark let go with another one of his patented second runs, clipping American leader Phil Mahre (silver medal) by a more realistic half second.

An interesting footnote to Stenmark's 1980 dual-gold Olympic performance was that several months before the Olympics, Stenmark was concentrating on some serious downhill training above Val Senales in the Italian Alps when he took a brutal tumble that didn't come to a halt until some 200 yards later.

Veteran Swedish skier Ingemar Stenmark clears a gate on his way to a win during a World Cup special slalom competition in Sestriere, Italy, in 1986.

Helicoptered to Bolzano, Italy, Stenmark—from his hospital bed (predating Schwartzenegger by some 10 years)—stated, "I'll be back." —*P.S.*

Mahres on Skis

Phil Mahre, without a doubt, is the most successful American alpine skier to date.

With two Olympic medals, a gold in slalom from the 1984 Olympics in Sarajevo, Yugoslavia (twin brother Steve won the silver), and a silver in the 1980 Lake Placid Games, Mahre is the only American male alpine skier to have medaled twice in the Olympics.

But more impressive than his Olympic performances, to Mahre at least, are his World Cup overall titles in 1981, 1982, and 1983.

"This, to me, is just another victory," said Mahre after his gold-medal slalom run in Sarajevo.

Mahre's comments, though painfully honest and seeming ungracious, stood very true at Sarajevo. First off, the two top World Cup slalom specialists that year, Luxembourg's Marc Girardelli (1985, 1986, 1989, and 1991 World Cup champion) and the legendary Ingemar Stenmark (who had won six World Cup slalom races heading into the 1984 Olympics) were both absent from the race.

And second, the Sarajevo slalom course took its toll on the world's top skiers like no other course in the history of the Olympics. Close to half (seven, to be exact) of the top 15 seeded racers were disqualified due to crashes or missed gates.

Still, Mahre, the second American male to win an Olympic gold medal at those Games (Bill Johnson won the downhill three days earlier) remains as our country's most successful amateur skier.

Born in 1957, four minutes before Steve, Phil grew up with his brother in White Pass, Washington, at the foot of the Dairy Queen peaks of the Cascade Mountain range. And if it weren't for Phil's accomplishments, Steve would have very well been one of our country's greatest amateur skiers.

Besides his three World Cup overall titles and two Olympic medals, Phil also won the United States Championships seven times. After hanging up the skis for several years, Mahre returned to the professional skiing scene where he's finished second overall in two of the last three years on the US Pro Tour. —P.S.

Pirmin Zurbriggen

Of the 1,793 athletes heading into the 1988 Calgary Winter Olympics, one had a "realistic" chance of winning five gold medals. Pirmin Zurbriggen, then 25, was Switzerland's hope to repeat Frenchman Jean-Claude Killy's sweep of alpine gold at the 1968 Grenoble Winter Games. By 1988 a sweep involved five medals rather than Killy's three, with super giant slalom and the downhill/slalom combined medal added to the program post-Killy.

Going into the Games, Zurbriggen was one of only two skiers ever to win four World Cup overall titles. Italian Gustav Thoni did it first and now Luxembourg's Marc Girardelli has done it since. In the World Cup season leading into the 1988 Games, Zurbriggen was plagued with a respiratory problem and won only two of 16 races he entered. But one of the two victories came in the pre-Olympic downhill at Schladming, Austria, which moved him into first place in the World Cup standings, ahead of Italy's Alberto Tomba.

The downhill was the opening event at Calgary. Zurbriggen's chief competitor and fellow countryman, Peter Mueller, drew the number-one starting position. Coincidentally, Zurbriggen drew number 14—the same number Killy had worn at Grenoble. Zurbriggen rode the turny downhill to near perfection, edging teammate Mueller for the gold. France's Franck Piccard took the bronze.

The following day, in the downhill/slalom combined event—an event that Zurbriggen had the best chance of winning out of all of them—he took a half-second lead after the first run. Needing just to ski an easy, clean run to lock up his second gold medal, Zurbriggen hooked a tip on a gate two-thirds of the way through his slalom run, slammed, and was disqualified from the race.

After a respectable fifth in the super-G, in which 33 of the 94 racers blew out of the course, Zurbriggen captured the bronze medal in giant slalom, two seconds behind Tomba.

Zurbriggen skied for two more years on the World Cup circuit, retiring before the 1990–91 season. Although he didn't come through the Calgary Games laden with gold, his place in skiing history is assured, given his World Cup and Olympic successes. —P.S.

Medalists

Alpine Skiing—Men's Downhill

1992	1. Patrick Ortlieb, Austria, 1:50.37
	2. Franck Piccard, France, 1:50.42
	3. Guenther Mader, Austria, 1:50.47
1988	1. Pirmin Zurbriggen, Switzerland, 1:59.63
	2. Peter Mueller, Switzerland, 2:00.14
	3. Franck Piccard, France, 2:01.24
1984	1. William Johnson, USA, 1:45.59
	2. Peter Mueller, Switzerland, 1:45.86
	3. Anton Steiner, Austria, 1:45.95
1980	1. Leonhard Stock, Austria, 1:45.50
	2. Peter Wirnsberger, Austria, 1:46.12
	3. Steve Podborski, Canada, 1:46.62
1976	1. Franz Klammer, Austria, 1:45.73
	2. Bernhard Russi, Switzerland, 1:46.06
	3. Herbert Plank, Italy, 1:46.59
1972	1. Bernhard Russi, Switzerland, 1:51.43
	2. Roland Collombin, Switzerland, 1:52.07
	3. Heini Messner, Austria, 1:52.40
1968	1. Jean-Claude Killy, France, 1:59.85
	2. Guy Perillat, France, 1:59.93
	3. Jean-Daniel Datwyler, Switzerland, 2:00.32
1964	1. Egon Zimmermann, Austria, 2:18.16
	2. Leo Lacroix, France, 2:18.90
	3. Wolfgang Bartels, West Germany, 2:19.48
1960	1. Jean Vuarnet, France, 2:06.0
	2. Hans-Peter Lanig, West Germany, 2:06.5
	3. Guy Perillat, France, 2:06.9
1956	1. Toni Sailer, Austria, 2:52.2
	2. Raymond Fellay, Switzerland, 2:55.7
	3. Andreas Molterer, Austria, 2:56.2
1952	1. Zeno Colo, Italy, 2:30.8
	2. Othmar Schneider, Austria, 2:32.0
	3. Christian Pravda, Austria, 2:32.4
1948	1. Henri Oreiller, France, 2:55.0
	2. Franz Gabl, Austria, 2:59.1
	3. Karl Molitor, Switzerland, 3:00.3
	3. Ralph Olinger, Switzerland, 3:00.3
1924-1936	Not held

Alpine Skiing—Men's Slalom

1992	1. Finn Christian Jagge, Norway, 1:44.39
	2. Alberto Tomba, Italy, 1:44.67
	3. Michael Tritscher, Austria, 1:44.85
1988	1. Alberto Tomba, Italy, 1:39.47
	2. Frank Woerndl, West Germany, 1:39.53
	3. Paul Frommelt, Liechtenstein, 1:39.84
1984	1. Phil Mahre, USA, 1:39.41
	2. Steven Mahre, USA, 1:39.62
	3. Didier Bouvet, France, 1:40.20
1980	1. Ingemar Stenmark, Sweden, 1:44.26
	2. Phil Mahre, USA, 1:44.76
	3. Jacques Luethy, Switzerland, 1:45.06
1976	1. Piero Gros, Italy, 2:03.29
	2. Gustav Thoni, Italy, 2:03.73
	3. Willy Frommelt, Liechtenstein, 2:04.28
1972	1. Francisco Fernandez Ochoa, Spain, 109.27
	2. Gustav Thoni, Italy, 110.28
	3. Roland Thoni, Italy, 110.30
1968	1. Jean-Claude Killy, France, 99.73
	2. Herbert Huber, Austria, 99.82
	3. Alfred Matt, Austria, 100.09
1964	1. Pepi Stiegler, Austria, 131.13
	2. Bill Kidd, USA, 131.27
	3. James Heuga, USA, 131.52
1960	1. Ernst Hinterseer, Austria, 128.9
	2. Hias Leitner, Austria, 130.3
	3. Charles Bozon, France, 130.4
1956	1. Toni Sailer, Austria, 194.7
	2. Chiharu Igaya, Japan, 198.7
	3. Stig Sollander, Sweden, 200.2
1952	1. Othmar Schneider, Austria, 120.0
	2. Stein Eriksen, Norway, 121.2
	3. Guttorm Berge, Norway, 121.7
1948	1. Edi Reinalter, Switzerland, 130.3
	2. James Couttet, France, 130.8
	3. Henri Oreiller, France, 132.8
1924-1936	Not held

Alpine Skiing—Men's Giant Slalom

1992 1. Alberto Tomba, Italy, 2:06.98
2. Marc Girardelli, Luxembourg, 2:07.30
3. Kjetil Andre Aamodt, Norway, 2:07.82
1988 1. Alberto Tomba, Italy, 2:06.37
2. Hubert Strolz, Austria, 2:07.41
3. Pirmin Zurbriggen, Switzerland, 2:08.39
1984 1. Max Julen, Switzerland, 2:41.18
2. Jurij Franko, Yugoslavia, 2:41.41
3. Andreas Wenzel, Liechtenstein, 2:41.75
1980 1. Ingemar Stenmark, Sweden, 2:40.74
2. Andreas Wenzel, Liechtenstein, 2:41.49
3. Hans Enn, Austria, 2:42.51
1976 1. Heini Hemmi, Switzerland, 3:26.97
2. Ernst Good, Switzerland, 3:27.17
3. Ingemar Stenmark, Sweden, 3:27.41
1972 1. Gustav Thoni, Italy, 3:09.62
2. Edmund Bruggmann, Switzerland, 3:10.75
3. Werner Mattle, Switzerland, 3:10.99
1968 1. Jean-Claude Killy, France, 3:29.28
2. Willy Favre, Switzerland, 3:31.50
3. Heini Messner, Austria, 3:31.83
1964 1. François Bonlieu, France, 1:46.71
2. Karl Schranz, Austria, 1:47.09
3. Pepi Stiegler, Austria, 1:48.05
1960 1. Roger Staub, Switzerland, 1:48.3
2. Pepi Stiegler, Austria, 1:48.7
3. Ernst Hinterseer, Austria, 1:49.1
1956 1. Toni Sailer, Austria, 3:00.1
2. Andreas Molterer, Austria. 3:06.3
3. Walter Schuster, Austria, 3:07.2
1952 1. Stein Eriksen, Norway, 2:25.0
2. Christian Pravda, Austria, 2:26.9
3. Toni Spiss, Austria, 2:28.8
1924–1948 Not held

Alpine Skiing—Men's Super Giant Slalom

1992 1. Kjetil Andre Aamodt, Norway, 1:13.04
2. Marc Girardelli, Luxembourg, 1:13.77
3. Jan Einar Thorsen, Norway, 1:13.83
1988 1. Franck Piccard, France, 1:39.66
2. Helmut Mayer, Austria, 1:40.96
3. Lars-Boerje Eriksson, Sweden, 1:41.08

Alpine Skiing—Men's Combined (Downhill and Slalom)

1992 1. Josef Polig, Italy, 14.58
2. Gianfranco Martin, Italy, 14.90
3. Steve Locher, Switzerland, 18.16
1988 1. Hubert Strolz, Austria, 36.55
2. Bernhard Gstrein, Austria, 43.45
3. Paul Accola, Switzerland, 48.24
1952–1984 Not held
1948 1. Henri Oreiller, France, 3.27
2. Karl Molitor, Switzerland, 6.44
3. James Couttet, France, 6.95
1940–1944 Not held
1936 1. Franz Pfnur, Germany, 99.25
2. Gustav Lantschner, Germany, 96.26
3. Emile Allais, France, 94.69

WOMEN'S ALPINE EVENTS

▼

HIGHLIGHTS

In 1948 US skier Gretchen Fraser won the giant slalom and took a silver in the combined (an event discontinued afterward until 1988) behind Austrian Trude Jochum-Beiser, who also took a silver in the downhill. The downhill gold medalist that year was Hedy Schlunegger of Switzerland. Four years later US skier Andrea Mead Lawrence won some rare gold for the US when she placed first in the slalom and giant slalom, despite a lack of snow. Jochum-Beiser was back for a gold in the downhill. Austria's 1952 silver medalist in the giant slalom, Dagmar Rom, was a film actress.

fact: A skier tries to avoid being airborne in the downhill because time spent in the air increases the distance she must travel. To keep from being pitched skyward by bumps, she pre-jumps them by pulling her skis off the snow just before they hit the bumps.

Canada's Lucille Wheeler captured a bronze in the downhill in 1956, behind gold medalist Madeleine Berthod of Switzerland. A Swiss pharmacy student, Renée Colliard, won the gold in the slalom and German Ossi Reichert captured top honors in the giant slalom.

Another Canadian, Anne Heggtveit, took the slalom in 1960, while US skier Penny Pitou came away with silvers in the downhill and giant slalom and her teammate Betsy Snite brought the US a third silver in the slalom. Heidi Biebl of Germany took the downhill gold and Yvonne Rüegg of Switzerland triumphed in the giant slalom by 0.1 seconds.

At the 1964 Games, Austria swept the women's downhill at Innsbruck, pleasing the home crowd. US skier Jean Saubert tied France's Christine Goitschel for the giant slalom silver behind Goitschel's sister Marielle; Saubert also picked up the bronze in the slalom behind the Goitschel sisters, with Christine taking the gold. Marielle Goitschel returned in 1968 to capture the slalom gold in Grenoble. That year Canada's Nancy Greene skied to the gold in giant slalom, by a huge margin of 2.64 seconds, and took a silver in the slalom. The downhill gold went to Olga Pall of Austria.

Twenty-two-year-old Petra Kronberger flies through the air on her way to a first-place finish in the downhill portion of the women's alpine combined event at Albertville.

quote: "Fourth is absolutely the worst place to finish in the Olympics." —Julie Parisien, who missed a slalom medal at Albertville by five hundredths of a second.

At Sapporo in 1972 US skier Barbara Cochran was a surprise gold in the slalom by 0.02 seconds, while teammate Susan Corrock snatched a bronze in the downhill. That year Annemarie Moser-Pröll of Austria settled for silvers in the downhill and giant slalom, due to upset victories by Swiss newcomer Marie Theres Nadig. Moser-Pröll retired from skiing before the 1976 Olympics, but eventually went back on the circuit to claim the downhill gold in Lake Placid.

At Innsbruck in 1976 West German Rosi Mittermaier took golds in the downhill and the slalom, earning a chance to be the first female skier to achieve an Olympic slam. But Kathy Kriner captured the giant slalom for Canada by a slim margin of 0.12 seconds. The only skiing medal won by the US at Innsbruck was Cindy Nelson's bronze in the downhill. Liechtenstein's Hanni Wenzel came away with a bronze in the slalom. Four years later, in Lake Placid, Wenzel took the gold in slalom and giant slalom, and the silver in the downhill behind Moser-Pröll. Wenzel's haul of two golds and a silver equalled the feat of Rosi Mittermaier in the previous Olympics. Wenzel's brother brought their tiny principality a silver medal in 1980 as well.

fact: When skiers Hanni and Andreas Wenzel between them earned four medals at the 1980 Games, the wins brought the principality of Liechtenstein one medal for every 6000-some people. (A comparable ratio for the US would yield 36,000 medals.)

Wenzel was ruled out of Olympic competition in 1984 for technicalities relating to her amateur status. At Sarajevo American Debbie Armstrong took a gold in women's giant slalom from the Europeans. 1984 also smiled on some newcomers, Italy's Paoletta Magoni, gold medalist in the women's slalom, and Switzerland's Michela Figini, who won the women's downhill in 0.05 seconds, becoming the youngest skier ever to take a gold.

Four years later Figini earned a silver in the super-G. Also in 1988, Canada's Karen Percy took a bronze in the super-G and another bronze in the downhill, while Swiss skier Brigitte Oertli captured two silvers. Her teammate, Vreni Schneider, won two golds in 1988, the fifth woman alpine skier to have won two golds in the same Games. West German Marina Kiehl won a surprise gold in the downhill that year. Sentimental favorite Christa Kinshofer-Güthlein of West Germany took a silver in giant slalom, to add to the slalom silver she won at

Austria's Anita Wachter in action in the second run of the women's combined slalom at the Calgary Games. Wachter won a bronze medal in the 1988 women's combined event, then captured a silver in the event at Albertville, where she also tied for third place in the giant slalom.

Lake Placid in 1980. Also competing in 1988 was Spain's Blanca Fernandez-Ochoa, a member of the family that produced the men's slalom gold medalist in 1972.

Albertville Highlights

"There's a tickle in my stomach," said Austrian Petra Kronberger about going into a race, "Then I pull everything together and hurl myself down." Kronberger hurled in a big way at Albertville, capturing the combined thanks to an awe-inspiring downhill run. Even two first-place slalom runs didn't allow Anita Wachter, the 1988 Games gold medalist, to vie for gold.

Kronberger dominated the slalom, as well. Not that anyone was surprised: she had won an unprecedented five women's Alpine disciplines in the World Cup from December 1990 to January 1991. Annelise Coberger, on the other hand, was a surprise: blistering into second place with the fastest second run time, the New Zealander pocketed silver—the first Winter medal ever captured by a skier from the Southern hemisphere (and New Zealand's first Winter medal). US skier Julie Parisien—wearing a mask to protect dental work resulting from a downhill collision—placed fourth in the event, only .05 seconds away from the podium.

Calgary native Kerrin Lee-Gartner and Alaskan Hilary Lindh shared top honors, respectively, in the downhill event, while Veronika Wallinger added a bronze medal to Austria's Albertville spoils. The giant slalom, meanwhile, spoiled the best laid plans of a number of alpine women: Petra Kronberger fell on the course, as did Switzerland's medal hopeful Vreni Schneider. Pernilla Wiberg—more than one second ahead of silver-medaling US skier Diann Roffe—made off with Sweden's first-ever women's alpine medal.

Italy's Deborah Compagnoni also fell in the giant slalom—tearing ligaments so severely that she'd be out of competition for several months—but not until after she had captured the super G title. In honor of her victory, the Italian paparazzi, impressed by her aggressive style, conferred her with the highest Italian honor—that of comparing her to Tomba—by dubbing her "Tombagnoni." Compagnoni's win was Italy's second gold medal success in women's alpine events at the Games.

Fraser and Mead: The USA's First Alpine Medals

Back in 1948 at St. Moritz, Switzerland, the year alpine skiing was fully introduced to the Winter Olympics, American Gretchen Fraser raced to a gold medal in the slalom, the USA's first medal in alpine skiing. On a gorgeous Swiss afternoon in the Alps, Fraser (who drew the No. 1 starting position) skied to near perfection, leading a pack of European skiers—four of whom were within one-tenth of a second of the American's lead.

"We in the grandstands watched the girl racers slowly climbing up the long, steep slope in the beautiful setting of Survretta for the last ordeal to decide who would win the gold medal," wrote the US women's team manager Alice Kiaer in her 1948 Olympic report. As Fraser stood at the starting gate, communication between the start and finish line failed for 17 minutes—which can seem like hours to a racer concentrating on their run. When finally given the green light, Fraser skied flawlessly, edging Switzerland's Antoinette Meyer and Austria's Erika Mahringer for the gold. Fraser also went on to win a silver medal in the slalom/downhill combined event.

Along with Fraser on that 1948 Olympic team was 15-year-old Andrea Mead.

There are other, more recognizable names in the history of American women's skiing (like Suzy "Chapstick" Chaffee). And other skiers have put forth better numbers on the World Cup circuit. But you'd be hard pressed to find a better performance by any American skier than that of Andrea Mead Lawrence's showing in the 1952 Winter Olympics in Oslo.

On snow hauled in from other areas of Norway (what amounted to about 100 train cars of it) and packed down by hundreds of soldiers and volunteers, the 19-year-old Mead Lawrence skied to a two-gold performance in the slalom and giant slalom events. Said Gretchen Fraser, the team manager that year, "As captain of the team she [Mead Lawrence] was a great help to me and an inspiration to the rest of the team. She is the finest type of sportswoman we could have to represent this country." —*P.S.*

Hanni Wenzel

When people talk of alpine skiing powerhouses, their attention naturally wanders to places like Austria, Switzerland, Sweden, and Norway. So it was no wonder that in 1980 at the Lake Placid Games people had a hard time pronouncing Liechtenstein (lick-ten-shtine). What they didn't have a hard time pronouncing, though, was the tiny country's most famous athlete—Hanni Wenzel.

Bottom line, at the 1980 Games, Wenzel matched the greatest Olympic skiing performance ever put forth by a woman. Her gold medal sweep in slalom and giant slalom, coupled with her silver in downhill, duplicated West German Rosi Mittermaier's 1976 Innsbruck Games first near-perfect alpine sweep.

The giant slalom, in which the strong German team of Maria Epple (1980 World Cup giant slalom champ) and teammate 19-year-old Christa Kinshofer (who won five World Cup giant slalom's leading up to the Olympics) were the heavy favorites, was not supposed to be Wenzel's strongest event. Although she had finished in the top 10 in every giant slalom that season, Wenzel did not seem to have what it would take to put together a medal-winning performance. That was, until she won the last World Cup giant slalom before the Olympics by over five seconds!

The next technical event, slalom, was dominated during the year by the Austrians. They had finished 1–2–3 in the previous World Cup season. In the 1980 season, no fewer than six skiers had won in the eight races. An Austrian 20 year old was to be on the Olympic victory stand twice, and so was Wenzel. The bronze medalist at Innsbruck in the slalom, Wenzel tore through the tough course at Lake Placid to win by a second and a half.

The big race of the 1980 Games was Wenzel's weakest event, the downhill. None of the pre-Olympic publications counted her even near medal contention. So when the times were put into the books, James Major, former World Cup Editor for *Skiing* magazine put it this way: "Anne-Marie Moser's (Austria) gold was the victory of the favorite, Wenzel's silver the upset, and Marie-Theres Nadig's (Switzerland) bronze a defeat."

That Olympic year was a very special one for Wenzel. Not only did she match the greatest Olympic skiing achievement ever by a woman, she also won the World Cup overall title. And she got to share in the celebration with her brother Andreas, who also medaled at the 1980 Games (silver in giant slalom) and won the men's World Cup overall title. —*P.S.*

Petra Kronberger

The news came as a shock to the ski world, especially to the Europeans. Quite possibly the most dominant female skier ever to snap into a set of bindings was calling it quits.

At what many would consider the post-prime age of 23, three-time overall World Cup champion Petra Kronberger of Austria decided to retire prior to the 1992–93 World Cup season.

On December 29, 1992, the Austrian Ski Union issued this press release: "I have reached everything possible in the world of ski racing," Kronberger said. "I know that many will say 'Petra is crazy to renounce all that money' .... My health is more important."

Born in the country town of Pfarrwerfen, Kronberger, a self-described "country girl," was never much for the limelight associated with World Cup skiing. After capturing her third consecutive overall Cup title in 1992, Kronberger addressed the skiing press by saying "I'm happy."

Still, to some, talk is cheap, and Kronberger surely proved that with her skiing.

Take, for instance, the 1990 season. At 20 years old, Kronberger placed her name into the skiing record books as she became the first woman to win in every discipline during the course of a single season. During that season Kronberger out-scored 10 other nations—singlehandedly. And she basically had the overall-points championship wrapped up by the New Year.

It was at season's end, however, that Kronberger's career began to close. A crash at the World Championships in Saalbach, Austria, forced her out for the rest of the year. And although she came back the following year to capture her third consecutive overall title—including gold medals in the downhill combined and slalom at the Albertville Games—the pain in her knee was just too much.

Though Kronberger's reign was brief, it was destined to be impressive. In her rookie debut in 1988 Kronberger scored an impressive 15th at the tough Leukerbad, Switzerland course. Three World Cup titles and two Olympic golds

Austrian Petra Kronberger lights up the podium with a smile as she collects the 1992 women's alpine combined gold medal at Meribel.

later, the Austrian country girl will undoubtedly be remembered as one of the all-time greats. —*P.S.*

Alpine Skiing—Women's Downhill

1992
1. Kerrin Lee-Gartner, Canada, 1:52.55
2. Hilary Lindh, USA, 1:52.61
3. Veronika Wallinger, Austria, 1:52.64

1988
1. Marina Kiehl, West Germany, 1:25.86
2. Brigitte Oertli, Switzerland, 1:26.61
3. Karen Percy, Canada, 1:26.62

1984
1. Michela Figini, Switzerland, 1:13.36
2. Maria Walliser, Switzerland, 1:13.41
3. Olga Charvatova, Czechoslovakia, 1:13.53

1980
1. Annemarie Moser-Pröll, Austria, 1:37.52
2. Hanni Wenzel, Liechtenstein, 1:38.22
3. Marie-Theres Nadig, Switzerland, 1:38.36

1976
1. Rosi Mittermaier, West Germany, 1:46.16
2. Brigitte Totschnig, Austria, 1:46.68
3. Cynthia Nelson, USA, 1:47.50

1972
1. Marie-Theres Nadig, Switzerland, 1:36.68
2. Annemarie Proell, Austria, 1:37.00
3. Susan Corrock, USA, 1:37.68

1968
1. Olga Pall, Austria, 1:40.87
2. Isabelle Mir, France, 1:41.33
3. Christl Haas, Austria, 1:41.41

1964
1. Christl Haas, Austria, 1:55.39
2. Edith Zimmermann, Austria, 1:56.42
3. Traudl Hecher, Austria, 1:56.66

1960
1. Heidi Biebl, West Germany, 1:37.6
2. Penny Pitou, USA, 1:38.6
3. Traudl Hecher, Austria, 1:38.9

1956
1. Madeleine Berthod, Switzerland, 1:40.7
2. Frieda Danzer, Switzerland, 1:45.4
3. Lucile Wheeler, Canada, 1:45.9

1952
1. Trude Jochum-Beiser, Austria, 1:47.1
2. Annemarie Buchner, West Germany, 1:48.0
3. Giuliana Minuzzo, Italy, 1:49.0

1948
1. Hedy Schlunegger, Switzerland, 2:28.3
2. Trude Beiser, Austria, 2:29.1
3. Resi Hammerer, Austria, 2:30.2

1924-1936 Not held

Alpine Skiing—Women's Slalom

1992
1. Petra Kronberger, Austria, 1:32.68
2. Annelise Coberger, New Zealand, 1:33.10
3. Blanca Fernandez Ochoa, Spain, 1:33.35

1988
1. Vreni Schneider, Switzerland, 1:36.69
2. Mateja Svet, Yugoslavia, 1:38.37
3. Christa Kinshofer-Guetlein, West Germany, 1:38.40

1984
1. Paoletta Magoni, Italy, 1:36.47
2. Perrine Pelen, France, 1:37.38
3. Ursula Konzett, Liechtenstein, 1:37.50

1980
1. Hanni Wenzel, Liechtenstein, 1:25.09
2. Christa Kinshofer, West Germany, 1:26.50

3. Erika Hess, Switzerland, 1:27.89

1976
1. Rosi Mittermaier, West Germany, 1:30.54
2. Claudia Giordani, Italy, 1:30.87
3. Hanni Wenzel, Liechtenstein, 1:32.20

1972
1. Barbara Cochran, USA, 91.24
2. Daniele Debernard, France, 91.26
3. Florence Steurer, France, 92.69

1968
1. Marielle Goitschel, France, 85.86
2. Nancy Greene, Canada, 86.15
3. Annie Famose, France, 87.89

1964
1. Christine Goitschel, France, 89.86
2. Marielle Goitschel, France, 90.77
3. Jean Saubert, USA, 91.36

1960
1. Anne Heggtveit, Canada, 109.6
2. Betsy Snite, USA, 112.9
3. Barbi Henneberger, West Germany, 116.6

1956
1. Renée Colliard, Switzerland, 112.3
2. Regina Schopf, Austria, 115.4
3. Yevgenia Sidorova, Soviet Union, 116.7

1952
1. Andrea Mead Lawrence, USA, 130.6
2. Ossi Reichert, Germany, 131.4
3. Annemarie Buchner, Germany, 133.3

1948
1. Gretchen Fraser, USA, 117.2
2. Antoinette Meyer, Switzerland, 117.7
3. Erika Mahringer, Austria, 118.0

1924-1936 Not held

Alpine Skiing—Women's Giant Slalom

1992
1. Pernilla Wiberg, Sweden, 2:12.74
2. Diann Roffe, USA, 2:13.71
3. Anita Wachter, Austria, 2:13.71

1988
1. Vreni Schneider, Switzerland, 2:06.49
2. Christa Kinshofer-Güethlein, West Germany, 2:07.42
3. Maria Walliser, Switzerland, 2:07.72

1984
1. Debbie Armstrong, USA, 2:20.98
2. Christin Cooper, USA, 2:21.38
3. Perrine Pelen, France, 2:21.40

1980
1. Hanni Wenzel, Liechtenstein, 2:41.66
2. Irene Epple, West Germany, 2:42.12
3. Perrine Pelen, France, 2:42.41

1976
1. Kathy Kreiner, Canada, 1:29.13
2. Rosi Mittermaier, West Germany, 1:29.25
3. Daniele Debernard, France, 1:29.95

1972
1. Marie-Theres Nadig, Switzerland, 1:29.90
2. Annemarie Proell, Austria, 1:30.75
3. Wiltrud Drexel, Austria, 1:32.35

1968
1. Nancy Greene, Canada, 1:51.97
2. Annie Famose, France, 1:54.61
3. Fernande Bochatay, Switzerland, 1:54.74

1964
1. Marielle Goitschel, France, 1:52.24
2. Christine Goitschel, France, 1:53.11
3. Jean Saubert, USA, 1:53.11

1960
1. Yvonne Ruegg, Switzerland, 1:39.9
2. Penny Pitou, USA, 1:40.0
3. Giuliana Chenal-Minuzzo, Italy, 1:40.2

1956
1. Ossi Reichert, West Germany, 1:56.5

197

2. Josefine Frandl, Austria, 1:57.8
3. Dorothea Hochleitner, Austria, 1:58.2
1952 **1.** Andrea Mead Lawrence, USA, 2:06.8
2. Dagmar Rom, Austria, 2:09.0
3. Annemarie Buchner, Germany, 2:10.0
1924-
1948 **Not held**

Alpine Skiing—Women's Super Giant Slalom

1992 **1.** Deborah Compagnoni, Italy, 1:21.22
2. Carole Merle, France, 1:22.63
3. Katja Seizinger, Germany, 1:23.19
1988 **1.** Sigrid Wolf, Austria, 1:19.03
2. Michela Figini, Switzerland, 1:20.03
3. Karen Percy, Canada, 1:20.29

Alpine Skiing—Women's Combined (Downhill and Slalom)

1992 **1.** Petra Kronberger, Austria, 2.55
2. Anita Wachter, Austria, 19.39
3. Florence Masnada, France, 21.38
1988 **1.** Anita Wachter, Austria, 29.25
2. Brigitte Oertli, Switzerland, 29.48
3. Maria Walliser, Switzerland, 51.28
1952-
1986 **Not held**
1948 **1.** Trude Beiser, Austria, 6.58
2. Gretchen Fraser, USA, 6.95
3. Erika Mahringer, Austria, 7.04
1940-
1944 **Not held**
1936 **1.** Christl Cranz, Germany, 97.06
2. Kathe Grasegger, Germany, 95.26
3. Laila Schou Nilsen, Norway, 93.48

Trivia Quiz

1. Which of these two alpine disciples became an Olympic event first?

A) Giant Slalom. **B)** Super-G.

2. Who is the program director for the US Ski Team?

A) Billy Kidd. **B)** Phil Mahre. **C)** Dennis Agee. **D)** Gerald Ford.

3. Which American men's team member scored the most World Cup points last season?

A) Phil Mahre. **B)** A.J. Kitt. **C)** Tommy Moe. **D)** Matt Grosjean.

4. The reigning Wold Cup women's champ is:

A) Anita Wachter. **B)** Katja Seizinger. **C)** Petra Kronberger. **D)** Carole Merle.

5. And for the men?

A) Paul Accola. **B)** Marc Girardelli. **C)** Alberto Tomba. **D)** Guenther Mader.

6. The downhill combined event, used to decide the best all-around skier, is a combination of these two events:

A) Downhill/super-G. **B)** Downhill/giant slalom. **C)** Downhill/slalom.

7. The last American woman to win a gold medal in alpine skiing was:

A) Debbie Armstrong. **B)** Cindy Nelson. **D)** Susan Corrock. **d.)** Penny Pitou.

8. And for the men?

A) Phil Mahre. **B)** Billy Kidd. **C)** Bill Johnson. **D)** Steve Mahre.

9. Alberto Tomba's nickname is:

A) The Beast. **B)** Fatso. **C)** Rocky. **D)** La Bomba.

198

10. Where is the home of America's Downhill?

A) Colorado Springs. **B)** Aspen. **C)** Stowe. **D)** Park City.

Skiing—Alpine

SKIING—FREESTYLE

WARM-UP

Americans first popularized freestyle skiing back in the late 1960s and early 1970s. Called "hot-dogging," it was a free-form exhibition that threw caution to the wind—and rules out the door. Throughout the 1970s and into the early 1980s, the sport received harsh press due to the danger and injuries involved. Competitions, once prevalent in the early days of the sport, became numbered due to escalating insurance premiums.

fact: Inverted aerials—backflips on skis done off small, steep ramps—were banned from freestyle contests in the late 1970s.

Those closely involved with the sport, understanding its incredibly high excitement level and ability to draw spectators whose numbers are rivaled by only those of the alpine World Cup, sought official recognition for the sport, receiving it in 1979 from the International Ski Federation.

A demonstration sport in Calgary, freestyle skiing—comprising moguls, aerials, and ballet, plus a combined event—became a full-medal sport in Albertville, even though medals are awarded only for the mogul events.

fact: Freestyle skiers use shorter skis and longer, stronger poles than alpine skiers.

In recent years, the US has dominated the world, capturing its sixth straight Nations Cup title following the 1991 season and winning seven medals at the 1991 World Freestyle Ski Championships in Lake Placid, New York.

Two-foot ponytail in tow, New Jersey girl Donna Weinbrecht lands a spread eagle on her way to the first-ever women's freestyle gold at the 1992 Olympic Games.

The mogul freestyle event made its full-medal debut during the 1992 Olympics. The event consists of carefully calculated high-speed turns on a heavily moguled slope (a slope pestered with snow bumps).

fact: Freestyle competitors are scored on the basis of form and technique in the moguls (50%), the degree of difficulty and performance of two acrobatic moves (25%), and, of course, speed (25%).

In the first round, all skiers run down the course. Judges rate the competitors on their speed and on the quality and technique of their turns and aerials. Of the seven judges' scores, the high and low are discarded. The top 16 men and the top eight women then move to the finals. The finals are either a one-run or a dual-format competition. During a dual-mogul event, athletes compete directly against one another. The winner of the run advances to the next round in the competition.

Snowboarding

The sport that has taken the worldwide ski industry by storm over the last couple years looks to be just moments away from full Olympic status.

Snowboarding, kind of a cross between skiing and surfing, will be known as a "cultural exhibition" sport at the Lillehammer Games. In a nutshell, that means it will be a demonstrational sport without the official title. It also means that it will, in all likelihood, become a full-blown medal sport at the 1998 Games.

One of the main reasons for the sport's rise in popularity has been its attraction with younger athletes. As one kid put it, "I know a lot of people who used to ski, but I don't know anybody who used to snowboard."

Coincidentally, FIS president Marc Hodler's grandson is an avid snowboarder, and word has it that grandpa's taken a liking to the sport which has been some what frowned upon in the past by skiing's upper crust. FIS—the Fédération Internationale de Ski—is the governing body of Olympic and World Cup skiing.

Alpine snowboarding pretty much follows in the tracks of skiing in that its events are run through similar giant slalom and slalom courses and are timed exactly the same way—which would make the crossover to Olympic status quite simple.

The freestyle portion of the sport resembles that of the aerial event in World Cup freestyle skiing, which will be a medal event at Lillehammer. The snowboarders, riding in a ditch-like trough known as a halfpipe, are judged on their maneuvers based on air time and degree of difficulty—much the same way as the Olympic aerial skiing event is judged.

As it stands now, US Skiing, which oversees the US Ski Teams and Olympic development programs, has given its full support to developing the sport of snowboarding. And the FIS is looking into the international supervising and developmental end of snowboarding as well.

Snowboarding will surely get its share of coverage at the 1994 Lillehammer Games. And by 1998, those strange-looking vehicles born in America's northeast will undoubtedly be dueling it out for Olympic gold.

One side note: The demonstrational sport of speed skiing, showcased at the Albertville Games for the first time, has been dropped from the Olympic roster.

HOPEFULS

For the last eight years, since they've been keeping freestyle statistics, the World Cup Freestyle Nations Cup has come to rest at season's end in the same spot—the US freestyle office in Park City, Utah. And the country that founded the sport of freestyle skiing, or hot-dogging as it's affectionately known, will boast a host of favored athletes heading into Lillehammer.

fact: Some freestyle moves have names like the Rudy, the Post Toastie, the Thumper, and the Bucher spin.

Leading the way for the US men's team will be Minnesota native Trace Worthington. One of the best combination-event (aerials and ballet) skiers on the World Cup circuit, Worthington finished the 1993 season with a bang by winning the aerials event—along with the combined—at the grand finale at Lillehammer.

Joining Worthington on the A Team will be fellow aerial Kris Fedderson, who missed the end of the 1993 season with a broken hip suffered in a crash at Oberjoch, Germany. The men's B Team will consist of mogul specialists Rick Emerson, James Moran, and Craig Rodman, as well as Ian Edmondson in ballet and Eric Bergoust in aerials.

fact: Freestyle ballet skiing resembles both figure skating and alpine skiing.

The women's best placer last year on the World Cup circuit was ballet specialist Ellen Breen. Breen medaled in all 11 World Cup ballet events last year, capturing

France's Edgar Grospiron, the first-ever men's moguls champion, steps into the limelight at Albertville.

the gold eight times. She capped off the season with a win at Lillehammer to help the US team capture the Nations Cup.

Joining Breen on the A Team will be Albertville moguls gold medalist Donna Weinbrecht, who's returning to the team after missing the 1993 World Cup season with a knee injury. Along with Weinbrecht will be three-event skier Kristie Porter, Nikki Stone (aerials), and Sharon Petzold (ballet). The B Team consists of mogul specialists Liz McIntyre, Rachael Savitt, and Anne Battelle, along with Stacy Blumer (aerials).

quote: "Someday, they may look back at me as the grandma of freestyle." —Donna Weinbrecht, first-ever women's freestyle gold medalist.

Other performers to keep an eye on are France's Edgar Grospiron, hometown gold-medalist at Albertville, and the Canadian men's team (known as the Canadian Air Force) of Lloyd Langlois, Nicholas Fontaine, Darcy Downs, Phillippe LaRoche, and Bernard Sevigny. Norway also has a women's mogul skier by the name of Stine Lise Hattestad who can be considered one of the favorites.

fact: In the gut flip, the skier plants her pole tips in the snow and the other ends against her abdomen and then launches herself into a forward full flip.

US Outlook: Breen is far and away our best shot at a first place, but since medals are not given in ballet, give the nod to Worthington in the aerials. A strong mogul contingent, led by Emerson's first place at last year's nationals at Breckenridge, could also figure in the medals.

Schedule

The tentative freestyle skiing schedule is as follows:

Tuesday, February 15
Elimination moguls

Thursday, February 17
Elimination aerials

Wednesday, February 16
Final moguls

Saturday, February 19
Final aerials

Nelson Carmichael, from Steamboat Springs, Colorado, lands a freestyle bronze medal for the US ski team.

HIGHLIGHTS

The morning was snowy and festive as freestyle skiing tumbled its way into the hallowed Olympic Games—accompanied by loud music and cheers from 10,000 enthusiastic spectators. The first Olympic golds in freestyle skiing went to Frenchman Edgar Grospiron and American Donna Weinbrecht, both world champions in the sport. France and the USA captured the other two men's medals, too, with Frenchman Olivier Allamand seizing the silver and Nelson Carmichael taking bronze. The Unified Team's Elizaveta Kojevnikova placed second in the women's moguls, though she made the fastest run at 39.47 seconds, and Norwegian Stine Lise Hattestad skied to third.

Medalists

Freestyle Skiing—Men's Moguls

1992   1. Edgar Grospiron, France, 25.81
        2. Olivier Allamand, France, 24.87
        3. Nelson Carmichael, USA, 24.82

Freestyle Skiing—Women's Moguls

1992   1. Donna Weinbrecht, USA, 23.69
        2. Elizaveta Kojevnikova, Unified Team, 23.50
        3. Stine Hattestad, Norway, 23.04

Trivia Quiz

1. What was the original term for freestyle skiing?

A) Moguls. B) Jumping. C) Hot-dogging. D) Flip City.

2. How many flips are now commonplace in the men's aerial competition?

A) One and a half. B) Two. C) Three. D) Four.

3. The move in which a mogul skier takes to the air and spins a full 360-degree turn before landing is called a:

A) Spin-O-Rama. B) Whirly Bird. C) Helicopter. D) Whooaaa!

4. Ballet skiers use:

A) Long skis and short poles. B) Medium skis and long poles. C) Short skis and long poles. D) Short skis and no poles.

5. Many of the aerial event experts on the US Freestyle Ski Team have a background in what sport?

A) Rugby. B) Gymnastics. C) Diving. D) Pole Vaulting.

208

6. The freestyle combined event uses which two events to find its best overall skier?

A) Moguls and ballet. B) Ballet and aerials. C) Moguls and aerials.

7. Team mogul skier Rick Emerson's nickname is:

A) Kooky. B) Emmo. C) The Clarkston Kid. D) Airborn.

8. Which American skier won a gold medal at the Albertville Games?

A) Chris Fedderson. B) Wayne Wong. C) Donna Weinbrecht. D) Suzy Chaffee.

9. In aerials, what do you call a 360-degree spin with your skis above your head?

A) A mistake. B) Mobius. C) Blind disaster. D) Inverted helicopter.

10. Which of these decides the winner of the mogul competition?

A) Speed. B) Number and quality of turns. C) Aerials. D) All of the above.

Answers: 1-a, 2-d, 3-c, 4-c, 5-b, 6-c, 7-d, 8-c, 9-b, 10-d

SKIING—NORDIC CROSS-COUNTRY

WARM-UP

S kiing has been practiced in northern Europe for centuries. The oldest known ski, found in a peat bog at Umea, Sweden, goes back nearly 45 centuries to 2500 BC. However, a Stone Age petroglyph in Rodoy, Norway showing a skier has been dated at 5000 BC, a sure sign that someone, now very old, was on skis more than 7,000 years ago. A sled runner about 10 feet long was pulled out of a Finnish bog and carbon-dated to 7000 BC, or 9,000 years ago. As Ted Bates notes in his book, *Nine Thousand Years of Skis*, "Where there were sled runners, there were probably skis." But thousands of years of relying on skis for transportation did not naturally give way to sport; only in the last century has it become a recreational and competitive sport.

Norwegian soldiers patrolled on skis as early as 960 AD, before the Vikings came to North America. Within two centuries of that time, Sweden maintained its own skiborne troops. In 1767, the Norwegian military began to stage races, while the first civilian race was held in 1843. As Scandinavians immigrated to the United States, they brought their ski heritage with them. The records of the early US ski competitions appear to have been taken from the Oslo or Stockholm telephone book, though, of course, telephones had not yet been invented.

fact: A cross-country skier consumes oxygen at a rate as high as 94.6 milliliters per kilogram of body weight per minute. That's more than 10 mpk higher than the best runner.

Norwegians introduced skiing to northern New England and the upper Midwest. In southern Wisconsin, Scandinavians are reported to have been skiing before 1840. Scandinavians also played a key role in importing skiing to the West, with competitions being held in California during the 1850s. The Scandinavians also brought their tradition of village sports clubs to the US, which encouraged recreational skiing.

In the US, competitive skiing began in earnest at the turn of the century. The first official national championship was held in 1904 in Ishpeming, Michigan and the National Ski Association (NSA) was formed a year later. (The NSA

The Unified Team's Lyubov Egorova catches her breath after winning the women's 15km classic-style cross-country race at Les Saisies, which she led from start to finish.

evolved into the US Ski Association, which became part of US Skiing in 1990.) In the early days, skiing invariably meant nordic: ski jumping and cross-country.

The Norwegian Ski Federation organized the first international ski congress in 1910, and annual meetings were held until World War I. In 1921, meetings resumed and rules for international events—only cross-country and jumping were recognized—were formulated. The NSA joined the congress in 1922.

In 1924, the group reorganized as the International Ski Federation, or Fédération Internationale de Ski (FIS), in time for the first Olympic Winter Games held at Chamonix, France. For the first three Olympics, only nordic events were staged, and those were only for men. Although women were part of the inaugural alpine event (the combined) in 1936, they did not compete in cross-country until 1952. In the US, the females did not participate in a national cross-country championship until 1967, when 13-year-old Alison Owen competed in a junior boys' race.

US skier Bill Koch revolutionized the sport in 1982 when he spread the word about a crisscross technique in which the skier actually skates on the skis, pushing off the inside edge of the weight-bearing ski.

The technique is thought to have first been used in 1971 by East German Gerhard Grimmer, racing in Holmenkollen, Norway. The snow conditions that day were strange, and skiers using the traditional parallel—or classic—technique had to continually rewax or change skis to maintain their kick. Grimmer won the race by a huge margin.

Skiers began experimenting with variations on Grimmer's technique, and Koch perfected and popularized it. Purists tried to ban this swifter style, but it was finally allowed in half the cross-country events held in 1988 at the Calgary Games. The men's 15km and 30km races and the women's 5km and 10km races were skied using the classic technique; the men's 50km and 4 x 10km relay races and the women's 20km and 4 x 5km relay races permitted any style, and the style of choice for both winners and contenders was skating.

Cross-country skiing produces the best-conditioned athletes in terms of overall fitness. Sweden's Sven-Ake Lundbäck, a 1972 gold medalist, was once tested as having an oxygen consumption rate as high as 94.6 milliliters per kilogram of body weight per minute; the best runners are in the low 80s. In 1988, Soviet cross-country skiers won eight of twelve medals, amid charges that they engaged in illegal blood-doping. This practice involves removing and storing a quantity of an athlete's blood prior to competition, then reinjecting it—or just the red blood cells—shortly before the event. The extra red blood cells increase endurance by carrying more oxygen to the muscles. It is an undetectable means of performance enhancement.

SPECTATOR'S GUIDE

In **cross-country** skiing, ski technique is combined with strength and endurance required to ski long distances over demanding terrain. Races for men are held over 10, 15, 30, and 50 kilometers, plus a 40km relay. Women compete in 5, 10, 15, and 30 kilometer events, as well as a 20km relay. The longest women's event was added in 1984 as a 20km run, then later lengthened to 30km.

The courses are laid out with a challenging mixture of uphill, downhill, and rolling terrain. The machine-prepared trails are 12–18 feet wide; grooves are set into them on most downhill sections. During the individual races, skiers are usually sent off at 30-second intervals in the individual races, although if there is a large field they could be started two at a time on parallel tracks.

fact: Cross-country events require great upper-body strength to double-pole across level terrain.

Cross-country skiers use two techniques: the classic, which requires the conventional form of parallel stride (the basic kick, pole, and glide technique), and skating (pushing off diagonally from the inside edge of the weight-bearing ski). In freestyle races, which place no restrictions on technique, competitors take advantage of skating, the faster technique. For each technique, specialized boots, skis, and poles have been developed.

The skis used for cross-country are very light and about half the width of those used in alpine, making them more flexible and better suited for the narrow nordic track. They are often referred to as "skinny skis."

fact: No one comes close to cross-country skiers in physiological tests of fitness.

The **nordic relay** races feature a uniform start, enabling the viewer to follow the race more easily. Since the races are run on relatively short courses, with each woman racing five kilometers and each man 10, the event is better followed by television than the longer events. The racers employ strategies common to bicycling and track and field, such as drafting off of one another, taking turns leading, and sprinting for the finish.

Bjorn Daehlie cleans up in the men's 50km freestyle cross-country race in Les Saisies, helping Norway to a clean sweep of the 1992 men's cross-country golds.

HOPEFULS

It doesn't take a rocket scientist to figure out that nordic skiing medals at Lillehammer will—again—be dominated by the Norwegians, Russians, and Swedes.

Two athletes who should reach the medals podium more often than not are Russia's Lyubov Egorova and Norway's Bjorn Daehlie—both of whom won nordic World Cup titles last year and a combined *nine* medals at the Albertville Games.

Egorova, who used to dream of being a ballerina, medaled in all five women's events at Albertville (three gold, two silver). She got some help along the way at the Games from teammate Elena Vialbe, who also kicked and poled to five medals (four bronze, one gold).

Daehlie struck for Albertville gold in the men's final pursuit, 50km and 4 x 10km relay. He and Egorova also won the 15km freestyle pursuit race which was in non-medal status at Albertville.

Both Egorova and Daehlie, coming off two of the more decisive World Cup overall titles in recent years (both won by around 50 points), should medal in the most events at Lillehammer. And given that the Norwegians are competing in front of the home snow crowd, keep an eye on Vegard Ulvang (third behind Daehlie in the 1993 World Cup overall) and top Norwegian women's skier Trude Dybendahl.

US Outlook: One word: Dim.

The United States, as good as we may be in baseball, basketball, and football, cannot put together a nordic program that can compete with Europe's best. Period.

There are a number of reasons for this, but it suffices to name one: money. Nordic skiers in the Scandinavian countries and Russia have the same commercial appeal as our top professional athletes.

Quick, name the top male and female nordic skiers in America. Name two nordic team members. One member?

Get the picture?

Though medals would mean money for the nordic program, which traditionally relies on the alpine program for much of its funding, don't count on them at Lillehammer or in the foreseeable future.

Our top entries, which will compete to break the top 20 at Lillehammer, should be Leslie Thompson, Nina Kemppel, and Nancy Fiddler for the women. And Ben Husaby, who was the cross-country skier featured on the Snickers television commercial, looks to be the best bet at a top-20 finish for the men.

Schedule

The tentative nordic cross-country skiing schedule is as follows:

Sunday, February 13
15km freestyle, women

Monday, February 14
30km freestyle, men

Tuesday, February 15
5km classical, women

Thursday, February 17
10km classical, men
10km freestyle, women

Saturday, February 19
15km freestyle, men

Monday, February 21
4x5km relay, women

Tuesday, February 22
4x10km relay, men

Thursday, February 24
30km classical, women

Sunday, February 27
50km classical, men

MEN'S CROSS-COUNTRY EVENTS

▼

HIGHLIGHTS

Norway's Thorleif Haug garnered three golds in 1924, taking the 15km, the 50km, and the combined. His countryman, Johan Gröttumsbraaten, claimed bronze medals in the 50km and the nordic combined and a silver medal in the 15km. He then captured the gold in the combined and the 15km in 1928, and returned for the combined gold in 1932. Another Norwegian, Hallgeir Brenden, captured the gold in the 15km in 1952 and 1956. Brenden was a lumberjack and farmer who was also Norway's steeplechase champion.

Finland's Veikko Hakulinen won seven Olympic medals beginning in 1952 with the 50km gold; he won silvers in that event during the next two Games, a gold in the 30km in 1956, a bronze in the 15km in 1960, and two relay medals, the silver in 1956 and the gold in 1960. The 1960 relay featured an exciting anchor leg by Hakulinen, in which he overtook the Norwegian skier in the final strides to win by three feet.

Sweden's legendary "king of the skis," Sixten Jernberg, won the 50km gold in 1956 and 1964. He also competed in the 15km for silver medals in 1956 and 1960 and a bronze in 1964. But Jernberg wasn't finished yet. In the 30km event, he skied for silver in 1956 and the gold in 1960, and helped Sweden to a bronze in 1956 and a gold in 1964 in the 4 x 10km relay. Jernberg won his final Olympic gold at Innsbruck on the day before his 35th birthday.

fact: Norwegian cross country multi-medalist Vegard Ulvang trains so effectively that his lungs absorb oxygen at almost twice the average rate. His resting heart rate is 35 beats per minute.

217

Norway's Vegard Ulvang celebrates a snowy victory as he crosses the finish line of the 10km cross-country event at the Albertville Games, winning his second gold medal of the Games.

Finn Ero Mäntyranta and Norwegian Harald Grönningen finished 1–2 in both the 15km and the 10km in 1964; they traded places in the 15km in 1968, and Mäntyranta took a bronze in the 30km at the Grenoble Games. In the relay Mäntyranta also won a gold in 1960, a silver in 1964, and a bronze in 1968. Grönningen claimed a relay silver in 1960 and a gold in 1968.

Sven-Ake Lundbäck of Sweden won the 15km gold at Sapporo in 1972, while the first Soviet to take an individual gold, Vyacheslav Vedenine, captured the 30km event. The 50m event was won in a very closely contested race by Pal Tyldum of Norway. In 1976 the Soviet skiers Nikolai Bayukoy and Yevgeny Beliaev negotiated a 1–2 sweep of the 15km event, confirming the Soviet threat.

The Swedish team long benefitted from the leadership of Thomas Wassberg; he won a gold medal in 1980 in the 15km event a scant one hundredth of a second ahead of Finland's Juha Mieto. Bulgaria received its first Winter Games medal in Lake Placid when Ivan Lebanov won a bronze in the 30km.

Sweden's Gunde Svan medaled in all four cross-country events in 1984 at the age of 22, and the Swedish men's team captured three golds that year. Finland's Harri Kirvesniemi took a bronze in the 15km in 1984, but by the 1980s the Soviet Union and East Germany had stepped in to redirect the medal flow. Soviet cross-country skier Nikolai Zimyatov skied for three gold medals at Lake Placid and added another in 1984. Soviet men captured four gold medals in 1988.

Albertville Highlights

Norway—a country with a population of only 4.2 million—has always had a field day in the cross-country events at the Games; Albertville was no exception. Norwegian skiers made a clean sweep of the gold medals in all five of the men's events, with Vegard Ulvang and Bjorn Daehlie sharing in most of the spoils: each contributed three gold and one silver to the Viking treasure trove.

But the Norwegian victories were not entirely predictable. Prior to the Albertville Games, Norway had never captured the 30km gold (the only gold to have eluded Norwegian skiers). Ulvang, who had taken home the 30km bronze from Calgary, laid to rest his national team's nemesis, capturing the first Norwegian 30km gold as teammates Bjorn Daehlie pocketed the silver and Terje Langli nabbed the bronze in the 10km event. Ulvang—known as "the Viking"—broke one of his poles more than 1600 feet from the line and still managed a gold-medal finish. In the 15km event, however, Ulvang settled for silver behind Daehlie, having been unable to practice the skating technique for three weeks prior to the Games thanks to a hip injury. And finally, the Norwegian team easily captured the 4 x 10km gold, its first relay medal since 1980.

Norwegians peopled the cross-country venue in droves, bearing flags, banners, horns, and cowbells; at home, the spirit was equally festive. At Kirkenes, Viking Ulvang's hometown, revelers tapped out the town's supply of champagne.

The Norwegians were not the only athletes with cause to celebrate. Italy managed five medals, of which Giorgio Vanzetta's 15km bronze was the first ever to have been won by a country other that Norway, Sweden, Finland, or the USSR. Sweden and Finland, meanwhile, were not banished from the podium, as Christer Majback captured the 10km bronze and the Finns made off with the relay bronze.

Bill Koch

The United States is not known as a nordic cross-country skiing powerhouse. The great majority of Americans do not use cross-country skis during the snowy months for transportation, preferring the freeway instead. The top American

Carrying the flag, cross-country skier Bill Koch leads the US delegation to the opening ceremonies at Albertville.

nordic skiers are not the athletes of choice for product promotion on TV and other media, as they are in the northern European countries. After all, the US has Michael Jordan and Bo Jackson.

In short, it's hard to be a cross-country star in the USA.

Before the 1976 Olympics in Innsbruck, no American cross country skier had ever been evenly remotely close to capturing an Olympic medal. America's best Olympic finish, a 15th, came in the 1932 Olympics in Lake Placid.

In 1976, with all the Olympic spectator and media attention on either Franz Klammer in the men's downhill or on the men's speedskating events, American Bill Koch, 20 years old at the time, from Guilford, Vermont, pulled off one of the most unexpected performances in Olympic history: a silver medal in the grueling 30km race (about 18 miles).

Koch, who actually led the 30km race at one point, had only competed in a few world-class races leading up to the Olympics and had only skied the 30km race twice.

The pre-race favorite, Thomas Magnusson, had left the Olympics to be with his family, following the death of his father the day before the race. This left two Soviet skiers, Serge Saveliev, a Russian soldier, and countryman Ivan Garanin, the veteran on the Soviet nordic team, as the picks for medals.

After Saveliev caught and passed Koch (he eventually went on to capture the gold and set an Olympic record time in the process), Koch put together a furious finishing kick that enabled him to keep pace ahead of Garanin and to trail the gold medal winner by little more than 28 seconds, which is equivalent to a few ski lengths in nordic racing.

Koch, who believed that he could pull off the best finish ever by an American, was nonetheless pleased with his historic effort. "To finish in the first ten was my goal," he said. "Of course, I'm even happier with the medal."

Headlines read "KOCH'S THE REAL THING," and "A SECOND FOR KOCH, A FIRST FOR THE USA." When asked about the lack of coverage at the finish line for his silver medal performance—none of the American press or ABC television reporters were on hand for the finish—Koch paused for a moment. "They'll be there next time," he said. —P.S.

Medalists

Nordic Skiing—Men's 10km Cross Country

1992 1. Vegard Ulvang, Norway, 27:36.0
2. Marco Albarello, Italy, 27:55.2
3. Christer Majback, Sweden, 27:56.4

Nordic Skiing—Men's 15Km Cross Country

1992 1. Bjorn Daehlie, Norway, 1:05:37.9
2. Vegard Ulvang, Norway, 1:06:31.3
3. Giorgio Vanazetta, Italy, 1:06:32.2
1988 1. Mikhail Deviatyarov, Soviet Union, 41:18.9
2. Pal Mikkelsplass, Norway, 41:33.4

3. Vladimir Smirnov, Soviet Union, 41:48.5

1984 1. Gunde Anders Svan, Sweden, 41:25.6
2. Aki Karvonen, Finland, 41:34.9
3. Harri Kirvesniemi, Finland, 41:45.6

1980 1. Thomas Wassberg, Sweden, 41:57.63
2. Juha Mieto, Finland, 41:57.64
3. Ove Aunli, Norway, 42:28.62

1976 1. Nikolai Bazhukov, Soviet Union, 43:58.47
2. Yevgeny Beliaev, Soviet Union, 44:01.10
3. Arto Koivisto, Finland, 44:19.25

1972 1. Sven-Ake Lundbäck, Sweden, 45:28.24
2. Fedor Simashov, Soviet Union, 46:00.84
3. Ivar Formo, Norway, 46:02.68

1968 1. Harald Gronningen, Norway, 47:54.2
2. Eero Mantyranta, Finland, 47:56.1
3. Gunnar Larsson, Sweden, 48:33.7

1964 1. Eero Mantyranta, Finland, 50:54.1
2. Harald Gronningen, Norway, 51:34.8
3. Sixten Jernberg, Sweden, 51:42.2

1960 1. Haakon Brusveen, Norway, 51:55.5
2. Sixten Jernberg, Sweden, 51:58.6
3. Veikko Hakulinen, Finland, 52:03.0

1956 1. Hallgeir Brenden, Norway, 49:39.0
2. Sixten Jernberg, Sweden, 50:14.0
3. Pavel Kolchin, Soviet Union, 50:17.0

1952 1. Hallgeir Brenden, Norway, 1:01:34.0
2. Tapio Makela, Finland, 1:02:09.0
3. Paavo Lonkila, Finland, 1:02:20.0

1948 1. Martin Lundstrom, Sweden, 1:13:50.0
2. Nils Ostensson, Sweden, 1:14:22.0
3. Gunnar Eriksson, Sweden, 1:16:06.0

1936 1. Erik-August Larsson, Sweden, 1:14:38.0
2. Oddbjorn Hagen, Norway, 1:15:33.0
3. Pekka Niemi, Finland, 1:16:59.0

1932 1. Sven Utterstrom, Sweden, 1:23:07.0
2. Axel T. Wikstrom, Sweden, 1:25:07.0
3. Veli Saarinen, Finland, 1:25:24.0

1928 1. Johan Grottumsbraaten, Norway, 1:37:01.0
2. Ole Hegge, Norway, 1:39:01.0
3. Reidar Odegaard, Norway, 1:40:11.0

1924 1. Thorleif Haug, Norway, 1:14:31.0
2. Johan Grottumsbraaten, Norway, 1:15:51.0
3. Tapani Niku, Finland, 1:26:26.0

Nordic Skiing—Men's 30Km Cross Country

1992 1. Vegard Ulvang, Norway, 1:22:27.8
2. Bjorn Daehlie, Norway, 1:23:14.0
3. Terje Langli, Norway, 1:23:42.5

1988 1. Alexei Prokurorov, Soviet Union, 1:24:26.3
2. Vladimir Smirnov, Soviet Union, 1:24:35.1
3. Vegard Ulvang, Norway, 1:25:11.6

1984 1. Nikolai Zimiatov, Soviet Union, 1:28:56.3
2. Alexandr Zavyalov, Soviet Union, 1:29:23.3
3. Gunde Anders Svan, Sweden, 1:29:35.7

1980 1. Nikolai Zimiatov, Soviet Union, 1:17:02.80

2. Vassily Rochev, Soviet Union, 1:27:34.22
3. Ivan Levanov, Bulgaria, 1:28:03.87

1976 1. Sergei Saveliev, Soviet Union, 1:30:29.38
2. Bill Koch, USA, 1:30:57.84
3. Ivan Garanin, Soviet Union, 1:31:09.29

1972 1. Vyacheslav Vedenine, Soviet Union, 1:36:31.15
2. Pal Tyldum, Norway, 1:37:25.30
3. Johs Harviken, Norway, 1:37:32.44

1968 1. Franco Nones, Italian, 1:35:39.2
2. Odd Martinsen, Norway, 1:36:28.9
3. Eero Mantyranta, Finland, 1:36:55.3

1964 1. Eero Mantyranta, Finland, 1:30:50.7
2. Harald Gronningen, Norway, 1:32:02.3
3. Igor Voronchikin, Soviet Union, 1:32:15.8

1960 1. Sixten Jernberg, Sweden, 1:51:03.9
2. Rolf Ramgard, Sweden, 1:51:16.9
3. Nikolai Anikin, Soviet Union, 1:52:28.2

1956 1. Veikko Hakulinen2, Finland, 1:44:06.0
2. Sixten Jernberg, Sweden, 1:44:30.0
3. Pavel Kolchin, Soviet Union, 1:45:45.0

1924-1952 Not held

Nordic Skiing—Men's 50Km Cross Country

1992 1. Bjorn Daehlie, Norway, 2:03:41.5
2. Maurilio De Zolt, Italy, 2:04:39.1
3. Giorgio Vanzetta, Italy, 2:06:42.1

1988 1. Gunde Anders Svan, Sweden, 2:04:30.9
2. Maurilio De Zolt, Italy, 2:05:36.4
3. Andy Gruenenfelder, Switzerland, 2:06:01.9

1984 1. Thomas Wassberg, Sweden, 2:15:55.8
2. Gunde Anders Svan, Sweden, 2:16:00.7
3. Aki Karvonen, Finland, 2:17:04.7

1980 1. Nikolai Zimiatov, Soviet Union, 2:27:24.60
2. Juha Mieto, Finland, 2:30:20.52
3. Alexandr Zavyalov, Soviet Union, 2:30:51.52

1976 1. Ivar Formo, Norway, 2:37:30.05
2. Gert-Dietmar Klause, East Germany, 2:38:13.21
3. Ben Soedergren, Sweden, 2:39:39.21

1972 1. Pal Tyldum, Norway, 2:43:14.75
2. Magne Myrmo, Norway, 2:43:29.45
3. Vyacheslav Vedenine, Soviet Union, 2:44:00.19

1968 1. Ole Ellefsaeter, Norway, 2:28:45.8
2. Vyacheslav Vedenine, Soviet Union, 2:29:02.5
3. Josef Haas, Switzerland, 2:29:14.8

1964 1. Sixten Jernberg, Sweden, 2:43:52.6
2. Assar Ronnlund, Sweden, 2:44:58.2
3. Arto Tiainen, Finland, 2:45:30.4

1960 1. Kalevi Hamalainen, Finland, 2:59:06.3
2. Veikko Hakulinen, Finland, 2:59:26.7
3. Rolf Ramgard, Sweden, 3:02:46.7

1956 1. Sixten Jernberg, Sweden, 2:50:27.0
2. Veikko Hakulinen, Finland, 2:51:45.0

3. Fedor Terentyev, Soviet Union, 2:53:32.0
1952 1. Veikko Hakulinen, Finland, 3:33:33.0
2. Eero Kolehmainen, Finland, 3:38:11.0
3. Magnar Estenstad, Norway, 3:38:28.0
1948 1. Nils Karlsson, Sweden, 3:47:48.0
2. Harald Eriksson, Sweden, 3:52:20.0
3. Benjamin Vanninen, Finland, 3:57:28.0
1936 1. Elis Wiklund, Sweden, 3:30:11.0
2. Axel T. Wikstrom, Sweden, 3:33:20.0
3. Nils-Joel Englund, Sweden, 3:34:10.0
1932 1. Veli Saarinen, Finland, 4:28:00.0
2. Vaino Liikkanen, Finland, 4:28:20.0
3. Arne Rustadstuen, Norway, 4:31:53.0
1928 1. Per-Erik Hedlund, Sweden, 4:52:03.0
2. Gustaf Jonsson, Sweden, 5:05:30.0
3. Volger Andersson, Sweden, 5:05:46.0
1924 1. Thorleif Haug, Norway, 3:44:32.0
2. Thoralf Stromstad, Norway, 3:46:23.0
3. Johan Grottumsbraaten, Norway, 3:47:46.0

Nordic Skiing—Men's 4 x 10Km Relay

1992 1. Norway, 1:39:26.0, Terje Langli, Vegard Ulvang, Skjeldal, Bjorn Daehlie
2. Italy, 1:40:52.7, Pulie, Marco Albarello, Giorgio Vanzetta, Silvio Fauner
3. Finland, 1:41:22.9, Kuusisto, Harri Kirvesniemi, Rassanen, Isometsa
1988 1. Sweden, 1:43:58.6, Jan Ottosson, Thomas Wassberg, Gunde Anders Svan, Torgny Morgen
2. Soviet Union, 1:44:11.3, Vladimir Smirnov, Vladimir Sakhnov, Mikhail Deviatyarov, Alexei Prokurorov
3. Czechoslovakia, 1:45:22.7, Radim Nyc, Vaclav Korunka, Pavel Benc, Ladislav Svanda
1984 1. Sweden, 1:55:06.30, Thomas Wassberg, Benny Tord Kohlberg, Jan Bo Otto Ottoson, Gunde Anders Swan
2. Soviet Union, 1:55:16.50, Alexandre Batuk, Alexandr Zavyalov, Vladimir Nikitin, Nikolai Zimiatov
3. Finland, 1:56:31.40, Kari Ristanen, Juha Mieto, Harri Kirvesniemi, Aki Karvonen
1980 1. Soviet Union, 1:57:08.46, Vassily Rochev, Nikolai Bazhukov, Yevgeny Beliaev, Nikolai Zimiatov
2. Norway, 1:58:45.77 Lars Erik Eriksen, Per Aaland, Ove Aunli, Oddvar Bra
3. Finland, 2:00:00.18 Harri Kirvesniemi, Pertti Teurajarvi, Matti Pitkanen, Juha Mieto
1976 1. Finland, 2:07:59.72, Matti Pitkanen, Juha Mieto, Pertti Teurajarvi, Arto Koivisto
2. Norway, 2:09:58.36 Pal Tyldum, Einar Sagstuen, Ivar Formo, Odd Martinsen
3. Soviet Union, 2:10:51.46 Yevgeny Beliaev, Nikolai Bazhukov, Sergei Saveliev, Ivan Garanin
1972 1. Soviet Union, 2:04:47.94, Vladimir Voronkov, Yuri Skobov, Fedor Simashov, Vyacheslav Vedenine

2. Norway, 2:04:57.06, Oddvar Bra, Pal Tyldum, Ivar Formo, Johs Harviken
3. Switzerland, 2:07:00.6, Alfred Kalin, Albert Giger, Alois Kalin, Eduard Hauser
1968 1. Norway, 2:08:33.5, Odd Martinsen, Pal Tyldum, Harald Gronningen, Ole Ellefsaeter
2. Sweden, 2:10:13.2, Jan Halvarsson, Bjarne Andersson, Gunnar Larsson, Assar Ronnlund
3. Finland, 2:10:56.7, Kalevi Oikarainen, Hannu Taipale, Kalevi Laurila, Eero Mantyranta
1964 1. Sweden, 2:18:34.6, Karl-Ake Asph, Sixten Jernberg, Janne Stefansson, Assar Ronnlund
2. Finland, 2:18:42.4, Vaino Huhtala, Arto Tiainen, Kalevi Laurila, Eero Mantyranta
3. Soviet Union, 2:18:46.9, Ivan Utrobin, Gennady Vaganov, Igor Voronchikin, Pavel Kolchin
1960 1. Finland, 2:18:45.6, Toimi Alatalo, Eero Mantyranta, Vaino Huhtala, Veikko Hakulinen
2. Norway, 2:18:46.4, Harald Gronningen, Hallgeir Brenden, Einar Ostby, Haakon Brusveen
3. Soviet Union, 2:21:21.6, Anatoli Shelyukin, Gennady Vaganov, Aleksei Kuznetsov, Nikolai Anikin
1956 1. Soviet Union, 2:15:30.0, Fedor Terentyev, Pavel Kolchin, Nikolai Anikin, Vladimir Kuzin
2. Finland, 2:16:31.0, August Kiuru, Jorma Kortalainen, Arvo Viitanen, Veikko Hakulinen
3. Sweden, 2:17:42.0, Lennart Larsson, Gunnar Samuelsson, Per-Erik Larsson2, Sixten Jernberg
1952 1. Norway, 2:20:16.0, Heikki Hasu, Paavo Lonkila, Urpo Korhonen, Tapio Makela
2. Norway, 2:23:13.0, Magnar Estenstad, Mikal Kirkholt, Martin Stokken, Hallgeir Brenden
3. Sweden, 2:24:13.0, Nils Tapp, Sigurd Andersson, Enar Josefsson, Martin Lundstrom
1948 1. Sweden, 2:32:08.0, Nils Ostensson, Nils Tapp, Gunnar Eriksson, Martin Lundstrom
2. Finland, 2:41:06.0, Lauri Silvennoinen, Teuvo Laukkanen, Sauli Rytky, August Kiuru
3. Norway, 2:44:33.0, Erling Evensen, Olav Okern, Reidar Nyborg, Olav Hagen
1936 1. Finland, 2:41:33.0, Sulo Nurmela, Klaes Karppinen, Matti Lahde, Kalle Jalkanen
2. Norway, 2:41:39.0, Oddbjorn Hagen, Olaf Hoffsbakken, Sverre Brodahl, Bjarne Iversen
3. Sweden, 2:43:03.0, John Berger, Erik A. Larsson, Artur Haggblad, Martin Matsbo
**1924-
1932** **Not held**

The Unified Team's Raisa Smetanina poses at Albertville with her record
tenth medal, a gold medal in the women's 4 x 5km cross country team relay.
At the age of 39 years and 352 days, she was the oldest female Winter Games
gold medalist.

WOMEN'S CROSS-COUNTRY EVENTS

▼

HIGHLIGHTS

Claudia Boyarskikh of the USSR swept all three women's nordic events in 1964. In 1968 Swedish skier Toini Gustafsson took the 5km and 10km gold and earned a silver with the fastest leg in the relay. Skiing for the USSR, Galina Kulakova claimed four gold, two silver, and two bronze medals from 1968 to 1980; she was 37 when she was awarded her last medal. Not to be outdone, her teammate, Raisa Smetanina, totalled up three gold medals (in the 10km in 1976, and the 5km and relay in 1980), five silver medals (in the 5km in 1976, the relay in 1980, the 10km and 20km in 1984, and the 10km in 1988), and one bronze (in the 20km in 1988). She thus tied for the most decorated competitor in the history of the Winter Games.

quote: "It's a hard battle. It gets harder with the years," says Russian cross-country skier Raisa Smetanina, who holds a record 10 medals and is the oldest gold medalist in the history of the Games.

Finland's Marja-Liisa Hämäläinen competed in the 1976 and 1980 Olympics without medaling, but finally skied for three gold medals in 1984, in the 5km, 10km, and 20km races. That made her the first woman ever to win three individual gold medals in cross-country. She also took a bronze in the relay. In 1988 her 19-year-old countrywoman, Marjo Matikainen, who had also won a relay bronze in 1984, was the only non-Soviet skier to finish in the top five in the 10km race, taking a bronze; her strong third leg in the 4 x 5km relay brought Finland another bronze.

Albertville Highlights

Thirteen days before her fortieth birthday, the Unified Team's Raisa Smetanina pocketed a gold medal; competing in her fifth Winter Games, Smetanina became the oldest woman to win a Winter Games gold medal. Not that it was easy: "It's a hard battle," she claimed. "It gets harder with the years." Nor was it Smetanina's first gold medal: in all, she's harvested ten medals since 1976, of which four are gold.

Smetanina's 25-year-old teammate, Lyubov Egorova, a relative outsider, made a major contribution to the Unified Team's medal haul, winning golds in the 15km, the pursuit, and the relay, and silvers in the 30km and 5km. And the Unified Team, whose skiers were shut out of the medals in the men's events,

Italy's Stefania Belmondo skates away with the women's 30km freestyle cross-country event at Les Saisies.

pocketed the relay gold, while Norway settled for a silver, its only medal in the women's events.

Finland's Marjut Lukkarinen came out of nowhere to capture the 5km gold and the 15km silver, while the Unified Team's heavily favored Elena Valbe was forced to settle for bronze medals in the four individual events. Italy, the only other country to medal in the women's events at Albertville, captured the relay bronze while Stefania Belmondo, whose skating form is legendary, nabbed the 30km gold.

Nordic Skiing—Women's 5Km Cross Country

1992
1. Marjut Lukkarinen, Finland, 14:13.8
2. Lyubov Egorova, Unified Team, 14:14.7
3. Elena Valbe, Unified Team, 14:22.7
1988
1. Marjo Matikainen, Finland, 15:04.0
2. Tamara Tikhonova, Soviet Union, 15:05.3
3. Vida Ventsene, Soviet Union, 15:11.1
1984
1. Marja-L. Haemaelainen, Finland, 17:04.0
2. Berit Aunli, Norway, 17:14.1
3. Kvetoslava Jeriova, Czechoslovakia, 17:18.3
1980
1. Raisa Smetanina, Soviet Union, 15:06.92
2. Hilkka Riihivuori, Finland, 15:11.96
3. Kvetoslava Jeriova, Czechoslovakia, 15:23.44
1976
1. Helena Takalo, Finland, 15:48.69
2. Raisa Smetanina, Soviet Union, 15:49.73
3. Nina Baldycheva, Soviet Union, 16:12.82
1972
1. Galina Kulakova, Soviet Union, 17:00.50
2. Marjatta Kajosmaa, Finland, 17:05.50
3. Helena Sikolova, Czechoslovakia, 17:07.32
1968
1. Toini Gustafsson, Sweden, 16:45:2
2. Galina Kulakova, Soviet Union, 16:48.4
3. Alevtina Kolchina, Soviet Union, 16:51.6
1964
1. Claudia Boyarskikh, Soviet Union, 17:50.5
2. Mirja Lehtonen, Finland, 17:52.9
3. Alevtina Kolchina, Soviet Union, 18:08.4
1924-1960 Not held

Nordic Skiing—Women's 10Km Cross Country

1992
1. Lyubov Egorova, Unified Team, 40:07.7
2. Stefania Belmondo, Italy, 40:31.8
3. Elena Valbe, Unified Team, 40:51.7
1988
1. Vida Ventsene, Soviet Union, 30:08.3
2. Raisa Smetanina, Soviet Union, 30:17.0
3. Marjo Matikainen, Finland, 30:20.5
1984
1. Marja-L. Haemaelainen, Finland, 31:44.2
2. Raisa Smetanina, Soviet Union, 32:02.9
3. Brit Pettersen, Norway, 32:12.7
1980
1. Barbara Petzold, East Germany, 30:31.54
2. Hilkka Riihivuori, Finland, 30:35.05
3. Helena Takalo, Finland, 30:45.25
1976
1. Raisa Smetanina, Soviet Union, 30:13.41

2. Helena Takalo, Finland, 30:14.28
3. Galina Kulakova, Soviet Union, 30:38.61
1972
1. Galina Kulakova, Soviet Union, 34:17.82
2. Alevtina Olunina, Soviet Union, 34:54.11
3. Marjatta Kajosmaa, Finland, 34:56.48
1968
1. Toini Gustafsson, Sweden, 36:46.5
2. Berit Mordre, Norway, 37:54.6
3. Inger Aufles, Norway, 37:59.9
1964
1. Claudia Boyarskikh, Soviet Union, 40:24.3
2. Eudokia Mekshilo, Soviet Union, 40:26.6
3. Maria Gusakova, Soviet Union, 40:46.6
1960
1. Maria Gusakova, Soviet Union, 39:46.6
2. Lyubov Baranova-Kosyreva, Soviet Union, 40:04.2
3. Radja Eroshina, Soviet Union, 40:06.0
1956
1. Lyubov Kosyreva, Soviet Union, 38:11.0
2. Radja Eroshina, Soviet Union, 38:16.0
3. Sonja Edstrom, Sweden, 38:23.0
1952
1. Lydia Wideman, Finland, 41:40.0
2. Mirja Hietamies, Finland, 42:39.0
3. Siiri Rantanen, Finland, 42:50.0
1924-1948 Not held

Nordic Skiing—Women's 15Km Cross Country

1992
1. Lyubov Egorova, Unifed Team, 42:20.8
2. Marjut Lukkarinen, Finland, 43:29.9
3. Elena Valbe, Unifed Team, 43:42.3

Nordic Skiing—Women's 20-30Km Cross Country

1992
1. Stefania Belmondo, Italy, 1:22:30.1
2. Lyubov Egorova, Unified Team, 1:22:52.0
3. Elena Valbe, Unified Team, 1:24:13.9
1988
1. Tamara Tikhonova, Soviet Union, 55:53.6
2. Anfisa Restsova, Soviet Union, 56:12.8
3. Raisa Smetanina, Soviet Union, 57:22.1
1984
1. Marja-L. Haemaelainen, Finland, 1:01:45.0
2. Raisa Smetanina, Soviet Union, 1:02:26.7
3. Anne Jahren, Norway, 1:03:13.6

Nordic Skiing—Women's 4 x 5Km Relay

1992
1. Unified Team, 59:34.8, Elena Valbe, Raisa Smetanina, Larisa Lasutina, Lyubov Egorova

2. Norway, 59:56.4, Solveig Pedersen, Inger Helene Nybraten, Trude Dybendahl, Elin Nilsen
3. Italy, 60:25.9, Vanzetta, Manuela Di Centa, Paruzzi, Stefania Belmondo

1988 1. Soviet Union, 59:51.1, Svetlana Nagueikina, Nina Gavriliuk, Tamara Tikhonova, Anfisa Reztsova
2. Norway, 1:01:22.0, Trude Dybendahl, Marit Wold, Anne Jahren, Marianne Dahlmo
3. Finland, 1:01:53.8, Pirkko Maatta, Marja Liisa Kirvesniemi, Marjo Matikainen, Jaana Savolainen

1984 1. Norway, 1:06:49.70, Inger Helene Nybraaten, Anne Jahren, Brit Pettersen, Berit Aunli
2. Czechoslovakia, 1:07:34.70, Dagmar Schvubova, Blanka Paulu, Gabriela Svobodova, Kvetoslava Jeriova
3. Finland, 1:07:36.70, Pirkko Maatta, Eija Hyytiainen, Marjo Matikainen, Marja-L. Haemaelainen

1980 1. East Germany, 1:02:11.10, Marlies Rostock, Carol Anding, Veronica Hesse-Schmidt, Barbara Petzold
2. Soviet Union, 1:03:18.30, Nina Badlycheva, Nina Rocheva, Galina Kulakova, Raisa Smetanina
3. Norway, 1:04:13.50, Brit Pettersen, Anette Boe, Marit Myrmael, Berit Aunli

1976 1. Soviet Union, 1:07:49.75, Nina Baldycheva, Zinaida Amosova, Raisa Smetanina, Galina Kulakova
2. Finland, 1:08:36.57, Liisa Suihkonen, Marjatta Kajosmaa, Hilkka Kuntola, Helena Takalo
3. East Germany, 1:09:57.95, Monika Debertshauser, Sigrun Krause, Barbara Petzold, Veronika Schmidt

1972 1. Soviet Union, 48:16.15, Lyubov Mukhatcheva, Alevtina Oljunina, Galina Kulakova
2. Finland, 49:19.37, Helena Takalo, Hilkka Kuntola, Marjatta Kajosmaa
3. Norway, 49:51.49, Inger Aufles, Aslaug Dahl, Berit Lammedal-Mordre

1968 1. Norway, 57:30.0, Inger Aufles, Babben Enger-Damon, Berit Mordre
2. Sweden, 57:51.0, Britt Strandberg, Toini Gustafsson, Barbro Martinsson
3. Soviet Union, 58:13.6, Alevtina Kolchina, Rita Aschkina, Galina Kulakova

1964 1. Soviet Union, 59:20.2, Alevtina Kolchina, Eudokia Mekshilo, and Claudia Bojarskikh
2. Sweden, 1:01:27.0, Barbro Martinsson, Britt Strandberg, Toini Gustafsson
3. Finland, 1:02:45.1, Senja Pusula, Toini Poysti, Mirja Lehtonen

1960 1. Sweden, 1:04:21.4, Irma Johansson, Britt Strandberg, Sonja Ruthstrom-Edstrom
2. Soviet Union, 1:05:02.6, Radja Eroshina, Maria Gusakova, and Lyubov Baranova-Kosyreva
3. Finland, 1:06:27.5, Siiri Rantanen, Eeva Ruoppa, Toini Poysti

1956 1. Finland, 1:09:01.0, Sirkka Polkunen, Mirja Hietamies, Siiri Rantanen
2. Soviet Union, 1:09:28.0, Lyubov Kosyreva, Alevtina Kolchina, Radya Eroshina
3. Sweden, 1:09:48.0, Irma Johansson, Anna-Lisa Eriksson, Sonja Edstrom

1924-
1952 **Not held**

Trivia Quiz

1. Which American skier revolutionized the skating technique at the 1976 Innsbruck Olympics?

A) Spider Nylund. **B)** Bill Koch. **C)** Eric Heiden. **D)** Zeb Seaborg.

2. Who won five medals (three gold, two silver) at the Albertville Games?

A) Elena Viable. **B)** Lyubov Egorova. **C)** Elin Nilsen. **D)** Stefania Belmundo.

3. Skating skis differ from traditional nordic skis in what way?

A) They're longer and flex more softly. **B)** Shorter and stiffer.

4. Nordic skis are sometimes referred to as:

A) Marathon skis. **B)** Sticks. **C)** Skinny skis. **D)** Granola skis.

5. The oldest know set of skis, found in a peat bog in Sweden, dated back to this time:

A) 2500 BC. **B)** 5000 BC. **C)** 1447. **D)** 1448.

228

6. Where were the first US nordic championships held?

A) Lake Tahoe, New Mexico. B) Ishpeming, Michigan. C) Lake Placid, New York. D) Columbus, Ohio.

7. The name and location of the USA's largest nordic race is:

A) The Vasa, Michigan. B) The Birkebeiner, Wisconsin. C) The Tour of Anchorage, Alaska. D) The California Gold Rush, California.

8. The wax on the base of the ski, underneath the skier's boot, is known as what?

A) Glide wax. B) Climbing wax. C) Turning wax. D) Kick wax.

9. How long is the longest Olympic nordic race?

A) 30 kilometers. B) 40 kilometers. C) 50 kilometers. D) 60 kilometers.

10. The nordic program director for the US Ski Team is:

A) Gunde Svan. B) Bill Koch. C) Sixten Jernberg. D) Alan Ashley.

Skiing—Nordic Cross-Country

Answers: 1-b, 2-b, 3-b, 4-c, 5-a, 6-b, 7-b, 8-d, 9-c, 10-d

SKIING—NORDIC SKI JUMPING AND NORDIC COMBINED

WARM-UP

In 1882, Norwegian immigrants built a ski jump in Berlin, New Hampshire, not far from the Canadian border. When explorer Fridtjof Nansen of Norway visited Berlin in 1890, the club became very excited, and, in his honor, renamed itself. The Nansen Ski Club staged jumping meets into the 1970s and remains the oldest continuously operating club in the nation. In Minnesota, the St. Paul club began in 1885; a year later the Red Wing Ski Club was formed. In 1887, the Ishpeming (Michigan) Ski Club met for the first time.

During this period, skis became more functional. Ranging up to 14 feet in length and made from ash, pine, hickory, and oak, some boards weighed up to 25 pounds. Bindings usually were simply a loop over the front part of the foot. Heel bindings were unheard of until Norwegian jumper Sondre Norheim, a poor sharecropper from the district of Telemark, designed an effective binding made from twisted birch root, officially displaying them at a jumping meet in 1866. The new bindings revolutionized alpine and nordic skiing.

fact: Ski manufacture is so quirky that no ski factory can produce two pairs of skis that are identical.

Norheim's contributions to skiing extended beyond bindings. In 1850, Norheim became the first person to make a parallel turn. In 1860, he made the first officially measured jump. And Norheim is also credited with developing the telemark turn, named for his home county. Used by jumpers as a means of stopping after landing, the telemark is taken in a kneeling position with one ski moving forward until the tip of the other ski is touching the boot.

The first major jumping meet was held at Husebybakken in Oslo in 1879, and produced a winning jump of 66 feet. Within 20 years, that distance had nearly doubled, to 117 feet. In 1917 a Norwegian immigrant, Henry Hall, jumped 203 feet at Steamboat Springs, Colorado. As with the other nordic sports, skiing came to the US via Scandinavian immigrants, and two former students of Norheim were among the early champions. Mikkel Hennm set an American record of 102 feet at Redwing, Minnesota, in 1891, and two years later, his brother Jorjus extended that mark by a foot.

When the Winter Olympics began in 1924, skiing events were classified as "special" (as if a specialist competed) and "combined." Competitions included one "special" jumping event, two "special" cross-country races, and the "combined" event, consisting of a separate 18km ski race and jumping competition. Six Americans participated, with US jumper Anders Haugen winning the bronze medal in the 70-meter jump. Unfortunately for Haugen, the medal was awarded erroneously to Thorleif Haug of Norway. A scoring miscalculation wasn't discovered until a half-century later when Jakob Vaage, long-time curator of the Norwegian Ski Museum, and Norwegian Toralf Stroemstad, who had been silver medalist in nordic combined in 1924, were computing the various distance and style points. They found Haugen actually had finished third ahead of Haug. In 1974, Haugen accepted the bronze medal from Haug's daughter in a special ceremony held in Oslo, under the heading, "better late than never."

One of the most honored US ski jumpers was Torger Tokle, a Norwegian who adopted the US in 1939. Tokle won 42 of the 48 meets he entered. In 1945, he was killed in action while serving with the 10th Mountain Division in Italy.

During the 1950s, large hill jumping became the hot trend in the sport. At the 1964 Olympics, the large hill (90 meters) was added to the program, joining the small hill (70 meter) leap, which had been part of the Winter Games since their inception.

▼
───────────────────────────────────

SPECTATOR'S GUIDE

A great crowd pleaser, ski jumping is one of the most spectacular of all Winter Olympic sports, employing speed and power in conjunction with the application of basic flight principles. Aerodynamics has become such a factor in ski jumping that, on the larger hills, jumpers actually speak of floating or gliding. Longer and heavier than alpine skis, jumping skis are made of wood, fiberglass, and epoxy. The skis are one-and-a-half times as wide and weigh up to 16 pounds each.

Ski jumps consist of an inrun (the approach), where virtually everyone has their own style and points are not deducted for form; the critical takeoff, occurring at the end of the inrun, the jumper timing his flight precisely, ski tips rising; the flight, with the jumper extending himself almost parallel to his skis, riding the air; the landing, when the jumper assumes the telemark position to allow the knees and hips to absorb the shock; and the outrun, the flat area where the skier decelerates and stops.

fact: In ski jumping, the competitor lands with one ski in front of the other, knees flexed, hips bent and arms straight out at the sides; this is the telemark position, named after a region in Norway where the sport originated.

Wind and velocity must be watched carefully to ensure that competitors are not blown off the landing or turned over in the air. When conditions are right, ski jumping is a very safe sport with a low incidence of injury. Contrary to how it appears on television, jumpers are usually not more than 10 feet in the air at any one time as their flight curve follows that of the hill. In the event of a fall, the athlete normally slides along the landing hills and harmlessly onto the flat.

Aside from the nordic combined, two individual jumping events are on the Olympic program, the 70-meter ("normal hills") and 90-meter ("large hills"). In 1988 a men's 90-meter team ski jumping competition was added. No jumping events for women are held. In the team jumping competition, each team is composed of four jumpers; the top three scores in each of two rounds are combined to give the total team score.

In the individual competitions, each competitor makes two jumps, earning points based on distance and form. These two elements are roughly equal in value in the scoring of the jump. While it is conceivable that the longest jump will not win, great distances are unusual without great form. But long jumps with bumpy landings can bring a score down.

fact: The length of a ski jumper's leap is still measured by the naked eye. Officials stand on either side of the hill, at one-meter intervals, watching the skiers feet as he lands; the official closest to the touchdown point raises his hand to indicate the distance of the jump.

The size of any jump is determined by the distance along the ground from the point of takeoff to a spot on the landing known as the norm point, which lies approximately two-thirds of the way to the point where the landing begins to pull out. Each of the five judges can award up to 20 points for a jump. High and low marks are thrown out, and the remaining scores added together to determine each jumper's final score. A perfect jump would be awarded a score of 60.

The jumpers are judged on the quality of their takeoffs, the smoothness of their air flights, and whether their landings are clean and safe. When a jump is executed correctly, the skier is in a complete forward-lean position with a slight bend at the hips and with arms feathered at his side to minimize drag. Skis should be parallel, with no extraneous movement, and this position is held until the point of landing. Points are deducted during the flight for such items as bent knees, hips, or back, poor body position, and improper positioning of skis.

fact: To capitalize on aerodynamics, ski jumpers hold their arms at their sides to form an airfoil, getting as much updraft as possible after takeoff from the slope.

An unsteady landing, or premature preparation to land, will also result in point deductions. Once the skier has landed, the judges watch for such infractions as touching the snow or skis or any other sign of an rocky landing.

The nordic combined is an exceedingly demanding test, requiring endurance for the cross-country and speed and power for the jumping. The nordic combined events include an individual 70-meter jump and 15km cross-country race as well as a team combined (three men to a team) featuring a 70-meter jump with a 30km relay race. Unlike the regular jumping competition, nordic combined permits each competitor to jump three times, with only the two best jumps counting toward the score. In the cross-country part of the race, times are converted to points based on a set of tables, and these points are added to the jumping points to determine the combined score.

HOPEFULS

Nordic Ski Jumping

Remember this name: Espen Bredesen.

The Norwegian caught fire during the latter part of the World Cup by winning a number of events, which included the prestigious Holmenkollen Nordic Ski Festival in front of his hometown fans in Olso.

Finishing fifth in the final World Cup standings, Bredesen will be looking forward to Lillehammer, where he will likely improve on his dead-last normal hill finish and second-to-last (because somebody crashed) finish on the large hill at Albertville.

According to US Jumping coach Alan Johnson, others to watch at Lillehammer include World Cup champion Andreas Goldberger of Austria, Japan's Noriaki Kasai, Czech Jaroslav Sakala, and, as a dark horse, Didier Mollard of France.

Finland's Toni Nieminen soars through the air on his way to win the gold medal in the 120m ski jumping event at Albertville. At the ripe old age of sixteen, Nieminen is the youngest gold medalist in the history of the Winter Games.

Noticeably absent from the top of last year's World Cup standings was Albertville Olympic champion Toni Nieminen.

According to Johnson, the Finnish teenager, who competed on the World Cup circuit last year, basically just had an off year. "I watched him compete at 10 or 12 different meets last year and I didn't see him doing anything different from the year before," Johnson said. Nieminen won the overall World Cup title during the Albertville Olympic year.

US Outlook: As in nordic skiing, don't count on any jumping medals coming home in our boys' pockets. "Relative to the rest of the jumping world," noted Johnson, "we're like a third-world country."

The USA's best hope lies in the nerve of veteran jumper Jim Holland. A native of Vermont, Holland laid down America's best finish in recent years with a second place at Thunder Bay, Ontario, in 1992. Holland also scored World Cup points in seven consecutive meets that year.

Last year a crash at Lahti, Finland, sent Holland back to the States with a broken wrist. He will undoubtedly be back to full strength at Lillehammer. Fellow Americans competing there with him include Bob Holme, Tad Langlois, and Randy Weber.

Nordic Combined

France's Fabrice Guy and Sylvain Guillaume—who captured the gold and silver, respectively, at Albertville—could team up again to lead the French in its individual assault on the Lillehammer nordic combined medals. Guy won the 1992 overall World Cup combined championship, while Guillaume finished seventh. Also figure in Norwegian homeboy Fred Lundberg, the 1991 overall World Cup combined champion, and Austrian Klaus Sulzenbacher, the 1992 overall runner-up.

The defending Albertville gold medal winners—Japan—should be considered as the favorite in the team combined event. The Norwegian silver-medalist team should also wind up on the medal podium.

US Outlook: If the United States is going to win a medal with anything associated with nordic skiing or jumping, it just may be with the combination of both.

At Albertville, the team of Tim Tetreault, Ryan Heckman, and Jim Holland flew to a fourth-place finish in the team jumping event, then dipped a bit in the 3 x 10km combined relay, finishing 10th.

Coach Alan Johnson is optimistic that the three can improve on their 10th-place overall Olympic finish and, possibly, bring home a medal. "Their cross country (skiing) has improved immensely, but their jumping was not as good as the previous year," Johnson said. "They just can't have as dismal of a year (jumping) as last year."

"A top five finish is not out of the question. And a medal is not out of the question."

Schedule

The tentative ski jumping schedule is as follows:

Sunday, February 20
70m, individual

Tuesday, February 22
90m, team

Friday, February 25
90m, individual

The tentative nordic combined schedule is as follows:

Friday, February 18
90m ski jumping

Saturday, February 19
15km cross-country

Wednesday, February 23
90m ski jumping, team

Thursday, February 24
3x10km cross-country, team

▼

HIGHLIGHTS

From 1924 to 1952 Norwegians won all six gold medals awarded in jumping. Norwegian Birger Ruud won two golds and a silver medal from 1932 to 1948; he was 36 when he won his last medal. He also won the downhill segment of the Alpine combined event in 1936. His brother Sigmund won a silver in 1928, and a third brother, Asbjorn, competed in 1948.

Finns, Germans, and Austrians began to practice on larger hills and rose to dominance after 1952. After trying to discourage jumping on large hills, the Norwegians finally joined the sport's trend and recaptured their medal prowess in 1964, when Toralf Engan won a gold and a silver in jumping and Torgeir Brandtzag took two bronzes. 1972 produced the oldest and youngest gold medalists: 28-year-old Yukio Kasaya of Japan in the 70m and 19-year-old Wojciech Fortuna of Poland in the 90m, which he won on the strength of his spectacular first jump.

fact: Ski jumpers attain speeds of about 60 mph; as much as 10% of drag while the jumper is airborne is caused by air molecules coming into contact with the surface of the body.

A pair of Austrian jumpers, Karl Schnabl and Toni Innauer, won the gold and silver medals, respectively, in the 90m event at Innsbruck in 1976; Toni was only 17 at the time. In 1980 it was Austrian Innauer for the gold in the 70m event while Jouko Tormänen of Finland captured the 90m gold. Finland's Matti Nykänen was already a legendary ski jumper when he competed in the 1984 Games—legendary for his temper tantrums and off-skis antics. But in 1984 he jumped for the gold at 90m and the silver at 70m, the first in Olympic history to do so. East German Jens Weissflog earned the 70m gold and the 90m silver. Back for more in 1988, Nykänen won another gold in the 70m, making him the first jumper in some 50 years to finish first in more than one Olympics, then captured the 90m gold to further his triumphant making of Olympic history.

Albertville Highlights

The V-formation proved to be the formula for success at Albertville. More than half of the 58 jumpers flew in V-formation, and all four of the gold medalists chose it over the classical mode, even though judges continued to award style demerits for the ungainly delta-wing style.

Conspicuously absent from the 1992 Games was England's "Eddie the Eagle," who, although championing the V-style, had finished dead last at Calgary.

Banners in the gallery queried, "Where's Eddie?", but no answer was forthcoming.

Austrian Ernst Vettori, who already had 14 World Cup victories under his belt, won his first Olympic victory in the 70m jump, while his teammate Martin Hollwarth slipped into second place. Just behind him was Finland's Toni Nieminen, who, winning the 70m bronze at the age of sixteen, became the youngest athlete to win a medal at the Winter Games. Seemingly intent on making a claim in the *Guinness Book of World Records,* Nieminen also contributed to the Finns' 90m team gold, to become the youngest gold medalist in the history of Games. But not by much: Nieminen was only one day younger than American record-holder William Fiske.

And again, in the 90m individual event, Finnish flyboy Nieminen outflew the competition with 239.5 points, forcing Austrian skiers, who took a silver in the team jump, to settle for silver and bronze medals.

The French team made sure that the top nordic combined medals didn't leave home. Fabrice Guy—who had the longest jump *and* the fastest 15km—easily captured the gold, while teammate Sylvain Guillaume—whose jump measured only 208'1"—managed to charge out of the thirteenth place by shaving precious seconds off his 15km time. Guillaume's incredible comeback forced Austrian Klaus Sulzenbacher—who landed a jump of 221'6"—to settle for third place.

In the team event, France mustered only a fourth-place showing, while the Japanese captured their first gold medal since the Sapporo Games. Although the Japanese team sent out Mikita, their weakest skier, first, they still turned in a relay time that was almost five minutes slower than the Norwegian team's. Their jump scores, however, were unbeatable: the Japanese team bested the Norwegian team's jumping score by some 75-odd points.

Matti Nykänen

Big air. Real big air.

Finland's Matti Nykänen, ski jumping's phenom of the 1980s, still stands out as one of the greatest to ever ride the sheet of air. His dual gold performance in the 70 and 90 meter events at the 1988 Calgary Olympics was the first ever Olympic jumping sweep. In the 70-meter jump, "Nukes" distanced himself from the silver medal by 17 points—which was a greater margin than between second and 10th place.

In a sport where all of the athletes are very close in size (Nykänen is actually on the larger end of the height curve at 5'10", but stretches that out at only 132 pounds), the domination by Nykänen leaves even the experts wondering. His inrun speed is well below average (54 mph for Nukes vs. the 58 mph average at Calgary), leading experts to believe he has the quickest takeoff reaction time, clocked at 0.12, in the sport. Nykänen also developed a style in which he throws himself slightly sideways in the air, grasping for more wind resistance, which allows him to get more "float" out of his jumps. Some folks even joke that the secret of his success is that he has bird bones, i.e., they're hollow.

Nykänen, on the other hand, sees his success in his attitude. "The secret is that I can trust myself so much on every jump," he said. "I think I can judge better than the others."

As attitude helped him rise to the pinnacle of his sport, attitude also forced him to crash—off the hill. Despite his four Olympic medals (he also took the 90m gold and 70m silver in Sarajevo) and numerous World Cup victories, Nykänen displayed a brash attitude that got him kicked off Finland's national team on more than one occasion.

As Mike Tyson is to American papers today, Nykänen was the topic of many Finnish tabloid headlines. "We sell a lot of magazines when we feature Matti," said gossip magazine *Seura* editor Isto Lysma. —*P.S.*

Medalists

Nordic Skiing—Men's 70m Ski Jumping (meters & score)

1992
1. Ernst Vettori, Austria, 88.0, 222.8
2. Martin Hollwarth, Austria, 90.5, 218.1
3. Toni Nieminen, Finland, 88.0, 217.0

1988
1. Matti Nykänen, Finland, 229.1
2. Pavel Ploc, Czechoslovakia, 212.1
3. Jiri Malec, Czechoslovakia, 211.8

1984
1. Jens Weissflog, East Germany, 90.0-87.0, 215.2
2. Matti Nykanen, Finland, 91.0-84.0, 214.0
3. Jari Puikkonen, Finland, 81.5-91.5, 212.8

1980
1. Anton Innauer, Austria, 87.2-87.7, 266.30
2. Manfred Deckert, East Germany, 88.2-88.2, 249.20
2. Hirokazu Yagi, Japan, 87.2-87.1, 249.20

1976
1. Hans-Georg Aschenbach, East Germany , 84.5-82.0, 252.0
2. Jochen Dannenberg, East Germany, 83.5-82.5, 246.2
3. Karl Schnabl, Austria, 82.5-81.5, 242.0

1972
1. Yukio Kasaya, Japan, 84.0-79.0, 244.2
2. Akitsugu Konno, Japan, 82.5-79.0, 234.8
3. Seiji Aochi, Japan, 83.5-77.5, 229.5

1968
1. Jiri Raska, Czechoslovakia, 79.0-72.5, 216.5
2. Reinhold Bachler, Austria, 77.5-76.0, 214.2
3. Baldur Preiml, Austria, 80.0-72.5, 212.6

1964
1. Veikko Kankkonen, Finland, 80.0-79.0, 229.9
2. Toralf Engan, Norway, 78.5-79.0, 226.3
3. Torgeir Brandtzaeg, Norway, 79.0-78.0, 222.9

1960
1. Helmut Recknagel, East Germany, 93.5-84.5, 227.2
2. Niilo Halonen, Finland, 92.5-83.5, 222.6
3. Otto Leodolter, Austria, 88.5-83.5, 219.4

1956
1. Antti Hyvarinen, Finland, 81.0-84.0, 227.0
2. Aulis Kallakorpi, Finland, 83.5-80.5, 225.0
3. Harry Glass, East Germany, 83.5-80.5, 224.5

1952
1. Arnfinn Bergmann, Norway, 67.5-68.0, 226.0
2. Torbjorn Falkanger, Norway, 68.0-64.0, 221.5
3. Karl Holmstrom, Sweden, 67.0-65.5, 219.5

1948
1. Petter Hugsted, Norway, 65.0-70.0, 228.1
2. Birger Ruud, Norway, 64.0-67.0, 226.6
3. Thorleif Schjelderup, Norway, 64.0-67.0, 225.1

1936
1. Birger Ruud, Norway, 75.0-74.5, 232.0
2. Sven Eriksson, Sweden, 76.0-76.0, 230.5
3. Reidar Andersen, Norway, 74.0-75.0, 228.9

1932
1. Birger Ruud, Norway, 66.5-69.0, 228.1
2. Hans Beck, Norway, 71.5-63.5, 227.0
3. Kaare Wahlberg, Norway, 62.5-64.0, 219.5

1928
1. Alf Andersen, Norway, 60.0-64.0, 19,208

239

2. Sigmund Ruud, Norway, 57.5-62.5, 18,542
3. Rudolf Burkert, Czechoslovakia, 57.0-59.5, 17,937

1924 1. Jacob Tullin Thams, Norway, 49.0-49.0, 18,960
2. Narve Bonna, Norway, 47.5-49.0, 18,689
3. Anders Haugen, Norway, 44.0-44.5, 18,000 (Thorleif Haug was awarded the medal. However, 50 years later, a mathematical error was discovered and Anders Haugen was declared the winner.)

Nordic Skiing—Men's 90m Ski Jumping (meters & score)

1992 1. Toni Nieminen, Finland, 123.0, 239.5
2. Martin Hollwarth, Austria, 120.5, 227.3
3. Heinz Kuttin, Austria, 117.5, 214.8
1988 1. Matti Nykänen, Finland, 118.5-107.0, 224.0
2. Erik Johnsen, Norway, 114.5-102.0, 207.9
3. Matjaz Debelak, Yugoslavia, 113.08-108.00, 207.7
1984 1. Matti Nykänen, Finland, 116.0-111.0, 231.2
2. Jens Weissflog, East Germany, 107.0-107.5, 213.7
3. Pavel Ploc, Czechoslovakia, 103.5-109.0, 202.9
1980 1. Jouko Tormanen, Finland, 96.7-96.4, 271
2. Hubert Neuper, Austria, 97.1-97, 262.40
3. Jari Puikkonen, Finland, 96.5-96.5, 248.50
1976 1. Karl Schnabl, Austria, 97.5-97.0, 234.8
2. Anton Innauer, Austria, 102.5-91.0, 232.9
3. Henry Glass, East Germany, 91.0-97.0, 221.7
1972 1. Wojciech Fortuna, Poland, 111.0-87.5, 219.9
2. Walter Steiner, Switzerland, 94.0-103.0, 219.8
3. Rainer Schmidt, East Germany, 98.5-101.5, 219.3
1968 1. Vladimir Beloussov, Soviet Union, 101.5-98.5, 231.3
2. Jiri Raska, Czechoslovakia, 101.0-98.0, 229.4
3. Lars Grini, Norway, 99.0-93.5, 214.3
1964 1. Toralf Engan, Norway, 93.5-90.5, 230.7
2. Veikko Kankkonen, Finland, 95.5-90.5, 228.9
3. Torgeir Brandtzaeg, Norway, 90.0-87.0, 227.2
1924-1960 **Not held**

Nordic Skiing—Men's 90m Team Ski Jumping

1992 1. Finland, 644.4, Ari Pekka Nikkola, Mika Laitinen, Laakkonen, Toni Nieminen
2. Austria, 642.9, Heinz Kuttin, Ernst Vettori, Martin Hollwarth, Andreas Felder
3. Czechoslovakia, 620.1, Goder, Jez, Jaroslav Sakala, Jiri Parma
1988 1. Finland, 634.4, Ari Pekka Nikkola, Matti Nykanen, Tuomo Ylipulli, and Jari Puikkonen
2. Yugoslavia, 625.5, Primoz Ulaga, Matjaz Zupan, Matjaz Debelak, and Miran Tepes
3. Norway, 596.1, Ole Eidhammer, Jon Kjorum, Ole Fidjestol, and Erik Johnsen

Nordic Skiing—Men's Combined (70m Jump, 15km)

1992 1. Fabrice Guy, France, 222.1, 44:28.1
2. Sylvain Guillaume, France, 208.1, 45:16.5
3. Klaus Sulzenbacher, Austria, 221.6, 45:34.4
1988 1. Hippolyt Kempf, Switzerland, 217.9; 38:16.8
2. Klaus Sulzenbacher, Austria, 228.5; 39:46.5
3. Allar Levandi, Soviet Union, 216.6; 39:12.4
1984 1. Tom Sandberg, Norway, 422.595
2. Jouko Karjalainen, Finland, 416.900
3. Jukka Ylipulli, Finland, 410.825
1980 1. Ulrich Wehling, East Germany, 432.200
2. Jouko Karjalainen, Finland, 429.500
3. Konrad Winkler, East Germany, 425.320
1976 1. Ulrich Wehling, East Germany, 423.390
2. Urban Hettich, West Germany, 418.900
3. Konrad Winkler, East Germany, 417.470
1972 1. Ulrich Wehling, East Germany, 413.340
2. Rauno Miettinen, Finland, 405.505
3. Karl-Heinz Luck, East Germany, 398.800
1968 1. Franz Keller, West Germany, 449.040
2. Alois Kalin, Switzerland, 447.990
3. Andreas Kunz, East Germany, 444.100
1964 1. Tormod Knutsen, Norway, 469.280
2. Nikolai Kiselev, Soviet Union, 453.040
3. Georg Thoma, West Germany, 452.880
1960 1. Georg Thoma, West Germany, 457.952
2. Tormod Knutsen, Norway, 453.000
3. Nikolai Gusakov, Soviet Union, 452.000
1956 1. Sverre Stenersen, Norway, 455.00
2. Bengt Eriksson, Sweden, 437.400

3. Franciszek Gron-Gasienica, Poland, 436.800
1952 1. Simon Slattvik, Norway, 451.621
2. Heikki Hasu, Finland, 447.500
3. Sverre Stenersen, Norway, 436.335
1948 1. Heikki Hasu, Finland, 448.800
2. Martti Huhtala, Finland, 433.650
3. Sven Israelsson, Sweden, 433.400
1936 1. Oddbjorn Hagen, Norway, 430.300
2. Olaf Hoffsbakken, Norway, 419.800
3. Sverre Brodahl, Norway, 408.100
1932 1. Johan Grottumsbraaten, Norway, 446.00
2. Ole Stenen, Norway, 436.050
3. Hans Vinjarengen, Norway, 434.600
1928 1. Johan Grottumsbraaten, Norway, 17.833
2. Hans Vinjarengen, Norway, 15.303
3. John Snersrud, Norway, 15.021
1924 1. Thorleif Haug, Norway, 18.906
2. Thoralf Stromstad, Norway, 18.219
3. Johan Grottumsbraaten, Norway, 17.854

Nordic Skiing—Men's Team Combined (70m Jump, 3x10km Relay)

1992 1. Japan, 645.1, 1:23:36.5, Mikata, Kono, Kenji Ogiwara
2. Norway, 569.9, 1:18:46.9, Apeland, Fred Lundberg, Elden
3. Austria, 615.6, 1:22:49.6, Klaus Ofner, Kreiner, Klaus Sulzenbacher
1988 1. West Germany, 629.8; 1:20:46.0, Thomas Mueller, Hans Pohl, Hubert Schwarz
2. Switzerland, 571.4; 1:15:57.4, Fredy Glanzmann, Hippolyt Kempf, Andreas Schaad
3. Austria, 626.6; 1:21:00.9, Hansjoerg Aschenwald, Guenther Csar, Klaus Sulzenbacher

Trivia Quiz

1. The ideal landing form in ski jumping is known as:

A) Telemark. B) Alpine. C) Skis first. D) Ka-Kwang.

2. Eddie "The Eagle" Edwards was from what country?

A) US B) Canada. C) Denmark. D) England.

3. The 1984 dual jumping gold-medal winner Matti Nykänen's nickname was:

A) Bird Bones. B) Air Time. C) Nukes. D) Fatti Matti.

4. The ABC Wide World of Sports "Agony of Defeat" guy was from what country?

A) Poland. B) Russia. C) Yugoslavia. D) Ireland.

5. The area where the steepness of the landing area starts to flatten out is called the:

A) Transition. B) The "Oh *%#@! point. C) K point. D) Critical point.

6. The noise-making instrument of choice used by European ski jumping fans is:

A) Air horn. B) Cowbell. C) Ref's whistle. D) Konk shell.

7. Bits of pine tree branches are stuck into the hill on and along the landing area for what reason?

A) To help officials judge distance. B) To add color and give the jumpers better depth perception. C) To break their outrun speed in case of a fall. D) To make it look like they're jumping over the tree tops.

8. *Jumpers on the large hill reach speeds of ___ mph on the inrun, before actually slowing down once they hit the air.*

A) 40 mph. **B)** 50 mph. **C)** 60 mph. **D)** 70 mph.

9. *The only World Cup skiing stop in the western hemisphere is where?*

A) Ishpeming, Michigan. **B)** Cleveland, Ohio. **C)** Summit County, Colorado. **D)** Thunder Bay, Ontario.

10. *Informal US ski jumping contests—using regular alpine recreational equipment—are called what?*

A) Crash and Burn Theater. **B)** Galendesprungs. **C)** C-YA Mr. Lift Ticket Shows. **D)** Knucklehead Days.

SPEEDSKATING

WARM-UP

The Vikings, Norsemen with a penchant for wandering and pirating, had much to do with the development of both skiing and its predecessor, skating. In England, Germany, Switzerland, and other countries with Viking settlements, archaeologists have found numerous ice skates of Viking manufacture. Scandinavian literature is full of allusions to skating on iron skates as early as 200 AD.

For centuries before this, the people of northern countries—such as Sweden, Finland, Norway, Russia, Holland, and Scotland—used skates made of polished animal bones for transportation over frozen lakes, rivers, canals, and icy fields. During the 14th century, people began to make skates with runners of highly waxed wood instead of bone. Since neither the bone nor the wood runners had sharp edges, early skaters propelled themselves by pushing a long pole against the ice.

fact: Speedskating is a national passion in the Netherlands.

Of the three forms of skating—speedskating, ice hockey, and figure skating—speedskating was the first to develop as a sport. More than 500 years ago, a form of speedskating gained popularity in the Netherlands, as racing down the frozen canals of Holland *à la* Hans Brinker became a public passion. But racing on ice wasn't a practical affair until all-iron skates were invented in Scotland in the 16th century; the sport became increasingly popular, and eventually, in 1742, enthusiasts formed the Skating Club of Edinburgh, the world's first such club. In 1850, the introduction of all-steel blades dramatically improved the skates. Unlike the iron blades, they were light and strong, and they maintained their sharp edge for months.

During the 18th century, speedskating developed into a national sport in Britain and the Netherlands. The first recorded speedskating competition took place on the Fens in England over a distance of 15 miles on February 4, 1763. Soon, skating clubs and tournaments spread throughout northern Europe. (Skating was exclusively an outdoor, winter sport until 1876, when an Englishman, W. A. Parker, invented an artificial ice surface.) Participants in the

243

China's Ye Qiaobo, who studied hours of videotapes of Bonnie Blair's form, races to a 500m silver medal at Albertville. Ye has since bested Bonnie in international competition in the 500m event.

tournaments were usually laborers, while the aristocrats tended to favor figure skating and placing bets on the speed racers. In 1879, the National Skating Association of Great Britain was founded, with the objective of protecting speedskating from the more unscrupulous promoters.

In 1885, the association adopted rules to stage all international races on a double track, with pairs racing over short, medium, and long distances. Seven years later, the International Skating Union (ISU) was formed in the Netherlands, and the following year Amsterdam hosted the first world championship. At the time, a skater had to win at least three of the four races (500, 1500, 5000, and 10,000 meters) to claim the world championship. Jaap Eden of Holland was the first "Champion of the World," a title that was known to win him a pint or two at the local pub. In 1908, the championship adopted a point system, turning to its current format in 1928.

In 1879, the first American competitors raced over courses of 10 and 20 miles; twelve years later, the US staged its first national championship. During the first half of this century, American skaters trained exclusively on frozen lakes, while skaters abroad were beginning to compete on refrigerated rinks. The Wisconsin Olympic Ice Rink opened in 1966 and was, until 1978, the only 400m refrigerated oval in North America; the rink, now transformed into the Pettit National Ice Center, boasts a number of notable alumnae, including the siblings Heiden and Bonnie Blair. Today, there are two 400m refrigerated rinks in the US, in Lake Placid, New York and in Butte, Montana; Canada houses another two rinks.

fact: The speedskater's body position—knees and waist bent, head lifted just enough to see down the track—is designed to reduce wind resistance. A top skater must have a least a 90-degree bend at the knee; Dan Jansen strokes through the 500m with a 78-degree bend, while short track skaters sit at a thigh-burning 70- to 75-degree angle.

Men's speedskating began as a Winter Olympic sport in 1924. Long track speedskating now features five events: 500, 1000, 1500, 5000, and 10,000 meters. The 1000m race is the newest addition for men, having been added in 1976. In 1960, women's speedskating joined the program as a full medal sport, with 500-, 1000-, 1500-, and 3000-meter races. In 1988, the Calgary Games featured the first women's Olympic 5000m race.

Short track speedskating—an exhibition event at the 1988 Games—was a full medal sport for the first time at Albertville, where a men's 1000m individual event and 5000m relay, and a women's 500m individual event and 3000m relay were added to the Winter roster. At Lillehammer, speedskaters will vie for two more short track medals: a men's 500m and a women's 1000m. Short track has been enjoying a spurt of new talent and growing popularity, and will appear this year for the first time in the Goodwill Games.

SPECTATOR'S GUIDE

With racers in their aerodynamic finery flying around the track at nearly 40 miles per hour, speedskating is the fastest an individual can move under her own power. Equipment is important to the sport. Racing skates have extra-long blades to allow for a longer glide without loss of speed; speedskate blades are half as long again as a hockey or figure skate, and are often just one thirty-second of an inch thick. The skintight speedskating uniforms, which cover the skater from head to toe in one piece, are designed to minimize wind resistance.

The skater's tuck cuts down on wind resistance, too. In a streamlined position, with her upper body virtually parallel to the ground, a skater keeps her head low and focuses down the track through the top of her eyes. Any slight imprecision in body position—elbows not streamlined against the body, head lifted a shade too high—can generate enough drag-time to separate medalists from also-rans.

The Olympics feature two distinct competitions, the long track and short track events. Held on an outdoor 400m track, **long track competition** pairs one skater against another. The shortest race—the 500m event—lasts just over 35 seconds, while the longest race—the 10,000m event—lasts about 12 lactic acid-building minutes.

Two skaters at a time compete head-to-head against the clock, and the ultimate winner is the skater with the fastest time at the end of the day. Speedskaters usually prefer to skate with the fastest skating partner possible: the faster the other person in the pair, the faster both times are likely to be.

The track features two separate lanes, with the inside lane shorter than the outside lane. Skaters race counterclockwise and must change lanes once each lap to ensure that the competitors in each race skate the same distance; a pre-race draw decides who skates first, and who starts on the inside lane. A flagman stands at the crossover point with a red and green flag and directs the leading skater to cross over first.

The start is critical to the race's outcome. Racers run on their skates, lurching toward the first turn with a furious duck walk; it isn't the most graceful expression of the sport. Some races are decided within the first 100 meters; Bonnie Blair wins her sprints in those first 100 meters.

Racing on a speedskating oval, skaters are almost constantly turning: a would-be medalist must not take more than 10 to 12 strokes between turns in order to remain competitive. A skater hits her top speed when she's coming out of a turn: as both legs stroke outward, to the right, the skater creates an inward force through the turn. Leaning into the 180-degree turns, she pivots her left leg against centripetal force (which accounts for why a speedskater's left leg is sometimes more than an inch bigger in circumference than the right leg). Coming out of the turn, this inward force translates to forward speed, and the skater slingshots out of the turn with a burst of forward momentum.

A skater who's struck the sweet spot hardly seems to be working: her movements are measured, fluid, methodical. It's poetry in motion. So what do you look for in a race? The subtle tells: are the skater's lap times consistent; is she taking a uniform number of strokes per lap; is she giving up any time by setting up a turn too late or cornering too wide? Look for signs that she's beginning to fade as her legs become leaden and her concentration wanes: she lets her elbows slip away from her back, ever so slightly; she lifts her head a little higher to see ahead; she doesn't fully extend her leg as she strokes; she grimaces.

Short track speedskating (fondly called "roller derby on ice") is held on a 111-meter indoor track and features pack races, with four to six skaters competing at the same time; skaters compete in elimination heats, quarterfinals, semifinals, and a final. Time doesn't determine winners in short track: first one across the line wins.

Short-track racers' equipment is a little different from that used by their long-track cousins. The boot, made of fiber glass, is higher cut, and the blade is offset and curved to help the skater navigate the tighter track.

Short track is highly strategic: skaters use tactics from track and cycling, including breakaways, drafting, and blocking. You may see a skater attempt to burn off the pack by charging into the lead. You may also see races that begin at an excruciatingly slow pace, where the skaters play a cat-and-mouse game to set themselves up for the gut-wrenching sprint for the finish line during the final three or four laps.

Position in the pack is important: a skater in the lead position encounters more wind resistance, while a skater at the back of the pack has more ground to cover and more obstacles to contend with.

Passing on a short track must be done cleanly and without body contact — that means no elbows to the ribs—which calls for excellent judgment and split-second timing. Judges can DQ a skater for a poorly executed pass, and a slight miscalculation can bring down a pack of skaters like so many dominoes. If the lead skater strays too far to the outside of the track markers, she leaves herself open to allow another skater to pass her on the inside. A skater wants to shave the corners as close as possible so that no one can make a pass on the inside; you'll probably see skaters touching their hands down on the inside of tight turns as they lean toward the ice.

In the relay, the four-person teams can alternate skaters any time they want, except that one person must skate the final two laps. The figurative relay baton is passed when one skater pushes—or shoves—a teammate into action. These exchanges make or break a relay; without a strong and efficient exchange, a team will lose fractions of seconds which can ultimately cost them the race. In order to maintain top speed through the exchange—which usually occurs every one and one-half to two laps—skaters must interact and communicate.

Norwegian world-champion speedskater Johann-Olav Koss claims his first Olympic gold medal in the 1500m race at Albertville. A mere .09 seconds separated the three medalists.

Men's Long Track

Lillehammer should feature a familiar cast of skaters from the class of '92. Dan Jansen, returning to the Games for his fourth go-round, has a passel of world records and titles to his name, but has yet to medal at the Olympics. Entering the Games for the second time as the hands-down fastest 500m record holder, Jansen has a good shot to medal in the 500m and 1000m events.

Igor Zhelezovski, who captured the 1993 1000m World Cup title, is considered to be one of Jansen's top rivals, now that 1992's 500m gold medalist, Jens-Uwe Mey, has retired. Chinese, Japanese, and Korean skaters also figure to make a bid for the medal podium in the shorter events; Japan's Yukinori Miyabe backed up his Olympic bronze medal with some impressive finishes in 1993, as did his compatriots Manabu Horii and Yasunori Miyabe. And South Korean Yoon-Man Kim's 1993 season proves that his 1000m silver at Albertville was no fluke.

The longer events could turn into old home week at the medals podium. Falco Zandstra, who hails from the Netherlands, topped off his 1992 Games 5000m silver medal by pocketing the 1993 Speedskating World Championship. Even more impressive, he beat out Norway's ice czar, Johann Olav Koss, who left Albertville a well-medaled man. Koss had a bad year in 1992, but, if he's healthy, should score some more precious metal on his home turf; after all, he beat his own world record in the 5000m, clocking 6:36.57 in a World Cup series final in the '93 season. Dutch skater Bart Veldkamp, who claimed both the World Cup 5000m and 10,000m titles, may have a good shot at defending his 1992 Games 10,000m title. And watch for Veldkamp's countryman, Rintje Ritsma—who enters Lillehammer as the reigning World Cup 1500m champion—to make a bid for the metric mile.

If there's one new name to remember for '94, it's Brian Smith. A freshman on the US Olympic team—he missed qualifying for the '92 Games by .100 second—the nineteen-year-old mesomorph is being touted as the Eric Heiden of generation X. In 1993, Smith turned in anything but generic performances, winning the national championships in the 1500m and 10,000m. In 1992, Smith smashed Heiden's US Junior All-Around record *and* the legendary skater's Senior Men's Short All-Around record. Granted, Heiden made history on an outdoor track while the Montana youngster skated indoors, but that doesn't take away from the fact that Smith was the first skater in thirteen years who successfully challenged the Great One's records.

Men's Short Track

The US men's team earned five spots at the 1994 Games through their performance at the 1993 Worlds in Beijing. A number of American men—

including Andy Gabel and Brian Arseneau—have posted some encouraging pre-Games results. Arseneau, you may remember, drew one of the most difficult qualifying heats in the first round of the '92 Games, and led for most of the race until he was disqualified at the end. His teammate Gable scored some points at the '94 Olympic venue, turning in a third-place 1000m finish at the 1993 Hamar Short Track Cup; earlier that season, at a short track meet at Chamonix, France, he stole first place in the 1000m from '92 Canadian medalist Freddy Blackburn. In any case, the US men's team—who came home from Albertville empty handed—will be looking forward to Lillehammer for a more positive Olympic experience.

Canadian skaters secured the maximum number of Olympic berths at Beijing, and should have a strong contingent in Norway. With two silver medals from Albertville, they could be on their way to becoming a force to be reckoned with in Olympic short track. Freddy Blackburn, the '92 silver medalist in the 1000m event, could make a bid to improve his standing, while brothers Marc and Sylvain Gagnon may vie for individual medals.

South Korean skaters, who claimed half of the Albertville short track medals, will undoubtedly stake their claim at Lillehammer. Ji-Hoon Chae—who captured an audacious win at the '93 Worlds by lapping the pack in the double metric mile (the 3000m)—could be destined for the Olympic podium if he doesn't run out of rocket fuel.

If the 1993 Worlds provide any clues to the outcome of the Lillehammer relays, New Zealand's talented team might test their mettle at Lillehammer; and don't count out the Italian team—powered by turbo-sprinter Mirko Vuillermin—who came in second at the Worlds.

The Heartbreak Kid

Dan Jansen became an Olympic star and media *cause célèbre* by not winning at the 1988 Winter Games in Calgary. Jansen went into the Games as a gold medal contender in the two shortest speedskating events, the 500 and 1000 meter races. He had placed fourth in the 500 meter race four years earlier in Sarajevo, just 0.16 seconds out of the medals. But three hours before his first race in Calgary, his sister, Jane Beres, died of leukemia. Jansen fell in both his races—an insurmountable obstacle at those distances.

One of the indelible images from 1988: Jansen skating aimlessly, head down, around and around the rink after his fall in the 500; his coach finally coming on the ice to put an arm on Jansen's shoulders and skate with him. Jansen was later given the Olympic Spirit Award.

Born June 17, 1965, in Milwaukee, Jansen was the youngest child in a family of nine. His brother, Mike, is a former world-class speedskater. In 1987, Jansen suffered from mononucleosis, but still finished third in the World Cup 500m and 1000m races. Because of that illness, too, it was decided that Jansen could not be a bone marrow donor for his sister, something Jansen had been willing to sacrifice his career for.

Dan Jansen skates a heavy-legged 1000m at Albertville. Jansen failed to medal at both the 1988 and 1992 Games, but has a good shot at the podium in 1994.

In 1988, though, separate from his Olympic spills, Jansen had already become World Sprint Champion, which he won in Milwaukee. But the next three years brought a string of fourth-place finishes at the World Sprint Championships. He won the overall men's title at the 1990 US International Speedskating Association, even though he skated with frostbitten toes.

Now gearing up for Lillehammer, Jansen has a good chance to medal in the 500m and 1000m events. Three weeks before the Albertville Games, Jansen broke the 500m world record which had been set at the Calgary Games by Germany's gold medalist Jens-Uwe Mey; Mey nonetheless prevailed at Albertville, where Japanese sprinters relegated Jansen to a fourth-place finish. Just over a year later, in Calgary, Jansen bettered his world record by .39 seconds, with a blistering time of 36.02 seconds.

Jansen's 500m resume is intimidating: he's a three-time world champion in the event, and he's run away with the US National Sprint title since 1990. Jansen had a promising season in 1993: At the World Cup Sprint in Baselgia Di Pine, Italy, Jansen captured the 500m title with a time of 36.63 seconds, and placed second behind Belarus's Igor Zhelezovski in the 1000m. And he was crowned 1992–93 500m champion of the seven-event World Cup competition. With Lillehammer's optimal ice conditions, and with a strong year behind him, D.J. stands to take some well-deserved medals home from the Games. —H.D.

Women's Long Track

Bonnie Blair will be looking to skate away with more gold medals and Olympic firsts, but Chinese skater Ye Qiaobo has her eye on the next step of the podium. Losing by a *combined* time of five hundredths of a second, Qiaobo settled for silver medals in the 500m and 1000m at Albertville. Preparing for the '92 Games, the Chinese skater made a study of Blair's near-perfect form, watching hours of videotapes of the Bonnie skating. She's an excellent student: since the 1992 Games, Qiaobo has edged out Blair in some major competitions. While Blair captured the 1000m World Cup title, Qiaobo slipped by her in the 500m in both the World Cup Championship and in the World Sprint Championship.

The shorter distance women's races at Lillehammer should be, in a word, awesome. Blair will be gunning for a three-peat, and may be shooting to break the 39-second barrier in the 500m as well. Qiaobo is a *very* motivated woman. And the indoor Hamar rink is the stuff that speedskating records are made of. There's no sure winner, but one thing is sure: it's gonna be fast.

The longer races at Lillehammer may give viewers a serious case of *déjà vu*. Germany's *ueber-fraulein* Gunda Niemann is once again the prohibitive favorite: after skating away from Albertville with two gold and one silver, she struck it rich at the 1992–93 World Cup Championships, capturing the 1500m, 3000m, and 5000m titles. Niemann's World Cup sweep was no surprise: in the first race of the series, she scalded the competition in the 1500m, winning by a two-second margin. When Gunda wins, Gunda wins big.

Germany's Heike Warnicke and Austria's Emese Hunyady—both of whom took home precious medals from Albertville—have posted some impressive World Cup standings since the 1992 Games, and may make another bid for the medals podium. Also showing promise in the longer distance events are Svetlana Bashanova of Russia and Hihaela Dascalu from Romania.

Women's Short Track

US women could strike gold again at the '94 Games, especially since 1992 500m gold medalist Cathy Turner has decided to take a sabbatical from her singing/acting/Ice Capading career in order to compete. Amy Peterson, who was on the 1992 silver medal relay team, shows a lot of promise in the individual sprints, having scored a silver in the 1000m and a gold in the 1500m events at the 1993 World Winter University Games in Poland. With a women's 1000m event added to the Lillehammer program, Peterson should have a good shot at an individual spot on the podium.

Having garnered its tenth-straight relay victory at the '93 Worlds, the Canadian team—which qualified the maximum number of skaters for the Games—will be aiming to defend their Olympic relay title at Lillehammer. If Nathalie Lambert skates at the Hamar ice rink, she could be hard to beat in the 1000m, one of her favorite races. Twelve years on the national team, Lambert—who captured the 1000m and 1500m titles at the '93 Worlds—has both power and speed, and is an outstanding tactician.

The Chinese women's team will doubtless be looking to Lillehammer to put Albertville out of their minds. Leading the women's relay in the semifinals at the '92 Games, the Chinese team suffered an untimely fall that prevented them from proceeding to the finals. At the '93 Worlds, China's relay team came in just behind the Canadian women, while Yanmei Zhang—who holds the 500m world record on the short track—captured the 500m title.

Bonnie Blair

"She is the best pure skater in the world, man or woman," boasts Peter Mueller, the US coach. Mueller may be biased, but the stopwatch isn't. Blair's resume consists of a litany of American records, world records, and Olympic firsts: her world-record 500m time, set at the Calgary Games, still stands; she holds the American records in the 500m, the 1000m, and the 1500m, and she holds the American women's record for Samalog points; she's tied with Dianne Holum, a former speedskater and Olympic coach, for being the most-medaled American female Winter Olympian. And the list continues to grow.

After placing eighth in the 500m event in the 1984 Olympics, Blair twice mounted the podium at Calgary, capturing the 500m gold and the 1000m bronze. In 1989 she won the World Sprint Championships, and at the following year's World Cup tournaments, she tied for first in the 500m event, won a silver in the 1000m, and placed fourth in the 1500m. Blair entered the Albertville Games having led the US Sprint Championships for seven consecutive years; and she had won a medal in nearly every international race she entered in 1991, including golds in about half of her 500m races.

At Albertville, she made history: the United States' only returning gold medalist, Blair became the first athlete from any country to win back-to-back 500s. Capturing the 1000m title as well, she became one of only two American athletes to medal twice in '92, pocketing more Winter gold medals than any other American woman. The only event to have eluded Bonnie's grasp was the 1500m. Abandoning her bid for a metric mile medal when it became clear she wouldn't win, Blair finished twenty-one places back in the pack.

"Champaign's favorite speeder" Bonnie Blair emotes effusively after setting a new world record for the women's 500m at the Calgary Games. Blair's time of 39.10 won her the gold medal.

Since the Albertville Games, The Corn Flakes cover girl has enjoyed tremendous celebrity (for a speedskater), skating over ice-filled NBC hallways on "Late Night with David Letterman" and drafting a van-full of hungry relatives for a McDonald's commercial. After winning the 1992 Sullivan Award (for the nation's top amateur athlete), Blair, who had four times been a finalist for the honor and apparently is not jaded by her growing coffer of awards, gushed, "I guess to win such an award is kind of beyond words." Only two other Winter Olympians—Dick Button and Eric Heiden—have landed a Sullivan, and Blair went up against some pretty stiff competition, including Kristi Yamaguchi. Blair also collected the USOC Woman Athlete of the Year award, making her the first speedskater to be so honored. But Blair's 1992 Oscar—given by a Norwegian group to the best speedskater in the world—is one of her most prized awards. The reason: Eric Heiden is the only other American to have captured a Norwegian Oscar.

In the 1993 season, Blair suffered some injuries and a serious case of role reversal in the 500m sprint—having been beaten in a few choice events by her Chinese nemesis Ye Qiaobo—but she's still in top form. Says the indomitable B-woman, "I figure as long as I'm still enjoying it and I'm able to keep on doing it, I'll do it."

And she could really do it right at Lillehammer. Should Blair successfully defend her 500m title, she'll be the first American athlete in any Olympics to win a gold medal in the same event in three consecutive Games. If she manages to grab a 1500m medallion in '94, she'll be the first American woman to medal in the event since Sheila Young captured a silver in 1976. And if conditions are right, this could be the year for Blair to break the women's 39-second barrier in the 500m. —*M.J.M.*

Cathy Turner

Just after winning the first-ever women's short track 500m gold medal, Cathy Turner revealed, "When I went into the last race, I was thinking that if I won a gold medal, I wouldn't have to skate again. And I won the gold medal, so...." A year and some months later, following a stint in the Ice Capades and a Hawaiian honeymoon, Turner sang a different tune, announcing her decision to take a break from her singing/songwriting/figure-skating/movie-starring career to prospect for more Olympic gold. Why? "Because I can," said the 5'2" Renaissance gal.

Post-Games fame, it seems, wasn't all it was cracked up to be, even though Turner was talking up book and movie contracts as soon as she skated off the Olympic oval. Although the sometime show girl did attract some endorsements and appearances—*and* she competed on "American Gladiators"—the million-dollar contracts weren't dropping at her doorstep. "It just doesn't happen," Turner lamented about post-Games fame and fortune. "I've been kind of disappointed."

255

US speedskater Cathy Turner revels in Old Glory after winning the first-ever gold medal in the women's 500m short-track event.

Turner's Olympic comeback story is the stuff that network broadcasters dream of: after an eight-year hiatus from the sport, and almost thirty years old, Turner, inspired by an article about Olympic speedskater/cyclist Connie Paraskevin-Young, decided to put her singing career on a back burner in order to lace up for the '92 Games. In speedskaters' lingo, "comeback" usually means a return to Olympic competition after a season or two of training like an animal in anonymity. Niki Newland, however—Turner's stage incarnation—hadn't been on skates in years, nor had she ever been an Olympian. But she did have plenty of moxie: "No matter what," she said of the long road to recovering her form, "I wasn't going to quit. I found myself. I was so happy. It was like coming home. No matter what, I was going to make it happen."

Turner made a lot of things happen. En route to Albertville, she became the top US performer at the World Championships, and was the American record-holder in both the 500m and the 1000m. And at Albertville, she definitely turned some heads. She, along with Bonnie Blair, was one of the only US athletes to return home with double medals. Turner, it seems, was no stranger to Blair, having trained with her at the West Allis oval in the late '70s, when the songstress was still dreaming of long-track fame.

Turner announced her decision to compete in the 1994 Games with only eight months to spare, even though her post-Albertville training hadn't exactly been kosher. Skating double salchows and axels in the Ice Capades may not be the typical speedskater's pre-Games regimen, but it's hard to argue with success. Turner's ballad, "Sexy, Kinky Tomboy," may never hit platinum, but if she has anything to say about it, they'll be singing her song at Lillehammer. —*M.J.M.*

Speedskating

Schedule

The tentative long track speedskating schedule is as follows:

Sunday, February 13
5,000m, men

Monday, February 14
500m, men

Wednesday, February 16
1,500m, men

Thursday, February 17
3,000m, women

Friday, February 18
1,000m, men

Saturday, February 19
500m, women

Sunday, February 20
10,000m, men

Monday, February 21
1,500m, women

Wednesday, February 23
1,000m, women

Friday, February 25
5,000m, women

The tentative short track speedskating schedule is as follows:

Tuesday, February 22
Finals, men and women

Saturday, February 26
Finals, men and women

Thursday, February 24
Finals, men and women

MEN'S SPEEDSKATING EVENTS

▼

HIGHLIGHTS

Speedskating was one of the original sports at the first Winter Games in 1924. Winning the 500m event, American Charles Jewtraw captured the first gold medal in speedskating; it was the first gold medal of the Winter Games. Finland collected the other three speedskating gold medals in 1924 as Clas Thunberg won both the 1500m and the 5000m and earned a silver behind compatriot Julius Skutnabb in the 10,000m; Skutnabb took a silver in the 5000m in 1924 and 1928. A 35-year-old Thunberg came back in 1928 to capture two more golds, tying with Norwegian Bernt Evensen in the 500m and successfully defending his title in the 1500m. Another Norwegian, Ivar Ballangrud, won the 5000m gold and the 1500m silver.

The 1932 Lake Placid Games were the only Olympics in which the American system of pack racing was allowed (until short track arrived); the European skaters were obviously disoriented. On the home ice, the US squad made a clean sweep; Irving Jaffee won the 5000m and the 10,000m, John Shea took the 500m and the 1500m, and Edward Murphy earned a silver in the 5000m. Frank Stack of Canada delivered the performance of his life in 1932, winning the bronze in the 10,000m; Stack continued to compete in Olympic speedskating for the next 20 years, finishing 12th in the 500m in 1952 at age 46.

Norwegian Ivar Ballangrud, one of the great skaters of all time, had to settle for a single silver in the 10,000 in 1932, but came back strong in 1936, his third Olympics, to become the first triple crown winner. He took the gold in the 500m, the 5000m, and the 10,000m, missing his bid for a Grand Slam when he placed second to compatriot Charles Mathisen in the 1500m. Norway and Sweden shared the next six consecutive 10,000m wins. In 1948 the speedskating golds went to three Norwegians and one Swede. Norwegian truck driver Hjalmar Andersen became the second triple crown winner in 1952, taking the gold in the 1500m, 5000m, and 10,000m. US skaters Kenneth Henry and Donald McDermott placed 1–2 in the 500m event.

Powerful skaters from the Soviet Union arrived in 1956, as Yevgeny Grishin won the 500m and tied with compatriot Yuri Mikhailov in the 1500m, and Boris Shilkov took the 5000m. The 10,000m went to Sigvard Ericsson of Sweden, just ahead of Norway's Knut Johannesen. Soviet skaters came back in full force in 1960: Grishin successfully defended his 500m crown and tied with Norway's Roald Aas in the 1500m, while Viktor Kosichkin claimed the 5000m. Johannesen captured the 10,000m, an event he'd silvered in at Cortina. Four years later the Norwegian led a surprise 1–2–3 sweep for his country in the 5000m, but Sweden's Jonny Nilsson defeated Johannesen in the 10,000 at Innsbruck.

fact: On ice that's too cold, gliding is impeded because the skateblade's friction can't create enough of that thin layer of water that makes skating possible; ice that's too warm allows too much water to form, and the resulting water resistance cuts down speed.

US men captured a gold medal in 1964 when Richard "Terry" McDermott, a barber from Flint, Michigan, scored an upset over veteran defending champion Grishin in the 500m. McDermott added a silver in 1968, losing his 500m title to Erhard Keller of West Germany, having drawn a poor position on rapidly deteriorating ice. Keller said he felt McDermott would have won the event if he'd skated earlier when the ice was still good, but the German retained his title in the 500m in 1972.

Sapporo's 1972 Games belonged to Ard Schenk of the Netherlands, who became another triple gold winner with victories in the 1500m, the 5000m, and the 10,000m; Schenk's win in the latter event ended the Scandinavian stranglehold on the 10,000m gold. At the 1976 Games a new men's distance was added, the 1000m, and US skater Peter Mueller (now coach of the US team) took the event's first gold; his teammate Dan Immerfall was a surprise bronze medalist in the 500m. Norway claimed two gold medals in 1976, in the 1500m and the 5000m, while the Soviets claimed a 500m victory and the 10,000m again went to the Netherlands.

When US speedskater Eric Heiden—coached by former US champion Dianne Holum—swept all five men's events in 1980, he was the only competitor ever to win five individual golds at a single Olympics (swimmer Mark Spitz's seven golds in 1972 included three relay medals). He started off by winning his weakest event, the 500m, then added the 5000m, and the 1000m; then he ran away with the 1500m, winning by almost a second and a half, even though he had lost his balance at one point. Finally, in the grueling 10,000m race, 25 laps around the track, Heiden claimed his fifth gold. Canada's Gaétan Boucher won a silver in 1980, then added two golds and a bronze in 1984, making him the most

Men's 10,000m speedskating gold medalist Bart Veldkamp of the Netherlands, center, joins silver medalist Johann Olav Koss and bronze medalist Geir Karlstad, both from Norway, on the Albertville podium. Veldkamp ended a 16-year medal drought for the Dutch in men's speedskating.

bemedaled Canadian Winter Olympian ever. Igor Malkov was only 19 in 1984 when he won the 10,000m event.

fact: The US Long Track Speedskating Team still reigns among the world's elite, as evidenced by its 26 Olympic medals in the last six Winter Games; 21 individual World Champions the past two decades; and 11 World Cup champions the past six years.

The US cherished high hopes for its men's speedskating team in 1988, but tragedy and illness took out favorites Dan Jansen and Nick Thometz (who is now the assistant national team coach). Only Eric Flaim was able to medal, taking a silver in the 1500m race. East German Jens-Uwe Mey captured the gold in the 500m and silver in the 1000m. Mey's 500m medal was the first gold the East German men's speedskating team had ever won; as politics would have it, it was also the last (Mey defended his title in 1992 as a member of a unified German team). In the 5000m and 10,000m events, Swedish skater Sven Tomas Gustafson captured the gold.

Only Canada's Nathalie Lambert remains standing as Cathy Turner from the US, Karine Rubini from France, and Japan's Nobuko Yamada collide during the quarter-final round of the women's 500m short track speedskating event at Albertville.

Albertville Highlights

Every one—including D.J.—had high hopes for Dan Jansen at Albertville. Only three weeks before the Games, in Davos, Switzerland, Jansen had reestablished the world record for the 500m; Jansen's scorching time of 36.41 bettered German Jens-Uwe Mey's Olympic and world record time (set on Calgary's record-inspiring ice) by .04 seconds. (Compare that to Eric Heiden's Olympic record-setting 500m time in 1980 of 38.03.) No one doubted Jansen's ability—his 500m record established him as the fastest sprinter of all time—but fate hadn't been inclined to treat him kindly at the Games. Jansen's tragic disappointment at Calgary was not entirely behind him: the press doggedly portrayed the '92 Games as Jansen's chance to "redeem" himself (as if heartbreak required redemption, and world titles weren't adequate accomplishment).

A few days before his first event, Jansen woke up with a debilitating neck cramp that kept him from practice. During the competition, the ice of the outdoor rink was subjected to spring-like rains and sunshine; the Albertville ice didn't favor record-breaking, nor did it favor power skaters such as Jansen. Skating in the second pairing of the 500m, Jansen watched as Jens-Uwe Mey bettered his time by .32 seconds; Mey, who was the 500m champion in Calgary, had won 31 out of 42 500m races during the four years preceding Albertville. Placing second and third were two relatively unknown Japanese skaters—Toshiyuki Kuroiwa and Junichi Inoue, respectively—whose quick-stroking style fared well on the Albertville ice.

In the longer distance races, Bart Veldkamp's 10,000m win captured the first Dutch speedskating gold since Piet Kleine was victorious in 1976. Norwegian Johann Olav Koss, who held the 10,000m record, came in three seconds behind Veldcamp to capture the silver, and later added a 1500m gold to his haul.

On the short track, the South Koreans dominated. Joon-Ho Lee set a world record in the 1000m semifinal, only to be bested by teammate Ki-Hoon Kim's gold-medal time. Canadian Freddy Blackburn settled for a silver medal, while Wilf O'Reilly—who was Calgary's champion in both demonstration distances *and* was the 1991 world champion—saw his hopes of a medal slip away when he fell in the sixth lap. In the 5,000m relay, the Korean team won a photo finish when Ki-Hoon Kim threw himself across the finish line just ahead of Canadian Michel Daignault. The British team, who held the previous year's World Championship gold and silver medals, were out of the medals, while the Japanese team skated away with the bronze.

The Heidens

Asked to name the most memorable incident of the 1980 Winter Olympics in Lake Placid, most Americans would probably recall the thrilling Soviet-toppling gold-medal performance by the young US hockey team. Coming in a close second, however, would be the performance of a quietly determined young speedskater from West Allis, Wisconsin, by the name of Eric Heiden.

But while the hockey victory was certainly dramatic, sports historians now agree that Heiden's performance was one of the greatest individual feats in Olympics history. "Perhaps the most vivid single image of the 1980 Winter Games," declared *Time* magazine, "was the sight of Eric Heiden's heroically muscled thighs molded in a skating skin of gold as he stroked his way to five Olympic golds, five Olympic records and one world record."

fact: When he was competing, Eric Heiden boasted a 32-inch waist and 29-inch thighs.

Such tributes were common for Heiden that winter's fortnight, but the jubilation he felt must have been tempered somewhat by the fate of his feisty speedskating sister, Beth, whose seventh, fifth, seventh, and third-place finishes in four events that same Olympiad were treated as a failure by an overzealous press, which had unreasonably projected her as a gold-medal winner as well. Still, Beth skated away from Lake Placid with one bronze medal, and by the mid-1980s this determined, multi-talented athlete had added a 1980 world bicycling championship and an NCAA cross-country skiing championship to her impressive trophy case.

Surely, the Heiden siblings are a duo who have always enjoyed new challenges. While they were growing up, Eric maintains, it was in fact Beth who provided the impetus to get him involved in speedskating. "There was many a time when Beth wanted to hit the ice, and I'd say, 'Aw, let's forget it today,'" Eric recalls. "But her tenacity would get the better of me—and that's what made the difference between success and failure." Like most kids from the northern Midwest, Eric played hockey as a boy and Beth was a figure skater, but by the time they reached adolescence both began to concentrate fully on speedskating.

Also arriving on the scene around that time was Dianne Holum, a 1972 gold medal winner-turned-University of Wisconsin student, who took a job coaching at the local speedskating club where the Heidens practiced. Quickly determining that Beth and Eric were serious about the sport, Holum put them on a rigorous training program that included bicycling, weightlifting, duck-walking for miles, and, of course, hours on the ice. While the regimen added a strong upper body and tree-like thighs to Eric's perfectly suited 6'1", 185-pound frame, the pint-sized Beth soon reached her physical limitations and so began to concentrate doubly hard on her technique and determination. In a sport dominated by Soviets and Europeans, the Heidens were an instant curiosity when they began competing in—and winning—international events, especially when Eric captured his first world championship at the age of 18.

"Americans had never thought they had the ability to win a world [speedskating] title," Holum said, "but Eric has shown them the way." In 1979, skating against women far bigger and stronger, Beth followed with her first world championship by adding an equal dose of guts to her flawlessly executed striding technique.

Thus, when the Heidens prepared to skate before their countrymen at the 1980 Winter Games, expectations were high that both would skate away with pockets full of gold. Eric by that time had been dominating men's speedskating for three years, rarely losing a race, and Beth was fresh from her world title a year previous. But what skating insiders knew at the time—and the press did not bother to understand—was that Beth's world championship had been based on *overall* performance in four events. At the Olympics, each event is awarded separately, and while Beth was excellent in all four, she was not particularly dominant in any. At Lake Placid she did take third in the 3,000 meter race, and indeed her overall performance was the best at the Games.

But when some members of the press chided her for not keeping pace with Eric, Beth, who was also skating on an injured ankle she told no one about, broke down. "I'm happiest when I skate for myself," she said, "but this year I have to skate for the press. The hell with you guys."

But expectations were surely not lost on Eric, who skated whole seconds off of world and Olympic record times in a sport where hundredths of a second can mean the difference between a champion and an also-ran. From the shortest

At the 1980 Lake Placid Games, Eric Heiden sports his five speedskating gold medals. Heiden's medal sweep inspired the Norwegian coach to say, "We just hope he retires."

Beth Heiden—pictured here winning a 500m event at Lake Placid in 1978—captured the bronze medal in the 3000m event at the 1980 Games.

sprints to the longest endurance races, at 500m, 1000m, 1500m, 5000m and 10,000m, Heiden dominated other racers, many of whom had prepared solely for one of the events. Comparing his feat to running helps to put Heiden's performance in perspective—it would be like the world's best sprinter turning around in two days and winning the marathon.

"In Norway, we say that if you can be good in the 5000 and 10,000, you can't do the 500," said Norwegian coach Sten Stenson at the time. "But Eric can do it. We have no idea how to train to take him. We just hope he retires."

Shortly after Heiden's gold-medal haul, Stenson received his wish. A private, intelligent 21 year old, Heiden looked forward to eschewing the media spotlight and returning to his original dream of becoming an orthopedic surgeon like his father. Beth, too, moved on to new challenges. Having trained extensively on a bicycle to complement her skating, Beth won a world championship in the sport in 1980. After becoming an honors physics student at the University of Vermont in the early 1980s, Beth took up cross-country skiing on a whim and soon found herself winning the NCAA championship in the 7.5km event. She later helped to develop extensive cross-country facilities in Michigan's Upper Peninsula.

Eric also took up competitive cycling after Lake Placid, but he found the going much rougher in his new sport. Although he was teased as being too big and clumsy to handle the fleet, lightweight cycles, Heiden did manage to muscle out a victory in the United States pro cycling championship in 1985. In 1986 he participated in the Tour de France, cycling's most prestigious event, and between semesters of pre-med study Heiden found time to provide television commentary for Olympic speedskating coverage.

But for a man who could easily have turned his Lake Placid gold medals into hard endorsement cash, Heiden has remained true to the spirit of amateur sport and did not exploit his incredible 1980 accomplishments. He passed on movie deals and an offer to record a song, and at age 28 entered Stanford Medical School. In 1991 Heiden graduated and began his residency as an orthopedic surgeon.

Throughout their stellar athletic and academic careers, both Eric and Beth Heiden have remained happy because they have never rested on their laurels. "We're not looking for money," Eric told a fawning media, as he said goodbye to that magical Lake Placid winter. "For me, next year will be a time to try things I've never done. I don't just skate and turn left. Sports aren't everything." —D.C.

Medalists

Long Track Speedskating—Men's 500m

1992
1. Jens-Uwe Mey, Germany, 37.14
2. Toshiyuki Kuroiwa, Japan, 37.18
3. Junichi Inoue, Japan, 37.26

1988
1. Jens-Uwe Mey, East Germany, 36.45 (WR,OR)
2. Jan Ykema, Netherlands, 36.76
3. Akira Kuroiwa, Japan, 36.77

1984
1. Sergei Fokitchev, Soviet Union, 38.19
2. Yoshihiro Kitazawa, Japan, 38.30
3. Gaétan Boucher, Canada, 38.39

1980
1. Eric Heiden, USA, 38.03 (OR)
2. Yevgeny Kulikov, Soviet Union, 38.37
3. Lieuwe De Boer, Holland, 38.48

1976
1. Yevgeny Kulikov, Soviet Union, 39.17 (OR)
2. Valery Muratov, Soviet Union, 39.25
3. Dan Immerfall, USA, 39.54

1972
1. Erhard Keller, West Germany, 39.44 (OR)
2. Hasse Borjes, Sweden, 39.69
3. Valery Muratov, Soviet Union, 39.80

1968
1. Erhard Keller, West Germany, 40.3
2. Richard McDermott, USA, 40.5
2. Magne Thomassen, Norway, 40.5

1964
1. Richard McDermott, USA, 40.1 (OR)
2. Alv Gjestvang, Norway, 40.6
2. Yevgeny Grishin, Soviet Union, 40.6
2. Vladimir Orlov, Soviet Union, 40.6

1960
1. Yevgeny Grishin, Soviet Union, 40.2 (EWR)
2. William Disney, USA, 40.3
3. Rafael Gratch, Soviet Union, 40.4

1956
1. Yevgeny Grishin, Soviet Union, 40.2 (EWR)
2. Rafael Gratch, Soviet Union, 40.8
3. Alv Gjestvang, Norway, 41.0

1952
1. Kenneth Henry, USA, 43.2
2. Donald McDermott, USA, 43.9

3. Gordon Audley, Canada, 44.0
3. Arne Johansen, Norway, 44.0
1948 1. Finn Helgesen, Norway, 43.1 (OR)
2. Kenneth Bartholomew, USA, 43.2
2. Thomas Byberg, Norway, 43.2
2. Robert Fitzgerald, USA, 43.2
1936 1. Ivar Ballangrud, Norway, 43.4 (EOR)
2. Georg Krog, Norway, 43.5
3. Leo Freisinger, USA, 44.0
1932 1. John A. Shea, USA, 43.4
2. Bernt Evensen, Norway
3. Alexander Hurt, Canada
1928 1. Bernt Evensen, Norway, 43.4 (OR)
1. Clas Thunberg, Finland, 43.4 (OR)
3. John O'Neil Farrell, USA, 43.6
3. Jaakko Friman, Finland, 43.6
3. Roald Larsen, Norway, 43.6
1924 1. Charles Jewtraw, USA, 44.0
2. Oskar Olsen, Norway, 44.2
3. Roald Larsen, Norway, 44.8
3. Clas Thunberg, Finland, 44.8

Long Track Speedskating—Men's 1,000m

1992 1. Olaf Zinke, Germany, 1:14.85
2. Yoon-Man Kim, Korea, 1:14.86
3. Yasunori Miyabe, Japan, 1:14.92
1988 1. Nikolai Gouliaev, Soviet Union, 1:13.03 (OR)
2. Jens-Uwe Mey, East Germany, 1:13.11
3. Igor Zhelezovsky, Soviet Union, 1:13.19
1984 1. Gaétan Boucher, Canada, 1:15.80
2. Sergei Khlebnikov, Soviet Union, 1:16.63
3. Kai Arne Engelstad, Norway, 1:16.75
1980 1. Eric Heiden, USA, 1:15.18 (OR)
2. Gaetan Boucher, Canada, 1:16.68
3. Vladimir Lobanov, Soviet Union, 1:16.91
1976 1. Peter Mueller, USA, 1:19.32 (OR)
2. Jorn Didriksen, Norway, 1:20.45
3. Valery Muratov, Soviet Union, 1:20.57

Long Track Speedskating—Men's 1,500m

1992 1. Johann Koss, Norway, 1:54.81
2. Adne Sondral, Norway, 1:54.85
3. Leo Visser, Netherlands, 11:54.90
1988 1. Andre Hoffmann, East Germany, 1:52.06 (WR,OR)
2. Eric Flaim, USA, 1:52.12
3. Michael Hadschieff, Austria, 1:52.31
1984 1. Gaétan Boucher, Canada, 1:58.36
2. Sergei Khlebnikov, Soviet Union, 1:58.83
3. Oleg Bogiev, Soviet Union, 1:58.89
1980 1. Eric Heiden, USA, 1:55.44 (OR)
2. Kai Arne Stenshjemmet, Norway, 1:56.81
3. Terje Andersen, Norway, 1:56.92
1976 1. Jan-Egil Storholt, Norway, 1:59.38 (OR)
2. Yuri Kondakov, Soviet Union, 1:59.97

3. Hans Van Helden, Netherlands, 2:00.87
1972 1. Ard Schenk, Netherlands, 2:02.96 (OR)
2. Roar Gronvold, Norway, 2:04.26
3. Goran Claeson, Sweden, 2:05.89
1968 1. Cornelis Verkerk, Netherlands, 2:03.4 (OR)
2. Ivar Eriksen, Norway, 2:05.0
2. Ard Schenk, Netherlands, 2:05.0
1964 1. Ants Antson, Soviet Union, 2:10.3
2. Cornelis Verkerk, Netherlands, 2:10.6
3. Villy Haugen, Norway, 2:11.2
1960 1. Roald Aas, Norway, 2:10.4
1. Yevgeny Grishin, Soviet Union, 2:10.4
3. Boris Stenin, Soviet Union, 2:11.5
1956 1. Yevgeny Grishin, Soviet Union, 2:08.6 (WR)
1. Yuri Mikailov, Soviet Union, 2:08.6 (WR)
3. Toivo Salonen, Finland, 2:09.4
1952 1. Hjalmar Andersen, Norway, 2:20.4
2. Willem van der Voort, Netherlands, 2:20.6
3. Roald Aas, Norway, 2:21.6
1948 1. Sverre Farstad, Norway, 2:17.6 (OR)
2. Ake Seyffarth, Sweden, 2:18.1
3. Odd Lundberg, Norway, 2:18.9
1936 1. Charles Mathiesen, Norway, 2:19.2 (OR)
2. Ivar Ballangrud, Norway, 2:20.2
3. Birger Wasenius, Finland, 2:20.9
1932 1. John A. Shea, USA, 2:57.5
2. Alexander Hurd, Canada
3. William F. Logan, Canada
1928 1. Clas Thunberg, Finland, 2:21.1
2. Bernt Evensen, Norway, 2:21.9
3. Ivar Ballangrud, Norway, 2:22.6
1924 1. Clas Thunberg, Finland, 2:20.8
2. Roald Larsen, Norway, 2:22.0
3. Sigurd Moen, Norway, 2:25.6

Long Track Speedskating—Men's 5,000m

1992 1. Geir Karlstad, Norway, 6:59.97
2. Falco Zandstra, Netherlands, 7:02.28
3. Leo Visser, Netherlands, 7:04.96
1988 1. Sven Tomas Gustafson, Sweden, 6:44.63 (WR,OR)
2. Leo Visser, Netherlands, 6:44.98
3. Gerard Kemkers, Netherlands, 6:45.92
1984 1. Sven Tomas Gustafson, Sweden, 7:12.38
2. Igor Malkov, Soviet Union, 7:12.30
3. Rene Schoefisch, East Germany, 7:17.49
1980 1. Eric Heiden, USA, 7:02.29 (OR)
2. Kai Arne Stenshjemmet, Norway, 7:03.28
3. Tom Erik Oxholm, Norway, 7:05.59
1976 1. Sten Stensen, Norway, 7:24.48
2. Piet Kleine, Netherlands, 7:26.47
3. Hans Van Helden, Netherlands, 7:26.54
1972 1. Ard Schenk, Netherlands, 7:23.61
2. Roar Gronvold, Norway, 7:28.18
3. Sten Stensen, Norway, 7:33.39
1968 1. Fred Anton Maier, Norway, 7:22.4 (WR)

2. Cornelis Verkerk, Netherlands, 7:23.2
3. Petrus Nottet, Netherlands, 7:25.5
1964 1. Knut Johannesen, Norway, 7:38.4
(OR)
2. Per Ivar Moe, Norway, 7:38.6
3. Fred Anton Maier, Norway, 7:42.0
1960 1. Viktor Kosichkin, Soviet Union, 7:51.3
2. Knut Johannesen, Norway, 8:00.8
3. Jan Pesman, Netherlands, 8:05.1
1956 1. Boris Shilkov, Soviet Union, 7:48.7
(OR)
2. Sigvard Ericsson, Sweden, 7:56.7
3. Oleg Goncharenko, Soviet Union,
7:57.5
1952 1. Hjalmar Andersen, Norway, 8:10.6
(OR)
2. Kees Broekman, Netherlands, 8:21.6
3. Sverre Haugli, Norway, 8:22.4
1948 1. Reidar Liaklev, Norway, 8:29.4
2. Odd Lundberg, Norway, 8:32.7
3. Gothe Hedlund, Sweden, 8:34.8
1936 1. Ivar Ballangrud, Norway, 8:19.6 (OR)
2. Birger Wasenius, Finland, 8:23.3
3. Antero Ojala, Finland, 8:30.1
1932 1. Irving Jaffee, USA, 9:40.8
2. Edward S. Murphy, USA
3. William F. Logan, Canada
1928 1. Ivar Ballangrud, Norway, 8:50.5
2. Julius Skutnabb, Finland, 8:59.1
3. Bernt Evensen, Norway, 9:01.1
1924 1. Clas Thunberg, Finland, 8:39.0
2. Julius Skutnabb, Finland, 8:48.4
3. Roald Larsen, Norway, 8:50.2

Long Track Speedskating—Men's 10,000m

1992 1. Bart Veldkamp, Netherlands, 14:12.12
2. Johann Koss, Norway, 14:14.58
3. Geir Karlstad, Norway, 14:18.13
1988 1. Sven Tomas Gustafson, Sweden,
13:48.20 (WR,OR)
2. Michael Hadschieff, Austria, 13:56.11
3. Leo Visser, Netherlands, 14:00.55
1984 1. Igor Malkov, Soviet Union, 14:39.90
2. Sven Tomas Gustafson, Sweden,
14:39.95
3. Rene Schoefisch, East Germany,
14:46.91
1980 1. Eric Heiden, USA, 14:28.13 (OR,WR)
2. Piet Kleine, Netherlands, 14:36.03
3. Tom Erik Oxholm, Norway, 14:36.60
1976 1. Piet Kleine, Netherlands, 14:50.59
(OR)
2. Sten Stensen, Norway, 14:53.30

3. Hans Van Helden, Netherlands,
15:02.02
1972 1. Ard Schenk, Netherlands, 15:01.35
(OR)
2. Cornelis Verkerk, Netherlands,
15:04.70
3. Sten Stensen, Norway, 15:07.08
1968 1. Johnny Hoglin, Sweden, 15:23.6 (OR)
2. Fred Anton Maier, Norway, 15:23.9
3. Orjan Sandler, Sweden, 15:31.8
1964 1. Jonny Nilsson, Sweden, 15:50.1
2. Fred Anton Maier, Norway, 16:06.0
3. Knut Johannesen, Norway, 16:06.3
1960 1. Knut Johannesen, Norway, 15:46.6
(WR)
2. Viktor Kosichkin, Soviet Union, 15:49.2
3. Kjell Backman, Sweden, 16:14.2
1956 1. Sigvard Ericsson, Sweden, 16:35.9
(OR)
2. Knut Johannesen, Norway, 16:36.9
3. Oleg Goncharenko, Soviet Union,
16:42.3
1952 1. Hjalmar Andersen, Norway, 16:45.8
(OR)
2. Kees Broekman, Netherlands, 17:10.6
3. Carl-Erik Asplund, Sweden, 17:16.6
1948 1. Ake Seyffarth, Sweden, 17:26.3
2. Lauri Parkkinen, Finland, 17:36.0
3. Pentti Lammio, Finland, 17:42.7
1936 1. Ivar Ballangrud, Norway, 17:24.3 (OR)
2. Birger Wasenius, Finland, 17:28.2
3. Max Stiepl, Austria, 17:30.0
1932 1. Irving Jaffee, USA, 19:13.6
2. Ivar Ballangrud, Norway
3. Frank Stack, Canada
1928 Event called off in the fifth race because
of the bad condition of the ice.
1924 1. Julius Skutnabb, Finland, 18:04.8
2. Clas Thunberg, Finland, 18:07.8
3. Roald Larsen, Norway, 18:12.2

Short Track Speedskating— Men's 1,000m

1992 1. Ki-Hoon Kim, Korea, 1:30.76
2. Frederic Blackburn, Canada, 1:31.11
3. Joon-Ho Lee, Korea, 1:31.16

Short Track Speedskating— Men's 5km Relay

1992 1. Korea, 7:14.02
2. Canada, 7:14.06
3. Japan, 7:18.18

WOMEN'S SPEEDSKATING EVENTS

▼

HIGHLIGHTS

Women's events joined the Olympic speedskating roster in 1960. That year Lydia Skoblikova of the Soviet Union garnered two gold medals in the 1500m and the 3000m, while teammate Klara Guseva captured the 1000m. Helga Haase of Germany reigned in the 500m. Skoblikova returned in 1964 to set an audacious precedent: the 24-year-old Siberian schoolteacher swept all four races in four successive days, the first four-gold-medal performance ever in the Winter Games. And, for good measure, Skoblikova set Olympic records in the 500m, the 1000m, and the 1500m. Melting ice made her six-tenths of a second slower than her own record in the 3000m; that event produced a surprise silver for North Korean skater Pil-Hwa Han, who also skated on bad ice.

The 500m event in 1968 had an unusual ending: the three American entries tied for second place behind Russia's Ludmila Titova. As a result, Dianne Holum, Jennifer Fish, and Mary Meyers each returned home with a silver medal. Holum also picked a bronze in the 1000m. At Sapporo in 1972 Holum became the first woman to bear the American flag during the opening ceremonies of a Winter Games, and she went on to capture the first US Olympic gold of that year, winning the 1500m. Holum padded her Olympic treasury with a fourth medal, a silver in the 3000m; 33-year-old Christina Baas-Kaiser of the Netherlands claimed the gold medal in that year's event. US skater Anne Henning was also a double medal winner, setting an Olympic record in the 500m and placing third behind Monika Pflug of West Germany in the 1000m.

fact: Speedskaters develop slowly; they need the stamina and musculature of a mature athlete to excel.

At Innsbruck in 1976, US skater Sheila Young became the first American ever to win three medals in one Winter Olympics, taking home a gold in the 500m, a silver in the 1500m, and a bronze in the 1000m. Young was also a world champion cyclist. Her speedskating teammate, Leah Poulos, captured a 1000m silver in 1976, behind Tatiana Averina of the Soviet Union, who also took the gold in the 3000m and bronzed in the 500m and the 1500m.

In 1980 Leah Poulos Mueller earned two silver medals for the US, in the 500m and the 1000m, while teammate Beth Heiden—under the tutelage of coach Dianne Holum—picked up a bronze in the 3000m. Canada's Cathy Priestner brought home a silver in the 500m. Women from the Netherlands completed a 1–2 sweep of the 1500m, while Soviet skater Natalia Petruseva captured the 1000m, and Bjorg Eva Jensen of Norway won the 3000m.

269

East German women began to dominate the skating scene in 1980. Karin Enke won a 500m gold at Lake Placid in 1980, and two golds and two silvers at the 1984 Games. Skating as Karin Kania at Calgary, she took a bronze in the 500m and silvers in the 1000m and 1500m races. Andrea Mitscherlich had taken a silver medal in the women's 3000m in 1976 at age 15; skating as Andrea Schoene in 1984, she sped to a gold in the 3000m and two silvers in the 1000m and 1500m. At the Calgary Games in 1988, this time as Andrea Ehrig, she captured silvers in the 3000m and 5000m races, and a bronze in the 1500m race. At Sarajevo, East German Christa Rothenburger claimed the gold in the women's 500m but had to settle for a silver in that event in 1988, when she captured the gold in the 1000m. Her countrywoman Gabi Zange emerged in 1988 to collect the bronze in the 3000m and the 5000m.

The indoor rink at the Calgary Games provided ideal conditions, and 1988 produced some record times. Bonnie Blair captured a gold in the 500m race—setting her still-standing world record of 39.10 in the 500m—and a bronze in the 1000m. The Netherlands enjoyed a good showing in women's speedskating at the 1988 Games when Yvonne van Gennip skated away with the gold in the 1500m, the 3000m, and the 5000m races.

Albertville Highlights

While the Albertville ice didn't set the stage for record-breaking times, Bonnie Blair stole the show with a number of Olympic records. Winning both the 500m and 1000m events, she became the first American woman to take home three gold medals from the Winter Games; she was also the first woman ever to win the 500m event in consecutive Games. The 1500m event proved to be Blair's sole failed bid for a medal; when her lap times made it clear that she wasn't bound for the top step of the podium, coach Peter Mueller had her turn off the afterburners. Twenty places ahead of Blair, German Jacqueline Boerner—recently recovered from having been hit by a car while training on her bicycle—captured the 1500m gold.

Ye Qiaobo came away from Albertville with China's first Winter Games medals, but not without a little disappointment. Forced to sit out the Calgary Games because of positive drug test results—for which the Chinese team doctor has since assumed the blame—Qiaobo had hoped to make Albertville a golden opportunity to redeem herself. Instead, she settled for silver medals in the 500m and 1000m, by a combined fifth of a second behind Blair. Fast becoming the hard-luck kid, Qiaobo claimed that the Unified Team's Elena Tiouchniakova had obstructed her on a lane changeover in the 500m event; the referees were unsympathetic, however, and, claiming that the impeded changeover had not affected the outcome of the race, refused her a do-over.

Gunda Niemann surprised no one when she ran away with the 3000m and 5000m events, adding another silver in the 1500m. The still-to-be-reckoned-with German team swept nine of the fifteen medals in all, making a clean sweep of the 5000m.

US speedskater Bonnie Blair shakes the hand of China's Ye Qiaobo, silver medalist, after winning the 1000m event at Albertville.

On the short track, media darling Cathy Turner enjoyed the limelight, pocketing the first-ever women's 500m gold—just .04 of a second ahead of China's Li Yan—and sharing in the US team's second place relay finish behind the Canadian women.

Although Turner had been slated to medal in the 500m, few expected her to strike gold. But when Canadian Sylvie Daigle—the four-time world champion—fell, Turner's chances increased. In fact, every one of the seven final races in the 500 featured a spill of some sort. Thinking that she had been nipped at the line by the Chinese skater, Turner skated around the oval with her head bowed disconsolately. When the scoreboards and announcers pronounced her the winner, however, it was showtime at the Olympic oval. Draped in Old Glory and waving an American flag, Turner, *cum* ice queen, played the champion to a "T."

Medalists

Long Track Speedskating— Women's 500m

1992
1. Bonnie Blair, USA, 40.33
2. Ye Qiaobo, China, 40.51
3. Christa Luding, Germany, 40.57
1988
1. Bonnie Blair, USA, 39.10 (WR,OR)
2. Christa Rothenburger, East Germany, 39.12
3. Karin Kania-Enke, East Germany, 39.24
1984
1. Christa Rothenburger, East Germany 41.02 (OR)
2. Karin Kania-Enke, East Germany, 41.28
3. Natalia Chive, Soviet Union, 41.50
1980
1. Karin Enke, East Germany, 41.78 (OR)
2. Leah Poulos Mueller, USA, 42.26
3. Natalia Petruseva, Soviet Union, 42.42
1976
1. Sheila Young, USA, 42.76 (OR)
2. Cathy Priestner, Canada, 43.12
3. Tatiana Averina, Soviet Union, 43.17
1972
1. Anne Henning, USA, 43.33 (OR)
2. Vera Krasnova, Soviet Union, 44.01
3. Lyudmila Titova, Soviet Union, 44.45
1968
1. Lyudmila Titova, Soviet Union, 46.1
2. Jennifer Fish, USA, 46.3
2. Dianne Holum, USA, 46.3
2. Mary Meyers, USA, 46.3
1964
1. Lydia Skoblikova, Soviet Union, 45.0 (OR)
2. Irina Yegorova, Soviet Union, 45.4
3. Tatiana Sidorova, Soviet Union, 45.5
1960
1. Helga Haase, East Germany, 45.9
2. Natalia Donchenko, Soviet Union, 46.0
3. Jeanne Ashworth, USA, 46.1
1936-
1956   **Not held**
1932
1. Jean Wilson, Canada, 58.0
2. Elizabeth Dubois, USA
3. Kit Klein, USA
1924-
1928   **Not held**

Long Track Speedskating— Women's 1,000m

1992
1. Bonnie Blair, USA, 1:21.90
2. Ye Qiaobo, China, 1:21.92
3. Monique Garbrecht, Germany, 1:22.10
1988
1. Christa Rothenburger, East Germany , 1:17.65 (WR,OR)
2. Karin Kania-Enke, East Germany, 1:17.70
3. Bonnie Blair, USA, 1:18.31
1984
1. Karin Kania-Enke, East Germany, 1:21.61 (OR)
2. Andrea Schoene, East Germany, 1:22.83
3. Natalia Petruseva, Soviet Union, 1:23.21
1980
1. Natalia Petruseva, Soviet Union, 1:24.10 (OR)
2. Leah Poulos Mueller, USA, 1:25.41
3. Sylvia Albrecht, East Germany, 1:26.46
1976
1. Tatiana Averina, Soviet Union, 1:28.43 (OR)
2. Leah Poulos, USA, 1:28.57
3. Sheila Young, USA, 1:29.14
1972
1. Monika Pflug, West Germany, 1:31.40 (OR)
2. Atje Keulen-Deelstra, Netherlands, 1:31.61
3. Anne Henning, USA, 1:31.62
1968
1. Carolina Geijssen, Netherlands, 1:32.6 (OR)
2. Lyudmila Titova, Soviet Union, 1:32.9
3. Dianne Holum, USA 1:33.4
1964
1. Lydia Skoblikova, Soviet Union, 1:33.2 (OR)
2. Irina Yegorova, Soviet Union, 1:34.3
3. Kaija Mustonen, Finland, 1:34.8
1960
1. Klara Guseva, Soviet Union, 1:34.1
2. Helga Haase, East Germany, 1:34.3

World-record holder Gunda Niemann, of Germany, digs in at the finish of the 3000m speedskating event at Albertville. Niemann captured the gold medal in both the 3000m and the 5000m events.

3. Tamara Rylova, Soviet Union, 1:34.8

1936-
1956   **Not held**
1932   **1.** Elizabeth Dubois, USA, 2:04.0
         2. Hattie Donaldson, Canada
         3. Dorothy Franey, USA
1924-
1928   **Not held**

Long Track Speedskating—
Women's 1,500m

1992   **1.** Jacqueline Boerner, Germany, 2:05.87
         2. Gunda Niemann, Germany, 2:05.92
         3. Seiko Hashimoto, Japan, 2:06.88

1988   **1.** Yvonne van Gennip, Netherlands, 2:00.68 (OR)
         2. Karin Kania-Enke, East Germany, 2:00.82
         3. Andrea Ehrig, East Germany, 2:01.49
1984   **1.** Karin Kania-Enke, East Germany, 2:03.42 (OR)
         2. Andrea Schoene, East Germany, 2:05.29
         3. Natalia Petruseva, Soviet Union, 2:05.78
1980   **1.** Annie Borckink, Netherlands, 2:10.95 (OR)
         2. Ria Visser, Netherlands, 2:12.24
         3. Sabine Becker, East Germany, 2:12.38
1976   **1.** Galina Stepanskaya, Soviet Union, 2:16.58 (OR)

273

2. Sheila Young, USA, 2:17.06
3. Tatiana Averina, Soviet Union, 2:17.96
1972 1. Dianne Holum, USA, 2:20.85 (OR)
2. Christina Baas-Kaiser, Netherlands, 2:21.05
3. Atje Keulen-Deelstra, Netherlands, 2:22.05
1968 1. Kaija Mustonen, Finland, 2:22.4 (OR)
2. Carolina Geijssen, Netherlands, 2:22.7
3. Christina Kaiser, Netherlands, 2:24.5
1964 1. Lydia Skoblikova, Soviet Union, 2:22.6 (OR)
2. Kaija Mustonen, Finland, 2:25.5
3. Berta Kolokoltseva, Soviet Union, 2:27.1
1960 1. Lydia Skoblikova, Soviet Union, 2:25.2 (WR)
2. Elvira Seroczynska, Poland, 2:25.7
3. Helena Pilejczyk, Poland, 2:27.1
1936-
1956 **Not held**
1932 1. Kit Klein, USA, 3:00.6
2. Jean Wilson, Canada
3. Helen Bina, USA

1924-
1928 **Not held**

Long Track Speedskating— Women's 3,000m

1992 1. Gunda Niemann, Germany, 4:19.90
2. Heike Warnicke, Germany, 4:22.88
3. Emese Hunyady, Austria, 4:24.64
1988 1. Yvonne van Gennip, Netherlands, 4:11.94 (WR,OR)
2. Andrea Ehrig, East Germany, 4:12.09
3. Gabi Zange, East Germany, 4:16.92
1984 1. Andrea Schoene, East Germany, 4:24.79 (OR)
2. Karin Kania-Enke, East Germany, 4:26.33
3. Gabie Schoenbrunn, East Germany, 4:33.13
1980 1. Bjorg-Eva Jensen, Norway, 4:32.13 (OR)
2. Sabine Becker, East Germany, 4:32.79
3. Beth Heiden, USA, 4:33.77
1976 1. Tatiana Averina, Soviet Union, 4:45.19 (OR)

2. Andrea Mitscherlich, East Germany, 4:45.23
3. Lisbeth Korsmo, Norway, 4:45.24
1972 1. Christina Baas-Kaiser, Netherlands, 4:52.14 (OR)
2. Dianne Holum, USA, 4:58.67
3. Atje Keulen-Deelstra, Netherlands, 4:59.91
1968 1. Johanna Schut, Netherlands, 4:56.2 (OR)
2. Kaija Mustonen, Finland, 5:01.0
3. Christina Kaiser, Netherlands, 5:01.3
1964 1. Lydia Skoblikova, Soviet Union, 5:14.9
2. Pil-Hwa Han, Democratic People's Republic of Korea, 5:18.5
2. Valentina Stenina, Soviet Union, 5:18.5
1960 1. Lydia Skoblikova, Soviet Union, 5:14.3
2. Valentina Stenina, Soviet Union, 5:16.9
3. Eevi Huttunen, Finland, 5:21.0

1924-
1956 **Not held**

Long Track Speedskating— Women's 5,000m

1992 1. Gunda Niemann, Germany, 7:31.57
2. Heike Warnicke, Germany, 7:37.59
3. Claudia Pechstein, Germany, 7:39.80
1988 1. Yvonne van Gennip, Netherlands, 7:14.13 (WR)
2. Andrea Ehrig, East Germany, 7:17.12
3. Gabi Zange, East Germany, 7:21.61

Short Track Speedskating— Women's 500m

1992 1. Cathy Turner, USA, 47.04
2. Li Yan, China, 47.08
3. Ok Sil Hwang, D.P.R. Korea, 47.23

Short Track Speedskating— Women's 3km Relay

1992 1. Canada, 4:36.62
2. USA, 4:37.85
3. Unified Team, 4:42.69

Trivia Quiz

1. **Olympic long track speedskating is held:**

A) on a 111-meter track, which can be either indoors or outdoors. **B)** on a 400-meter track, staged in pairs. **C)** on different sized tracks, depending on the event. **D)** on frozen, man-made straight canals.

2. Electric timing to .00 second:

A) was introduced to the Games and World Sprint Championships in 1972. **B)** was first used at the Games in 1964, to verify a three-way tie for silver in the men's 500 meters. **C)** has been used at the Games since 1962 but has never been used at the World Championships. **D)** was replaced in Albertville by .000 laser timing.

3. Short track speedskating is:

A) a contest against the clock, where the fastest time wins. **B)** a strategic race that may start at a snail's pace. **C)** a race of nerves, where skaters are allowed to shove other skaters out of their way. **D)** not for passive people.

4. A short track speedskater is cruising at top speed:

A) in both straightaways. **B)** in the exit of the second turn. **C)** one meter beyond the finish line. **D)** in only one of the straightaways.

5. In the 500 meters, American men:

A) have medaled in every Games since the event first appeared. **B)** have not medaled since 1980. **C)** have won every gold medal since 1980. **D)** have won more medals than American women since 1980.

6. Eric Heiden's coach for the 1980 Games at Lake Placid was:

A) Sheila Young, erstwhile cyclist and 1976 gold medalist. **B)** Erhard Keller, from West Germany, who won the gold in 1972 by setting an Olympic record in the 500 meters. **C)** Dianne Holum, 1972 gold medalist in the 1500 meters and author of *The Speedskating Handbook*. **D)** Bonnie Blair, *wunderkind*.

7. Short track speedskating was a medal sport for the first time:

A) at the first Games, in Athens in 1896. **B)** at the first Winter Games, in Chamonix, in 1924. **C)** at the ancient Roman Games, where polar bears were let loose among Christians. **D)** at Albertville, in 1992.

8. Long track speedskaters change lanes every lap:

A) to help them count laps. **B)** to break the monotony of skating in circles. **C)** to make sure both skaters cover the same distance. **D)** to wear the ice evenly.

9. The new kid on the block in world competition short track speedskating is:

A) Japan. **B)** Canada. **C)** Jamaica. **D)** Korea.

10. Short track skaters often wear brightly colored gloves:

A) because it makes them go faster. **B)** because it corresponds to their position in the pack. **C)** so their teammates can pick them out more easily. **D)** so that judges can spot violations more easily.

Answers: 1-b, 2-a, 3-b, 4-b, 5-b, 6-c, 7-d, 8-c, 9-d, 10-d

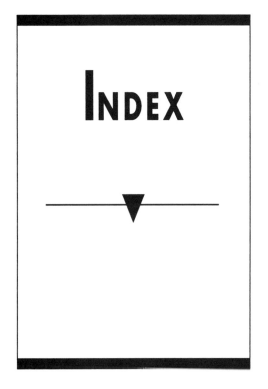

INDEX

INDEX

287